Career Management & Work–Life Integration

This book is dedicated to our families, who give our work meaning and purpose.

To our parents,

Ed and Florence Harrington

Anne and Robert Hall

To our wives,

Dr. Annie Soisson

Dr. Marcy Crary

And to our children,

Maggie, Hannah, and Dillon Harrington

Elizabeth, Chip, and Mary Lauran Hall

Career
Management
&Work–Life
Integration
Using Self-Assessment
to Navigate Contemporary Careers

Brad **Harrington**
Boston College

Douglas T. **Hall**
Boston University

SAGE Publications
Los Angeles • London • New Delhi • Singapore

Copyright © 2007 by Sage Publications, Inc.

All rights reserved. No part of this book may be reproduced or utilized in any form or by any means, electronic or mechanical, including photocopying, recording, or by any information storage and retrieval system, without permission in writing from the publisher.

For information:

Sage Publications, Inc.
2455 Teller Road
Thousand Oaks, California 91320
E-mail: order@sagepub.com

Sage Publications India Pvt. Ltd.
B 1/I 1 Mohan Cooperative
  Industrial Area
Mathura Road, New Delhi 110 044
India

Sage Publications Ltd.
1 Oliver's Yard
55 City Road
London EC1Y 1SP
United Kingdom

Sage Publications Asia-Pacific Pte. Ltd.
33 Pekin Street #02-01
Far East Square
Singapore 048763

Printed in the United States of America

Library of Congress Cataloging-in-Publication Data

Harrington, Brad.
Career management & work–life integration: Using self-assessment to navigate contemporary careers / Brad Harrington, Douglas T. Hall.
      p. cm.
Includes bibliographical references and index.
ISBN 978-1-4129-5410-5 (cloth)
ISBN 978-1-4129-3745-0 (pbk.)
    1. Career development. 2. Self-evaluation. 3. Vocational interests.
4. Work and family. 5. Quality of work life. 6. Vocational guidance.
I. Hall, Douglas T., 1940– II. Title. III. Title: Career management and work–life integration.

HF5381.5.H364 2008
650.1—dc22   2006102674

This book is printed on acid-free paper.

07   08   09   10   11   10 9 8 7 6 5 4 3 2 1

Acquisitions Editor:	Al Bruckner
Editorial Assistant:	MaryAnn Vail
Production Editor:	Diane S. Foster
Copy Editor:	Carol Anne Peschke
Typesetter:	C&M Digitals (P) Ltd.
Proofreader:	Ellen Brink
Cover Designer:	Candice Harman
Marketing Manager:	Nichole M. Angress

Contents

Preface

This book was originally developed as a companion to a course Brad teaches at Boston College called "Career Management and Work–Life Integration." It also contains material and exercises that Tim has used in his courses on career management and leadership over the years. These courses are targeted at graduate students in schools of management, but the materials presented are equally relevant to anyone faced with the challenge of succeeding in a career while trying to live a happy, well-balanced life. In today's fast-paced, ever-changing world that includes just about all of us. The book should also be of particular use to anyone who provides counseling and coaching to others in the process of making career choices, changes, and transitions. These advisors could include line managers, human resource professionals, career counselors, executive coaches, or even spouses, parents, and friends.

In recent years, much has been written about the profound changes occurring in the workplace and the workforce. The employer–employee contract has been dramatically altered as leading organizations have moved from practices of lifelong (or at least long-term) employment to a more free-agent approach to managing their workforce. This change has led to the establishment of a new career model that is increasingly organization independent. As individuals have come to depend less on their employers to provide stable career paths and job security, and as changes in the labor market call for more frequent job and even career changes, working people have come to realize that, as Cliff Hakim says in his 1994 book with the same title, we are all self-employed. Tim has called this concept of individually driven career management the *protean career*. Proteus was a god in Greek mythology who could change forms to adapt to threats.

The skills involved in navigating careers and maintaining work–life balance are now necessary for all individuals, regardless of the sector in which they are employed. Every sector—business, law, professional services, healthcare, government, and education—has seen unprecedented change in its career contract. This book will examine these changes and help readers develop critical competencies and skills needed to successfully manage their career development and maintain work–life integration in light of the changing landscape.

The career courses we teach are highly personal experiences. Unlike in most graduate courses in business, the focus begins in the most atypical place: with the individual. Course components include:

- A rigorous self-assessment process that helps students clarify their interests, values, skills, career goals, and aspirations in the context of their overall life. Students use this information to formulate themes clarifying their career goals and direction.

- An approach that helps students apply their self-assessment as a filter or focus to analyze the labor market, career options, and potential employers to identify and attain their desired career goals.

- A review of the knowledge and skills needed to manage and maintain successful career development and work–life integration over the individual's lifespan.

A self-assessment and career management course relies heavily on the use of exercises and instruments that increase students' self-awareness and understanding of the world of work. We have tried wherever possible to include these exercises in the book. Where this is not possible, we refer the reader to ways to access the exercises and instruments.

Our aim is to help readers develop their own view and reference points on what it means to be successful or to have a life that is balanced. We believe there is no such thing as actual success, at least not as judged by others. Success, like beauty, is in the eye of the beholder. No job title, compensation level, or set of material possessions can determine whether one evaluates his or her life as successful. This distinction is equally true of work–life balance. What constitutes an appropriate balance differs from person to person. We hope this book will give the reader a comprehensive understanding of the self, the changing workplace, the changing nature of work and careers, and the issues surrounding the elusive goals of career success and work–life balance, whatever the reader determines those two things to be.

We hope to help the reader move between observing and understanding the realities of what is happening in the external world of work and reflecting on his or her internal world (including personal goals, interests, values, and aspirations). It is the integration of the individual's aspirations and desires with a clear understanding of the dynamics of the labor market that allows one to achieve work, career, and life fulfillment.

Many works are available on the dynamics of the labor market, the changing nature of work and the workplace, the process of self-assessment, job search strategies, and the challenge of career management and work–life integration. Each is offered by a specialist from a particular field, such as economics, sociology, psychology, career development, and organizational theory, and focuses on one dimension of the whole equation. What seems to be lacking is one work that does an effective job of weaving together the whole story. We hope this book is an important first step.

This book can be used in a number of different ways and for different target audiences, including the following:

- *Individuals:* Individuals can use this book as a guide to managing their careers and their work lives. Although it would be ideal to have readers progress through this book in one process, it may be equally useful for the reader to refer to parts of this book when various career issues arise or at important points of career and life transition.

- *Colleges and universities for courses:* Professors can use this book as a text for classes in career planning and work and family balance. Unfortunately, it is still not the norm for most schools to offer classes on this subject, but we think that in light of the changes in the past two decades, such a class should be part of the curriculum in every university, not just in business schools. To facilitate the teaching process, we have developed a companion teachers' guide, complete with syllabus, course assignments, teaching slides, and author notes that follow the outline of the book. This set of materials should help with the planning and delivery of the course and offers suggestions from the authors' experience in guiding students through this process. The rewards for both teacher and student have been great.

- *College and university career planning centers:* This book could be helpful for career center staff and the students who are "customers" of the career office. Some career centers offer multiweek career seminars to students, and we think this book would be an excellent companion guide to such workshops.

- *Corporate career development programs:* Many organizations offer 1- to 2-day (or more) courses in career management and work–life planning. Although covering all the material outlined in this book would take far longer than most organizational training programs last, almost all activities and approaches outlined would work well for adults in the workplace. In addition, participants could do the exercises without the aid of an instructor or facilitator. This approach would allow the participants to complete assignments in their own time, when the topics are the most salient for them.

- *Special seminars for individuals and couples:* Many consultants offer career and life planning seminars for individuals or couples. We believe that this book would be an excellent resource for such seminars and that many of the exercises contained in it would provide a basis for discussion topics.

We hope this work contributes to the field and to the lives of working people and their employers, families, and communities.

Acknowledgments

This book is the result of a collaboration that dates back 20 years. We first met when Tim was teaching his career course at Boston University and Brad was leading the development of a global career management program for Hewlett-Packard. Brad was a frequent guest lecturer in Tim's class, describing how career concepts were being applied at one leading company. Our friendship and collaboration continued over the years until Tim served on Brad's (and later Brad's wife's) dissertation committee at Boston University.

We would like to express our indebtedness to many people. First, our profound thanks to Dr. Annie Soisson (Brad's wife) and Bob Gardella, who were the main editors for this book. Annie put in a great deal of time, and her writing and editing abilities added tremendously to the clarity of the book. Bob Gardella, who has authored an excellent book on job search (*The Harvard Business School Guide to Finding Your Next Job*) did extensive editing of this work and offered invaluable suggestions on format and content. He is an excellent resource in this field.

We would also like to express our appreciation for Brad's current and past colleagues at the Boston College Center for Work & Family. Since 1990, the center has passionately explored, researched, and educated organizations on the changing nature of work and the impact of these changes on employees, the workplace, families, communities, and society. The center's small staff has produced an excellent body of work on such diverse topics as flexible work options, the changing employment contract, dependent care, the impact of job loss on employees and their families, women's advancement, work–life programs for employees in low-wage occupations, and the relationship between employers, employees, and the community. The center's research serves as a consistent point of reference for this book.

We would like to thank Jackie James of the Center for Work & Family for her thoughts on the sections of the book dealing with the aging workforce. Sylvia DeMott, a graduate assistant at the center, provided assistance in developing, editing, and improving some portions of this material. She contributed to a number of sections, including the ones on job search, leaves and sabbaticals, and career stages. Elizabeth Hamilton, Ph.D. candidate at Boston College, contributed extensively to the section on telecommuting;

Rosalind Barnett, Ph.D., and Phil Mirvis, Ph.D., co-authored articles with Tim on reduced work hours and on the protean career and older workers, respectively. We sincerely appreciate their willingness to allow us to use some of their thoughts in this book.

We would also like to thank the corporate members of our respective organizations. Brad has received excellent support for his work from corporate partners of the Center for Work & Family, including members of the National Work and Family Roundtable, the Global Workforce Roundtable, and the New England Work & Family Association. Tim would like to acknowledge the support of the Boston University Executive Development Roundtable. Our interaction with these outstanding professionals has been a great source of information and inspiration on current organizational practices.

We would like to thank our partners at Sage, especially Al Bruckner, MaryAnn Vail, and Diane Foster, for their hard work, their encouragement, and their support. Their professionalism and expertise helped guide us through the process of getting this book to print.

Finally our thanks go to the students, faculty, staff, and administration of the Carroll School of Management at Boston College and of the Boston University School of Management who have supported and encouraged our work.

Understanding the New Career 1

THE BARNES FAMILY

John and Nancy Barnes have been married for 14 years, have two preteen children, and live in the Midwest. John is a 37-year-old executive at a high-technology company with a demanding job requiring frequent travel. Over the past year, he has traveled often to the West Coast corporate headquarters, and he has recently been offered a transfer to that location. The job prospect is exciting, and it would offer John high visibility and greater promotional opportunities.

In the meantime, Nancy, 38, holds a senior-level position with one of the area's largest hospitals. Nancy has been with her employer since she earned her graduate degree in healthcare administration 15 years ago. She has had some interrupted periods of employment over the years, taking leaves when the children were born. She also worked a reduced schedule for a short period of time when the children were very young but generally has stayed on the career track.

In the past few years, John and Nancy have discussed the possibility of one or both of them scaling back their work to be more available to their children, particularly after school. As their children approach the teenage years, they have come to realize that spending time with them is more necessary than ever. They have often discussed how quickly time is flying by and remarked that "the kids will be gone off to college before we know it."

Although John is excited about the position he has been offered, Nancy does not share his enthusiasm. She does not see how pursuing this promotion fits with their overall life plan (which, in fact, they have never clearly articulated). If scaling back is a priority, then this promotion and

1

move seem to be leading the Barneses in the wrong direction. Housing prices at the West Coast location are extremely high, and even with a promotion their overall financial picture would not improve. In addition, Nancy's career has finally reached a stage where she thinks she could ask for reduced hours without compromising her position at the hospital. Starting over in a new location may mean great things for John's career, but it will certainly change Nancy's situation, and it will mean that plans for scaling back are put on hold or perhaps even permanently altered.

How the situation will be resolved is unclear. At this point, the Barneses are having a difficult time sorting through their options. This dilemma is causing a high level of stress as John feels pressure to give his management team an answer to the exciting prospect they have offered him.

HELEN CASEY

Helen is a 41-year-old executive in a consulting firm. For the past 16 years, her life has focused primarily on her work. Always stimulating and demanding, Helen's job has been a source of enormous gratification and learning. She has traveled extensively, worked on challenging problems with world-class organizations, and even had the opportunity to spend 4 years living in Europe in a dream assignment. She thinks that professionally, since she graduated from a top-tier business school, her career has gone according to plan and has even exceeded her expectations.

However, for the past 4 or 5 years Helen has become increasingly dissatisfied with her life as a whole. While her career has flourished, her life outside work has not. Constant travel has made it difficult for Helen to develop her social life. She was married once, but when that marriage ended, she increased her focus on work. The transfer to Europe for 4 years was a great life experience, but it disrupted her life in ways she had not fully anticipated. When she was moved to Europe she was in her early 30s, and time still seemed to be on her side. By the time she returned, bought a home, and resettled into a stable pattern in the United States, she was in her late 30s and realized that her chances of becoming a parent were increasingly remote. Helen found this realization difficult to accept.

After reaching a high level in the firm, Helen finds herself with little drive to go further in the hierarchy. She has begun to dream of changing her life and career. She thinks about doing work that would focus her skills on a new adventure, perhaps starting her own business or working in a not-for-profit organization. Helen's success had made her financially secure, and now seems a good time to refocus her energies on something that would bring her greater joy and allow her to help others. Perhaps working with children would allow her to develop her nurturing side, even if she never has children of her own.

Helen has also decided to try to change her personal situation. She has begun the process for adoption and is looking forward, with some trepidation, to the possibility of being a mother. She has some concerns that making a career change while taking on the responsibilities of being a single parent might be unwise. On the other hand, staying in her present role will make parenting very challenging because of her long work hours and extensive travel. She thinks that the time to make a decision is now.

THE SMITH FAMILY

Stan and Ellen Smith have been married for 10 years. In their first years of marriage, both worked in the public sector, Ellen as a teacher and Stan as a social worker. They had both always loved the out of doors. They enjoyed hiking, camping, and skiing. However, when it came time to buy a home, they settled in the town where Stan grew up, a beautiful, upscale suburb of Washington, D.C. They purchased a small cottage, and although both were employed, they were able to enjoy their home, travel, and pursue their interest in the outdoors. They even put aside money for future home improvements. Life was busy but uncomplicated.

Ten years later, things are not so simple. The Smiths now have three children, and Ellen decided to stop working when her second child, Hannah, was born. Initially the loss of income, though noticeable, did not seem to be unmanageable. But as the family grew, so did expenses. Soon the small cottage wasn't big enough for their growing family. In preparation for the third child's arrival, the Smiths put an addition on their home. This decision gave them some much-needed space, but soon the new baby and the other growing children made the house again seem too small for their needs. Finances became an increasing challenge, and living on one income seemed no longer just difficult but nearly impossible. Both Stan and Ellen had agreed that for one of them to stay home while the kids were young was a priority, but they hadn't fully realized all the expenses and needs that went with having a family of five. The town where they live compounded the problem. With an average income in the upper 10% of the state, expectations were high. Even young children were involved in skiing, ballet, tennis, and gymnastics, often at an early age. Continuing on the present path became increasingly difficult in the short term, and the Smiths were equally worried about the long term. Saving for their children's education and their own retirement became greater concerns as they reached their late 30s. In addition, they both yearned to be in a more rural, less pressured environment.

There are a few obvious alternatives that the Smiths could consider. Ellen could return to work. Although many see teaching as an ideal career for parents of young children, teachers' schedules often are idealized by those not in the profession. When one includes prep work and time for correcting papers, teachers work longer days than most people assume. Also, teaching offers little flexibility. A teacher cannot simply go in late or leave for an hour in the middle of the day to attend children's school events, go to the doctor, or deal with small emergencies. In addition, the relatively low salary for teachers, coupled with the high cost of daycare and after-school care, means returning to teaching would create significantly more hassle without greatly improving their financial situation much.

Another option is to sell their house, which has appreciated dramatically, and move to a less expensive area. To make this move worthwhile, the Smiths will need to go a long distance from suburban Washington. This move may solve the financial situation but could create a number of other problems. First, Stan has been in his job for many years and would like to continue, but a move could mean that commuting time to his job would increase from 20 minutes each way to more than 2 hours a day, decreasing the time Stan can spend with his family. Second, they worry that the schools in rural areas will not be as good as those in their current location, raising the possibility of paying for private schools. Third, Stan's father, a widower who lives nearby, is getting older and increasingly relies on the Smiths for support. Finally, Ellen and Stan will be losing important support networks that include many close friends and Ellen and Stan's extended families.

The Smiths could also simply try cutting back and making it on one salary. But attempts to do so have proven difficult. And they believe there is not enough slack in their spending to allow these cuts to make a difference. Although both Stan and Ellen are committed to coming up with a solution, there are some difficulties. One is that each believes there is a better option, but their preferred options are not the same. For Ellen, the answer is clear: Sell the house and move to a lower-cost area. But for Stan the answer is to wait things out in their present home until Ellen can return to work when the youngest children are in school all day. It has been extremely difficult to find time to discuss this dilemma and come to consensus on the best option.

The Changing Landscape of Careers

These cases represent but a few of the many issues experienced by people who are several years into their careers. We start with these cases to give you a flavor of some of the topics we will be covering in this book. The challenges that these people face are hardly unusual. Integrating work and family is one of the most difficult challenges people face as they think about their current and future career options.

Today, the changing nature of work and the workplace and the changing nature of families have profoundly affected the nature and structure of careers. The forces that must be factored in include globalization; working parents; breakdown of the nuclear family; lack of extended family support due to geographic mobility; lack of high-quality daycare; burdensome costs of education, housing, and retirement; and caring for elderly parents who are living longer. All these forces, coupled with an unrealistic sense that we can have it all (or should try to do it all), seem to have come together to form a perfect storm of stress and confusion.

Anyone who works needs no expert to state the obvious: The world of work is in a state of unprecedented change. In today's organizations, change is a fact of life. Even organizations that for many years were static today change at a speed never before experienced. In very short periods of time, organizations are created, experience dramatic growth, merge or are acquired, downsize dramatically, reinvent themselves, or simply cease to exist.

Additionally, organizations have never before dealt with such a high degree of complexity. The impact of globalization, new technologies, joint ventures and strategic alliances, changing workforce demographics, and changing employee, customer, stockholder, and societal expectations are all making organizational management increasingly challenging. One of the major challenges for any organization is to better understand how to manage its changing workforce in the context of the changing organization.

The Changing Employment Contract: A Case Study

One of the most profound changes in the workplace that has occurred in recent years is the end of the old employment contract. Beginning in the mid-1980s, a fundamental shift has occurred in the employer–employee contract (sometimes also called the psychological contract). For a host of reasons, organizations have changed their stance regarding their commitment to maintain, or even try to maintain, the ongoing employment security of their workers. Brad's 20-year experience with Hewlett-Packard, which for many years was seen as one of the leading proponents of employment security in the United States, illustrates how much this foundational aspect of human resource practice has changed in the past 20 years.

Brad worked for Hewlett-Packard from 1980 to 2000. During much of this time, HP was viewed as one of the world's top companies, a leader in developing both top-notch products and highly skilled employees by offering progressive human resource practices and highly stable employment, especially for a high-technology firm. But beginning in the mid-1980s, business developments occurred that mirror how the employment contract was changing for many major employers in the United States and abroad.

HP enjoyed more than 40 years of highly stable employment. With very few exceptions, HP had promised employees job security based on job performance. In

(Continued)

(Continued)

effect, if an employee met his or her job expectations, he or she was implicitly guaranteed a job for life. By the mid-1980s, senior management saw a need to revise this contract. The growing impact of computers, new technology, and automation in manufacturing and the consolidation and centralization of operations made the promise of a job for life increasingly unrealistic. HP changed its stance from providing *job security* to providing *employment security,* the first sign that things were changing. Employment security still implied that HP would provide a job; it simply meant that any particular job might change or be eliminated (e.g., if technology rendered it obsolete). Soon it became apparent that even this promise would constrain the options available to the company to contain costs and remain more competitive.

Within a very short period in the 1980s more formal measures were put in place to address the changing workforce dynamics. At first, these initiatives reflected HP's paternalistic stance toward its employees: *The company will take care of you.* Extensive retraining programs were introduced to help displaced workers retool their skills from production jobs to administrative and clerical positions. New programs gave managers greater flexibility and financial support to move displaced employees to other divisions or geographic areas where jobs were in greater supply (assuming the employees were interested in moving). And for the first time, employees were offered generous severance or early retirement packages if they left voluntarily. Later, strategies aimed at getting employees to play a stronger role in the process began to emerge. Career management programs based on the work of Brad and his colleagues began cropping up across the company to ensure that employees played a more active role in planning and managing their careers.

Each change in HR policy was well articulated by the company as being both necessary in the changing economic landscape and consistent with the organization's core values. HP's management team was effective in communicating to employees that the change in employment practices was consistent with the "HP Way," HP's legendary corporate culture. Although cutting jobs was undesirable, management stressed that the approach demonstrated attention to the business's bottom line *and* respect for employees' needs. The company's efforts to balance these two sets of needs typified the company's culture and approach to doing business.

From that time until the end of the 1990s, HP's employment contract continued to evolve. Programs became increasingly nonvoluntary and aggressive. A host of new terms became a part of the company's human resource lexicon: *downsizing, outsourcing, flex force,* and *contingency workers.* At the same time, other new initiatives—flexible work options, telecommuting, alternative work schedules, job sharing, and voluntary leave programs—reflected responses to employee-driven needs for greater balance and control. Many of these changes were driven by employees looking for new alternatives to manage their careers (in the long term) and their day-to-day work–life balance (in the short term). It seemed that both the company and the employees were looking for the same thing: flexibility.

In addition to the changing employment relationship, profound changes in how people worked were driving this change in HP workforce management. The 24-7 economy, movement of jobs overseas, and expansion of global business organizations that led to more frequent and more distant business travel were making it harder for employees to be ideal parents and ideal workers simultaneously. The increasing number of women, two-career couples, and single-parent households in the workforce made flexibility a highly desirable characteristic of the organization. In surveys of employees, increasing flexibility became a prized organizational characteristic, often more valued than even compensation.

Just before Brad left HP, even larger changes were taking place. In 1999 the company decided to split into two separate organizations, creating a new company, Agilent Technologies, which, ironically, was made up of all of HP's original product lines (i.e., technical, scientific, and medical instrumentation). This meant that 45,000 employees (roughly a third of HP's staff) were working for a different organization, and HP became a computing and printing business. Then, a few years later, HP acquired Compaq Computers, which had itself acquired Digital Equipment Corporation in the late 1990s. Part of the strategy attached to the Compaq acquisition stated that HP would eliminate 15,000 jobs to cut costs and increase productivity. In just over 3 years, this 60-year-old company had gone from a 120,000-person instrument, computing, and printing firm to a nearly 150,000-employee printer and computer business. Approximately half of those employees had not worked for HP at the beginning of 2000.

In summary, in the mid-1980s HP was still committed to lifelong employment, by the 1990s it was in the throes of large scale reorganizations and redeployment, and by 2002 it had made a large divestiture and a major acquisition with the stated aim of large-scale downsizing. This reinforces how drastically the employment contract changed over a 20-year period. But HP's experience was hardly unique. As Louis Uchitelle states in the opening of his excellent recent work *The Disposable American: Layoffs and Their Consequences* (2006),

> More than two decades have passed since the modern layoff first appeared as a mass phenomenon in American life. Until that happened, companies tried to avoid layoffs. They were signs of corporate failure and a violation of acceptable business behavior. Over the years however, the permanent separation of people from their jobs, abruptly and against their wishes, gradually became the standard management practice, and in the late 1990s, we finally acquiesced. Acquiescence means giving up, seeing no alternative; we bowed to layoffs as the way things have to be. Now we justify them as an unfortunate necessity. (p. IX)

Brad's experience of the profound changes that have occurred in the world of work, on both organizational and personal levels, illustrates that the career–life equation has changed in a very palpable way in a short time. In light of the changes, instability, and unpredictability of life in modern organizations, equipping individuals with the skills and models needed to navigate their careers and maintain work–life balance is critical. Sound organizational policies can support staff in making and implementing good career decisions and managing work and life changes. But it is the individual, ideally with the support of his or her manager, who must take responsibility for navigating these changes. In today's turbulent environment, individuals must be skilled at crafting a career–life strategy that meets their needs, reflects their values and priorities, and contributes to the ever-changing needs of employers.

The Changing Nature of Families

As work and the workplace have changed dramatically over the past few decades, so has the American family and, specifically, who works in the American family. In the 1960s the stereotype of the American family developed, and it endures today. As Linda Waite and Mark Nielsen observe in "The Rise of the Dual-Earner Family, 1963–1997" (2001),

> During the 1950s and early 1960s the traditional family was king. Young men and women married early and had rather large families relatively quickly. Divorce was rare and unmarried childbearing unheard of. Young women worked before they were married and some continued working until their first child was born, but almost all mothers of infants left the labor force for an extended period and many did not return. Women earned much less than men because they had less education and training, because they almost all worked in "women's jobs," and because they either had just started working or would soon leave. (p. 23)

Using data from the 1963 and 1997 U.S. censuses, the authors point out just how much the world has changed. We have updated some of Waite and Nielsen's interesting statistics with information from the most recent U.S. Census and the Department of Labor. Some noticeable shifts include the following:

- In 1963, most adults were married (84% of women and 87% of men), and 91% of all children lived with two married parents. Only one child in 100 lived with a never-before-married parent. By 1997, one in three adults was not married. One man in five had never been married, and the percentage of women who had never been married nearly tripled, from 6% to 16%. This trend seems to be continuing. According to the 2000 U.S. Census, there was a 72% increase in the number of cohabiting couples over the decade from 1990 to 2000 (Kantrowitz et al., 2001).

- In 1963, only one woman in three worked full time, compared to 86% of men. Half of the women did not hold a paying job. By 1997, 57% of all women were working full time, and another 23% were working part time. The percentage of women who did not work at all shrunk to one in five (Waite & Nielsen, 2001). It is estimated that women will make up 48% of the total U.S. labor force in 2008 (U.S. Department of Labor, 2006).

- The category of married women changed the most in this period. In 1963, 42% of married women without children worked full time, but this number rose to 60% in 1997. Perhaps more significant was the change in married mothers. In 1963, only one in four worked full time. By 1997 the proportion working full time had more than doubled, to 49%, and less than one quarter of mothers were not employed (Waite & Nielsen, 2001, pp. 24–29). By 2005, two thirds of married women with children under the age of 18 were employed (U.S. Department of Labor, January 2006).

These statistics clearly show that the 1960s stereotype of the nuclear family with a male breadwinner and a stay-at-home mom no longer holds true. If it is a two-parent family, it is likely that both spouses work. Single-parent households are much more common today than 40 years ago. Even since 1990, the number of families headed by single mothers has increased by 25% to more than 7.5 million (Kantrowitz et al., 2001). Whether for reasons of professional development, financial need, insecurity, or the need for independence, parents in most families today are working.

What does this mean for working individuals and families? First, the notion that someone will be at home to take care of domestic tasks, child rearing, and community involvement is no longer the case for most of us. Issues of child care and after-school oversight of school-age children become matters of great concern for working parents. Second, the idea that a couple has one primary breadwinner and that career decisions would be the primary concern of one spouse is no longer the case. A decision made by one working spouse can have a profound effect on the career of the other. Finally, the stereotype of "women's jobs" and "men's jobs" has become largely a thing of the past. Women no longer limit their opportunities to fields such as education and nursing. But this reality challenges many of the norms that have long existed in traditionally male professions such as law, medicine, and corporate leadership. Unwillingness to rethink the expectations inherent in these roles has led to serious conflicts for working mothers as they try to advance in a system that does not support their dual role of worker and parent. These changes raise serious challenges not only for working parents but also for families, employers, community service providers, and society.

The New Careers

A few years ago, Tim wrote a book whose title said it all: *The Career Is Dead—Long Live the Career* (Hall & Associates, 1996). The redefinition of careers today reflects their changing nature. This does not mean that having a career is no longer possible but that they have changed radically. The notion of a career as a series of jobs, moving in an unfaltering path up the hierarchy in one particular organization, simply doesn't fit today's norm. So, some might ask, "Do we have careers anymore or simply a series of jobs?"

Careers are very much alive and well. They have simply taken a very different form. Before defining and illustrating this new form, let's discuss what might distinguish a job from a career. If the old employment contract and the traditional career path are increasingly things of the past, how can someone say they have a career today? In the early 2000s, Joy Pixley, a faculty member at the University of California at Riverside, studied the differences between a job and a career. Her research examined the views of 50 couples (i.e., 100 individuals) regarding this issue.

Pixley identified five factors that would lead a person to define his or her work as a career, not merely a series of jobs:

- *Emotional investment:* This includes the extent to which people say they care about their work, are intrinsically motivated, are personally invested in their work, or associate the work with their identity—in essence, seeing their work as something that they do for reasons other than simply making a living. This could also be the degree to which people think about their work during nonwork time and pour themselves into their work.

- *Time investment:* This form of personal commitment carries a very practical orientation. It is the amount of time one has invested in getting and keeping specialized education or skills, the number of work hours one spends, or continuity or stability in a job or occupation over a period of time. A person who has invested a great deal of time in college and graduate school or in professional certification programs will view his or her work as a career. Likewise, one who invests long hours at work but does not receive overtime pay might also be more likely to see his or her work as a career.

- *Progressive job changes and advancement:* People who see their jobs as leading them on a path of increased growth and responsibility would view themselves as having a career. Some participants in Pixley's study saw the lack of future advancement or growth as a reason for seeing their current work as a job rather than a career, even when they had experienced advancement in the past.

- *Income levels:* Occupations considered as careers typically pay more than jobs. However, a surprisingly small number of people in the study used this as the criterion to differentiate between and job and a career.

- *Income motivation:* Distinct from how much one earns is the notion of how motivated one is by income. Do people do a job because they get paid to do it, or do they have other reasons?

According to Pixley, people see themselves as having careers if they have strong emotional commitment to their work, have invested significant time in developing and maintaining their professional identity, earn reasonable compensation, and see their work as providing opportunities for future growth. Accordingly, many or most of us would see ourselves as having a career despite the fact that for many, identification with a particular organization is a thing of the past.

Our Career and Work–Life Model

The premise of this book is that careers still exist, but fewer and fewer occur within one organizational context (or even one particular industry). In addition, the changing nature of families has changed expectations for both men and women regarding what role they will aspire to in their workplace, what the balance will be between their work and nonwork roles, and how each of us ultimately defines success. Although it may have always been the case that each of us was responsible for managing our own career, today each individual must define his or her own view of success. We call this self-directed career model the protean career. In this new career model, some of the widely accepted conventional wisdom on careers has been changed, perhaps permanently (Table 1.1).

Table 1.1 Protean Versus Traditional Careers

Issue	Traditional Career	Protean Career
Who's in charge	Organization	Individual
Core values	Advancement	Freedom, growth
Degree of mobility	Low	High
Success criteria	Position, level, salary	Psychological success
Key attitudes	Organizational commitment	Work satisfaction, professional commitment

In this book, we base much of our thinking on this notion of the protean career. We assume that the individual is in charge of his or her career, is responsible for defining roles, boundaries, and balance, needs to navigate through many changes over the lifespan, and is the ultimate judge of his or her own success. Although we do not suggest that all careers are protean, we do see this as a significant shift in recent years as changes in society, employment, levels of education, family arrangements, and technology have revolutionized how we conceive of work and our careers.

The shift we observe toward more individually driven careers should not however be taken as a generalization that all careers and individuals adopt this career strategy. There are many people in all professions who continue to connect their careers strongly with an organizational identity. For them, following an organizational path is both desirable and preferable. Also, it is important to note that for those in low-wage work or those with limited education, the protean career may seem a somewhat abstract concept reserved for those of privilege. Many individuals and couples work tirelessly in order to meet the basic economic needs of their family. They may not often have a great degree of choice in mapping out a career strategy that maximizes their sense of fulfillment. Although we believe we should strive to help those at all economic levels make better, more informed vocational choices, we fully recognize that some people have a much greater range of choices than others.

The good news is that the remainder of this book follows a very logical and linear approach to careers. The bad news is that careers, especially these days, rarely follow such linear paths or logic. That said, we have sequenced the materials so that they can be followed and understood more easily (Figure 1.1).

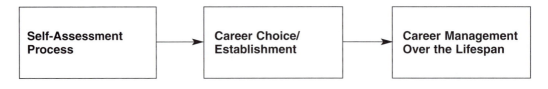

Figure 1.1   The Basic Framework of the Book

Chapter 2 of the book takes a step back from the externalities of the labor market and looks at the most important person in our discussion: you. The goal of the chapter is to help you generate a significant amount of useful information about you and your interests, goals, values, skills, and aspirations.

In chapter 3, this information is synthesized into a self-assessment profile that will be the foundation of plans for your career and work–life priorities. You will develop life themes that are grounded in the self-assessment materials you developed in chapter 2. You will also begin the process of determining what implications those themes have for your career and life choices.

Chapter 4 explores the challenges of making career choices. You will determine how to assess the labor market, develop the tools and the strategy needed to launch an effective job search, identify potential "ideal" employers, and think about how to make career decisions. In this section, we cover topics such as career information gathering, networking, and job search strategies.

In chapter 5 we lead you through many of the alternative ways to think about work today, from traditional, hierarchical roles to less conventional ways to structure your work life. We address ways to think about how your work life might meet your individual needs. We look at different contemporary career patterns. The new career contract has created more ways of thinking about and managing our careers. We explore these patterns in detail and discuss the upsides and downsides of these various approaches.

Chapter 6 explores specific issues and challenges in terms of work and family. First, we look at what unique career challenges are faced by women and by men. Although in recent years distinctions by gender have diminished, gender continues to have a large influence on how people view their careers and work–life issues. We discuss some of the unique challenges of working families today, specifically of dual-career couples. As we have discussed, making work and career decisions without understanding, weighing, and discussing the impact of these decisions on one's spouse, partner, family, or future family is a thing of the past. To provide a context for thinking about careers and career decision making in light of this reality, we explore the issues of operating in a dual-earner family. This information and the accompanying exercises provide a useful grounding for you to plan for your career over time.

Chapter 7 looks at various approaches individuals and organizations are using to meet the challenges presented by work and family. We review flexible work arrangements and family-friendly benefits and describe the advantages and challenges presented by various approaches.

Chapter 8 explores how careers evolve over time and over one's lifespan. Although such patterns are not nearly as stable or linear as they once were, the material gives the reader some basis on which to think about their work and their lives. Chapter 8 concludes with a summary of the key points of the book.

We hope this book offers a comprehensive view of the career process, from deciding what to do, to finding the place to do it, to succeeding over time. Always, we have tried to view careers in the context of one's overall life goals. Too often, career thinking and decision making are discussed outside that context, which is likely to lead to frustration and possibly failure in one's career or personal life (or both). We believe that reframing careers in a work–life context offers a more realistic view of how one thinks about and manages a career today and how one defines and achieves success.

For Further Reading

Bolles, R. (2007). *What color is your parachute? A practical manual for job-hunters and career-changers.* Berkeley, CA: Ten Speed Press.

Bronson, P. (2003). *What should I do with my life? The true story of people who answered the ultimate question.* New York: Random House.

Hakim, C. (1994). *We are all self-employed: The new social contract for working in a changed world.* San Francisco: Berrett-Koehler.

Uchitelle, L. (2006). *The disposable American: Layoffs and their consequences.* New York: Knopf.

The Self-Assessment Process 2

What lies behind you and what lies before you are tiny matters compared to what lies within you.

—Ralph Waldo Emerson

As we have stated, fundamental shifts have occurred in recent years from the organizational career to individually driven careers. Although it has always been the case that individuals in some professions needed to be entrepreneurs (e.g., many doctors, lawyers, and plumbers), many professionals have expected that their careers would play out in an organizational setting. Today, however, many of us have come to the conclusion that we are all self-employed. Despite employers' assertions that "people are our most important asset," the fact is that no one cares as much about your career as you do.

Because the new career contract is with oneself and not with an organization, it is essential to develop the competencies needed to navigate a career and a life of fulfillment and balance. People change jobs, organizations, and even careers with far greater frequency than ever before. In addition, the complexity and dynamism of the labor market are greater than ever. The kinds of jobs that can be constructed today challenge our traditional notions of what is possible. (A generation ago, few people would have believed it was possible to live in Boston and commute to a job in California.) In view of the high percentage of working couples today and the stresses of one's home life and children, there is little time to reflect. Taking time to get grounded in a clear sense of who we are, what we can and want to do, and what priorities will drive our decision making is extremely important.

The late Peter Drucker said that managing oneself has become a skill that everyone must possess in today's labor market. He observed that, in contrast to the past, where the ability to manage oneself was a skill needed and possessed by only a few exceptional individuals, today it is needed by nearly all. In the past, Drucker explained, because people followed careers that were prescribed by what their parents had done (e.g., farmers' children became farmers, carpenters' children became carpenters), there was little need to analyze one's own career interests, values, and options. Today, by contrast, we are faced with many choices that we need to sort through:

> Now, most of us, even those with modest endowments, will have to learn to manage ourselves. We will have to learn to develop ourselves. We will have to place ourselves where we can make the greatest contribution. And we will have to stay mentally alert and engaged during a 50-year working life, which means knowing how and when to change the work we do. (Drucker, 1999, pp. 65–66)

William Bridges, the author of *Job Shift* (1994) and *Transitions* (1980), has taken this message even further. In 1997 Bridges published *Creating You & Co.,* a book intended to help everyone "learn to think like the CEO of your own career." Bridges contends that jobs are increasingly becoming a thing of the past and that "more and more of the work that must be done today is being done by people who do not hold 'jobs' at the company that needs the work done" (Bridges, 1997, p. 8).

The Basic Areas of Self-Assessment

Critical to managing one's career and integrating work with the other parts of one's life is a clear self-awareness, or a sense of *identity*—knowing who we truly are. There are many different ways, both structured and unstructured, to come to know oneself. These include reflection, meditation, asking for feedback from others, psychotherapy, or just plain being self-aware. For the purpose of our career development work, let's assume that the best, or at least the most teachable, means for achieving this self-awareness is through a rigorous self-assessment process. This idea is hardly novel. Many career books, career courses, and guidance by professionals are based on this premise. The goal in this undertaking is to give you some insight and practice at the process of generating information about yourself and then using that information in a structured way to develop a comprehensive self-understanding.

There are many different things you could want to know about yourself to achieve an appropriate and complete level of self-understanding. The areas that seem to be the most frequently cited in career literature include the following:

- Understanding your background, your experiences, and the likes and dislikes that can be identified from a review of your history
- Clarifying your values
- Understanding your interests and passions
- Understanding your preferred lifestyle
- Identifying your life goals and personal vision
- Inventorying your skills

Drucker stresses many of the same points in "Managing Oneself." He states that the important areas to understand include the following:

- *What are my strengths?* Drucker thinks people need more insight in this area. He suggests that the use of feedback analysis (i.e., from oneself or from others) is the best way to develop this skill. He also suggests that it may take 2 to 3 years to develop a thorough self-understanding but that this is the most important understanding to develop.

- *How do I perform?* How one likes to work and works best is as important to Drucker as what one works at. He suggests that knowing how one gets things done is a matter of personality. In this area of self-awareness, he emphasizes the importance of knowing how you learn (e.g., by listening, by writing, by talking, alone or in a team).

- *What are my values?* How do I establish what is important to me in the way I operate and in the way my employer operates? If there is conflict between the two sets of values (the organization's and my own), can these be resolved? Drucker writes, "A person's values must be compatible with the organization's values. They do not need to be the same, but they must be close enough to co-exist" (1999, p. 70).

You can generate the information you need to get a handle on each area of self-assessment by using a number of structured exercises and instruments that this book will lead you through. For many of these activities, there is a high correlation between the time invested and the usefulness of the information.

For exercises or activities that rely on a review of one's background, as the Career Autobiography Exercise does, the more depth and detail provided, the greater the likelihood that the data can be mined for important clues about you and your motivations.

REFLECTING ON THE PAST

Perhaps paradoxically, before you plan for the future direction of your work, it helps tremendously to review your past experiences. Especially if you have significant work experience, there may be no source of career information that is more useful than learning from your past.

In most career counseling relationships, the counselor begins by asking the client (either verbally or in writing) to provide an in-depth historical background that provides a context for the counselor. This history often goes deep into the client's past and provides detailed information on things such as earliest childhood memories, parents and parental relationships, socioeconomic status, education, job history, and critical experiences that helped shape the client's views. One of the most useful parts of the self-assessment process is a detailed career autobiography. It will allow you to reflect on the entire range of experiences you have had, both work related and nonwork related, and later explore this document for important themes and trends.

The following are two alternative exercises for self-exploration: the development of an autobiography and a peak experiences exercise. The autobiography takes the most effort but can be the most enlightening. However, both are useful methods of self-discovery and probably the most important components of this process.

SELF-DISCOVERY EXERCISES

Alternative 1: The Career Autobiography

The Career Autobiography is a written interview that asks you to tell your story. If we could work directly with you as your career counselors, we would begin our first meeting by asking some open-ended questions that would help us learn as much as possible about your background, your influences, and the things that matter most to you. Because as you go through this book, you will be acting as your own career counselor, this exercise will provide you with the same background and detail. Writing your autobiography may seem strange, but you will understand your past much better when you have taken the time to write it down. And you will probably be surprised at the new insights into your own experiences that this autobiography will help you discover.

If the autobiography is typed (double spaced) it will probably take 15–20 pages to tell your story, but it could be much longer. The more fully you answer each question, the more useful the autobiography will be to you. Please answer each question in as much detail as possible before moving to the next question. As you address the subsequent questions, incorporate your answers into the text in the place you think is most appropriate chronologically (e.g., integrate answers about your earliest experiences into the beginning of your autobiography). This way, the final product should read as a chronological story.

In our experience, although completing the autobiography is one of the most valuable activities in a rigorous self-assessment process, it is also the most time-consuming. Therefore, we recognize that not everyone will complete this activity (unless they are required to do so as part of a course on the topic of career management). Although we recognize the challenge for many readers in completing such an in-depth activity, we encourage everyone to give it a try. Beyond its value for self-assessment purposes, we believe you will also find the process of writing your life's history to be enlightening. It will bring back many memories and remind you of many experiences from your life that you have not thought about for quite some time.

Career Autobiography Questions

1. Tell your life's story. Talk about who you are, where you've come from, what experiences you've had, and what has brought you to where you are today.

2. If you have not done so, add to your autobiography by going back to begin with your earliest recollections.

3. Talk about your working life. What kinds of work experiences have you had? (These can be paid experiences, volunteer work, student activities, or any leadership positions that have taken a lot of time.) What did you like or dislike about these experiences?

4. What have been the major turning points and transitions in your work life?

5. Who have been your influencers (e.g., parents, teachers, role models) in your school and work lives? Why were they so influential? What did your parents do for work? In what ways did their work and work experiences formulate or influence your thinking about work and careers?

6. What have been some of your most enjoyable work experiences? Why? What have been some roles that you have not enjoyed? Why?

7. Have there been a few peak experiences you have had in your life or work life? What about the experience, the environment, the team, or the situation made these particularly memorable?

Alternative 2: The Peak Experiences Exercise

Because not all readers will be able to complete the autobiography, the Peak Experiences Exercise can be used to get at some of the same information. In this activity you are asked to reflect on 5 to 10 experiences in your life that you would list as highlights. For each one, write why it felt like a peak experience. These experiences need not be times when you won an award in a sport or received an "A" for a school project (although these certainly may be viewed as peak moments). Rather, these should describe times when you felt particularly happy, successful, fulfilled, or at peace, or simply when you felt the most like yourself. Table 2.1 lists some examples from Brad.

(Continued)

(Continued)

Table 2.1   Sample of Completed Peak Experiences Exercise

Peak Experience	Description of the Experience	Why It Was a Peak Experience
1. The birth of our daughter Maggie	Maggie was our first child. The pregnancy included many scary moments where we thought things had gone wrong. Finally, after a trying pregnancy, I was in New Hampshire at a company off-site, about 140 miles from home. I received a call that Annie was on her way to the doctor 3 weeks ahead of schedule and "this was the moment." I drove like a crazy person and made it to the hospital just a short time before the delivery. We received an amazing outpouring of support from family, friends, and work colleagues.	1. There was a lot of fear throughout the pregnancy that things might not work out. When everything did, it was an amazing feeling of joy mixed with some relief. 2. I felt very centered. My mind was focused on one thing: the family and our new addition. That level of focus is a rare occurrence for me. There were no other distractions. I spent 2 weeks just being home with the family, not allowing work interruptions. 3. That weekend we received many gifts, flowers, and phone calls from loved ones. It made me appreciate how many people we were connected to in our lives.
2. Graduation after completing my doctorate	It was a special weekend. On Friday night, Annie hosted a fairly large gathering of my friends at our house to celebrate. On Saturday was the "hooding" ceremony at BU, which Annie and the girls attended. Sunday was graduation that my mother, brother, and sister and their spouses attended, and afterwards we had a nice dinner out with all of them.	1. I had worked 5 years on a doctorate, continuing to work, often full time. 2. I was inducted into two honor societies because of my academic performance. 3. I completed my dissertation, and it was accepted by my committee without revision. 4. I felt I had made up for my less stellar academic performance from my college days.
3. My years living in England	From 1988 to 1991, I lived in England. I loved almost everything about the experience, especially the opportunity to live in a foreign country and visit so many wonderful places in Europe. I also thrived	1. I proved something to myself regarding my ability to succeed in building a life for myself in a place where I knew no one starting out. 2. I had a great deal of quiet time and time for introspection. There were few distractions and not

Peak Experience	Description of the Experience	Why It Was a Peak Experience
	professionally during this period.	many responsibilities other than my work. 3. I had the opportunity to spend time appreciating the beauty of Europe, its arts, and its architecture. 4. I advanced my career and my professional reputation significantly through this experience.
4. My fist years coaching youth soccer	From 2001 to 2004, I coached girls' youth soccer for my daughters, Maggie and Hannah.	1. Having fun with a team of young kids as they got their first exposure to an organized sport. I resolved not to worry about winning and losing, and this made the experience pure fun. 2. Offering the kids gentle instruction and tips on the game (at which I was not necessarily an expert).

IDENTITY AS A CORE COMPETENCE

There are two meta-competencies in managing and sustaining the protean career: *identity* and *adaptability*. In this context identity is something akin to self-knowledge or self-awareness.

We can differentiate between *personal identity* and *social identity*. Personal identity consists of the parts of your self-image that are unique to you. Social identity consists of the portions of your identity that derive from being a member of a particular group, such as your gender, nationality, or race.

Related to the concept of social identities are multiple *subidentities*. "Each subidentity is the view of self in a particular social role (such as worker, mother, father, community member). The role represents the expectations held by significant others in the role set, while the subidentity represents self perceptions as one responds to these role expectations" (Hall, 2001, p. 25).

In many Western cultures, the development of one's personal sense of identity is closely tied to the establishment of one's career identity. Personal and professional identity often are very closely linked with one another, sometimes so much that the question "What do you do?" has become a socially acceptable ways of asking, "Who are you?" (Hall & Associates, 1996,

p. 170). Although many of us use our career as a surrogate for identity, the question of identity tries to get to the deeper question of "Who is the real me?" The concept of identity has two facets. One is the *content* of what you know about yourself (e.g., your particular values, interests, and goals). The other is your *skill in learning more about yourself*. What you are doing as you go through this book is helping you in both areas. You are learning more about yourself, and you are learning the *skills of self-assessment*, which are lifelong skills that you can use at any stage in your career.

THE IDENTITIES EXERCISE

When thinking about our identity, we can sometimes fall into the trap of oversimplifying the process (e.g., "I am an accountant," "I am a New Yorker," "I am a stay-at-home mother") or tend to accentuate one domain of our lives over others. As we have just suggested, in many modern cultures professional identity often is dominant.

For this exercise, take a few minutes to think about your primary sources of identity. Start with your work role but think about what other areas make up your other important subidentities.

1. First, simply list each of these identities.

2. Next, for each area, describe how this subidentity defines your self-concept.

3. Finally, describe how each influences your priorities and your actions, especially in relation to your work.

For example, if you listed one of your subidentities as parent, you might fill out that section of the table as shown in Table 2.2.

Table 2.2   Sample of Completed Identities Exercise

Areas of Identity	How Does It Define Your Self-Concept or Views?	How Does It Influence Your Priorities and Actions?
Parent	• Provides an enormous sense of pride and self-esteem. • Makes me think about my self-concept as less about me as an individual and more about my role as a family member. • Makes me see myself more in the role of provider.	• Plays a dominant role in occupying my time and energy. Other than work, most of my time is spent in domestic work or child rearing. • Helps (forces?) me to take a more balanced view of my work life.

Areas of Identity	How Does It Define Your Self-Concept or Views?	How Does It Influence Your Priorities and Actions?
	• My self-concept is influenced not only by how I behave and whether I succeed or fail but also by my spouse's and children's successes and setbacks.	• Affects my career in that I do not make career decisions without giving primary consideration to how it would affect my family. • At the same time, strengthens my commitment to earning enough to provide a good standard of living for my family.

The goal of this exercise is to help you think about two things. First, from the standpoint of your subidentities, how do your various roles influence how you see yourself, what you do, and how you do it? Second, from a social identity perspective, how does your affiliation with certain groups influence the way you act and the way you view the world? Table 2.3 is offered as a template, but you should feel free to create your own categories of subidentities.

Table 2.3   Identity Exercise Template

Areas of Identity	How Does It Define Your Self-Concept or Views?	How Does It Influence Your Priorities and Actions?
Professional or vocational role		
Employing organization		
Family roles		
Ethnic group or race		
Hobbies and avocations		
Community membership		

(Continued)

(Continued)

Areas of Identity	How Does It Define Your Self-Concept or Views?	How Does It Influence Your Priorities and Actions?
Religious affiliation		
Volunteer activities		
Political affiliation		
Socioeconomic group		

CLARIFYING YOUR VALUES

One of the most important determinants of career satisfaction relates to an individual's values and the degree to which those values can be expressed in one's chosen career. The *American Heritage Dictionary* (1996) defines values as "principles, standards, or qualities considered worthwhile or desirable, to regard highly, to rate according to relative estimate of worth or desirability" (p. 1972).

The terrible events of September 11, 2001, put the notion of values front and center in discussions of work and life. After that day, a number of trends became evident:

• People were asking questions about the work they had chosen. The fundamental questions of working for the right reasons seemed to resonate with many. People explicitly stated that doing work they believed in and work that benefited society had become a much higher priority.

• The kind of organization people worked for also took on new meaning. Suddenly, working for organizations in the public or the not-for-profit sector was seen as more attractive, even though compensation in these sectors often was lower than in the private sector. In addition, those in the private sector felt it was important to be affiliated with an organization that did more than simply make profits. Organizations that had a strong business ethic and those that were seen as "giving back" to society became more attractive.

• The issue of work–life balance took on new importance. Many people, in all walks of life, began to ask themselves whether their fundamental view of work had been blown out of proportion with respect to other elements of their lives.

Values consist of what one finds desirable or good. A person's values guide actions in two ways:

> First, they provide a kind of moral "road map" for the individual, representing internalized guidelines about morality or ethically good or bad ways to behave. Second, values indicate the attractiveness to the person of various objects, behaviors, and experiences, not so much in moral terms as in terms of amounts of pleasure (or frustration) they provide him. (Hall, 1976, p. 105)

The process of identifying and understanding one's values is an important step in the self-assessment process. *Values clarification* is the term used to describe the process of assessing the relative importance of values to an individual. There are at least two points to make about this process. The list of potential values is enormous. First, overemphasis on one value can lead to inappropriate career decisions. Human resource personnel often find that salary is a matter of the utmost concern for job seekers. Other issues such as work environment, managers, and work colleagues seem to be second-order priorities compared with salary. Surprisingly, even benefits that are of tangible financial value do not seem to carry nearly the weight with applicants that salary does.

Second, values often come into conflict with one another. It is easy to say that you value many things that sound worthwhile or noble: helping society, earning a lot of money, making contributions to your field, achieving work–life balance, operating with integrity, attaining high levels in the organization you work for, and so on. The issue one needs to wrestle with is, "When values conflict, which ones matter most?" What are the things you can't or won't compromise, because they are truly at the core of your identity?

Chris Argyris and Donald Schon present the notions of *espoused theory* and *theory-in-use* in their work on organizational learning. Espoused theory is the theory of action to which a person gives allegiance and communicates to others. Theory-in-use is the theory that actually governs a person's behavior. This theory-in-use may or may not be compatible with a person's espoused theory. Furthermore, the person may or may not be aware of the incompatibility of the two theories (Argyris & Schon, 1978, 1995). For example, it is often the case that managers publicly state their commitment to two lines of reasoning in their decision-making process that conflict with one another (e.g., "I believe in the abilities and intelligence of our management team" and "I believe in holding people accountable to their commitments and 'no-excuses' management"). Although Argyris uses the terms *espoused theory* and *theory-in-use* to describe a person's thought process, it is easy to apply this same notion in reference to values (e.g., "I give lip service to Value A but truly support Value B").

The desirability of certain values is influenced by the social environment and the surrounding culture, including the culture of one's relationships, one's employer, the community, or society at large. Therefore, certain values can be viewed as more socially acceptable than others. For example, in an organizational culture that puts a high emphasis on achievement, goal attainment, or status, it might be difficult (or perhaps even self-destructive from a career standpoint) to espouse values such as work–life balance or to not seek higher levels of responsibility. Likewise, it may be difficult in an environment that prides itself on teamwork and democratic management approaches to be overtly ambitious or visibly seek power.

In *Values and Teaching* (1966) Louis Rath identifies three basic factors of a value: prizing, choosing, and acting. We define these as follows:

1. *Prizing:* What do I espouse as a value?
   a. Do you feel strongly about and cherish a position on this issue?
   b. Do you speak in public about a prize position, affirming it with conviction when appropriate?

2. *Choosing* (reactive): When I am forced to make a choice, does the value generally carry a great deal of weight in my decision-making?
   a. Do you consider the alternatives available to you before taking a position?
   b. Do you examine the consequences of a position before taking it?
   c. Do you select a position independent of external pressures to feel, think, or act in a given way?

3. *Acting* (proactive): When I make my plan for the day, do I consistently look for ways to make time to exhibit this value in my actions?
   a. Do you back up your feelings and beliefs with action?
   b. Do you act on your feelings and beliefs consistently?

To understand this framework from a practical perspective, there is perhaps no easier example than one's approach to health and fitness. You might happily espouse the virtues of physical fitness as leading to an overall better standard of life (prizing). But when faced with a choice (choosing), such as the choice between completing a work project and exercising, you might almost always forgo exercise in favor of this other activity. The fact that the work project is important and consistent with other values (doing good work, earning a living) makes it easier to rationalize the incongruence between your espoused values and your actions.

EXERCISES IN VALUE CLARIFICATION

Alternative 1: Career Values Card Sort

A very effective and efficient way to clarify values is to use the Career Values Card Sort. This activity was developed by Richard Knowdell (1998), a well-known career counselor, and can be ordered through Career Trainer (http://www.CareerTrainer.com).

The cards contain a comprehensive list of many things a person might value in his or her work. For example, do you value security in your work? Adventure? Working independently? Helping society? Influencing people? After reviewing the list of more than 50 items, you can also add values that might apply to you but were not included in the cards.

Find a large space, such as your kitchen table, where you will have plenty of room to move the cards around. Then sort the cards into five columns—"Always Valued," "Often Valued," "Sometimes Valued," "Seldom Valued," and "Never Valued"—based on the extent to which you express each value in your everyday life. Is this something that you always value? Is it a value that you often express? Sometimes express? Seldom express? Or is it something that you never value and have little or no desire to express in your daily work and life? Feel free to move cards from one pile to another as you give the values more thought.

There is one rule in this sorting, however: You can put only eight value cards in the "Always Valued" pile. You will find it difficult to limit yourself to eight values in this top category, and you will probably put more there initially. One criterion to help you decide is the following: Is this a value that means so much to me that, if I couldn't express this value, I wouldn't be me? There is no limit to the number of cards that you can have in the other piles. When you are satisfied that the values in the "Always Valued" category represent the real you, the sorting is completed. Record a summary of your prioritized values.

Alternative 2: Developing a List of Values

Another value-clarifying exercise is to create your own set of value cards. Get a set of 40 blank notecards, or use the backs of business cards. (Actually, cards the size of business cards work very well.) Write the name of one thing you value highly on the back of each card. These can include things such as achievement, high status, money, leadership positions, travel, and free time. Identify your top eight values from the cards you have completed.

Now that you have clarified and prioritized your values, where do you go from there? Richard Knowdell (1998) suggests that one important way of applying your "Always Valued" values is to hold them up against a decision or problem that you are trying to work through. Here is a process for doing that. At the top of a page, describe a current career or life decision or choice that you are considering (Table 2.4). Examples might be the decision to look for a new job, to accept a particular job offer, to move to a certain location, or to marry a certain person. Then add the three column headers indicated in Table 2.4.

(Continued)

(Continued)

Table 2.4   Value Conflict Analysis

Career or Life Decision: _____

Top 8 Values	Value Fit (S, C, or NR)	Resolving Conflicts
1.		
2.		
3.		
4.		
5.		
6.		
7.		
8.		

Write your top eight values in the left-hand column. Now, for each value, ask yourself how that value fits with this decision. For example, say you are thinking about accepting a certain job offer, and the first value in your list is security. Would this new job offer provide you with a lot of security? If so, write an *S* in the middle column, indicating that this value *supports* making this decision. Or would you be working for a boss with a reputation for very high turnover in his group and for firing people for their first mistake? If so, write a *C* in the middle column, indicating that your value for security *conflicts* with this decision. Or would this job be so exciting to you and give you such good opportunities to succeed and get recognition that these benefits would make security far less salient to you in that position? In that case, for *Not Relevant,* write *NR*. Do this for each value.

Next, look over your entries for the middle column for each value. For each *C*, write in the right-hand column an idea for how you might resolve that conflict between the decision and that value. For example, in the case of a boss who creates insecurity, perhaps you could explore options for working in a different department, with a different boss.

Finally, look at the pattern of entries in your middle column. If you have a lot of *C*s, are you able to find reasonable ways to resolve these conflicts? If you have a lot of *S*s, what question does that raise for you? How about, "Why haven't I already acted on this decision?" And if you have a lot of *NR*s, what question does that raise? What does it mean that you are seriously considering a major life or career decision, but you are saying that this decision is not relevant to the values you hold most dear?

To conclude this value clarification exercise, complete the following sentence: "As a result of this exercise, I learned that I _____."

UNDERSTANDING YOUR INTERESTS AND PASSIONS

One of the most fundamental determinants of whether work will be enjoyable and meaningful is rooted in the notion of interests and passions. One could view these two terms (*interests* and *passions*) as either quite similar or very different depending on one's perspective. For us, these two concepts differ mainly in intensity. An interest taken to an extreme becomes a passion.

People like to do things that they are interested in, whether they are hobbies or paid work. Most successful people probably would say that their work is their interest; highly successful people often see their work as their passion. Poet Donald Hall refers to the state of *absorbedness* when describing how he feels when he is at work. In a passage from *Life Work* (1993) he describes in detail the joy of finding work that is an expression of oneself. He differentiates work from other forms of activity that generate income:

> Work, I make a living at it. Almost twenty years ago I quit teaching—giving up tenure, health insurance, and annual raises—as one of my children began college and the other was about to begin. I worked like crazy to pay tuitions and mortgages—but because I loved my work it was as if I did not work at all.
>
> There are jobs, there are chores, and there is work. Reading proofs is a chore; checking facts is a chore. When I edit for a magazine or a publisher, I do a job. When I taught school, the classroom fit none of these categories. I enjoyed teaching James Joyce and Thomas Wyatt too much to call it a job. The classroom was a lark because I got to show off, to read poems aloud, to help the young, and to praise authors or books that I loved. But teaching was not entirely larkish; correcting piles of papers is tedious, even discouraging, because it tends to correct one's sanguine notions about having altered the young minds arranged in the classroom's rows. Reading papers is a chore—and after every ten papers, I might tell myself I could take a break and read a Flannery O'Connor short story. But when I completed the whole pile, then I could reward myself with a real break. When I finished reading and correcting and grading and commenting on seventy-five essay-questions about a Ben Jonson or a Tom Clark poem, *then*—as a reward—I could get to work. (p. 4)

Finding one's passion is not always easy. Sometime the process is slow and evolving; at other times, it can be the result of a sudden jolt. As Richard Boyatzis and his colleagues wrote in "Reawakening Your Passion for Work," "We all struggle with the question of personal meaning throughout our lives. September 11, 2001, brought the issue into focus for many people all at once, but the impulse to take stock comes up periodically for most of us in far less dramatic circumstances. . . . The process is rarely easy, but we've found this type of awakening to be healthy and necessary. . . . Leaders cannot keep achieving new goals and inspiring people around them without understanding their own dreams" (Boyatzis, McKee, & Goleman, 2002, p. 5).

Boyatzis et al. suggest that the best ways to get in touch with your passions include reflecting on the past, defining your principles for living, and envisioning the future. Sound familiar? It should, as it closely resembles many of the activities we discussed in this chapter.

EXERCISES IN CLARIFYING INTERESTS

Alternative 1: The Strong Interest Inventory

For 80 years, the Strong Interest Inventory (SII) assessment has helped people find a link between their life interests and their life's work. Organizations have also used the SII to attract and develop talent. Generally regarded as the most respected and widely used career planning instrument in the world, the newly revised SII provides a wealth of information that includes the following:

- 6 updated general occupational themes: These themes, based on the work of John Holland, outline six personality types that align with occupations. The six themes are *Realistic* (the doers), *Investigative* (the thinkers), *Artistic* (the creators), *Social* (the helpers), *Enterprising* (the persuaders), and *Conventional* (the organizers).

- 30 basic interest scales that identify specific interest areas within each of the six themes, indicating areas and activities that are likely to be the most rewarding to you. These interest areas cover a broad spectrum of job-related roles, including sales, management, law, performing arts, writing, social sciences, counseling and helping, teaching, finance and investing, computers, research and medical sciences, technology, and entrepreneurship.

- 244 occupational scales: In this section, your scores on the inventory are compared with those of people who are happily and successfully employed in more than 120 jobs. These jobs cover a broad spectrum of positions in business, government, healthcare, the military, service occupations, and many more.

- Personal Style Scale: The newest version of the SII also has a five-element Personal Style Scale that can help you assess your style with reference to learning, leadership, risk taking, work style, and team orientation.

The SII's popularity is based on the fact that it has a very high degree of validity and reliability and on the richness of information it provides to its users. Unfortunately, the SII can be administered only by a licensed and certified counselor, who will help you interpret your results. Fortunately, many colleges, universities, and career coun-selors are trained to use this instrument, and it is a highly effective way to match your life interests with potential career options.

Alternative 2: The Campbell Interest and Skills Survey

The Campbell Interest and Skills Survey (CISS), developed by psychologist David Campbell (formerly of "Strong Campbell" fame), is a tool that can help you find the kind of work environment and roles that would be a good fit for you. Like the SII, the CISS measures your interests, or activities that you like to do. Interests are very sta-ble over the lifespan. Even interests that are measured at one point in life, say at age 17 in high school, correlate very highly (around .70) with interests measured as much as 20 years later. In addition to interests, the CISS also asks users to assess their skills, or activities that they are good at. You can arrange to take the CISS at https://www.profiler.com/cgi-bin/ciss/moreform.pl?client=ncs&page=intro.

When you review the results of your CISS, do not take the occupational descrip-tions too literally. Try to look for patterns and themes in your results. For example, do the occupations listed have certain qualities in common, such as a lot of people con-tact or a lot of investigative work? It is important to see what the underlying nature of all of the occupations is rather than looking at specific jobs.

In a similar way, if an occupation is listed that seems strange or unlikely for you, try to look beneath the surface to determine what features of that job might be the critical ones. For example, it is not uncommon for business school students to get a high score for Funeral Director. Not too many business school graduates become funeral directors, but consider what this works involves. A funeral director runs a small business and often has a lot of entrepreneurial qualities. There is a lot of people contact, the funeral director deals with a lot of stress and emotion, and good finan-cial and technical management skills are required. Jobs in marketing, operations management, and human resource management have a lot of overlap with this type of work. The online materials for the CISS provide more detailed information about how to interpret and use your own results.

Alternative 3: The Business Career Interest Inventory

The Business Career Interest Inventory (BCII), part of the self-assessment program called Career Leader®, developed by Timothy Butler and James Waldroop, is also a measure of interests, but it is more specialized, focusing on business careers. (The CISS covers all kinds of occupations.) Here is how the Web site for the BCII describes the process of using it:

- First you take our proprietary tests. Using the Business Career Interest Inventory (BCII) we help you define your "career interest universe." Your unique pattern of interests defines a *universe* of possible careers in which you could find a way

(Continued)

(Continued)

to express those interests. Then we use the Management and Professional Reward Profile (MPRP) to help you to *focus* that universe by assessing your values concerning the rewards you want to get back from your work. Lastly, we use an abilities assessment inventory, the Management and Professional Abilities Profile (MPAP), to help you focus still further by thinking in a systematic way about your business skill strengths and weaknesses and the implications of these strengths and weaknesses for different career paths.

- With all of the information in hand, we combine it and compare your integrated profile against the opportunities available (or not available) in more than 20 major business career paths, in order to recommend that you investigate those careers further. We then provide details about each career (what it's about, what interests you'll be able to express, which work rewards are typically available, and what skills are necessary), showing why we think a given career is (or is not) a good match for you.

- Then we use two ways of assessing your fit with critical elements of corporate culture, to make sure that you are able to find the right work environment in which to pursue your career. Lastly, we offer an assessment of potential career breakdowns, those "Achilles' Heels" that can derail you if you are not aware of them and adjust your forward progress accordingly (http://www.careerdiscovery.com/guided_tour.html).

SOURCE: Copyright © 1997–2006 Peregrine Partners.

If this instrument looks useful, please go http://www.careerdiscovery.com to take the BCII. (If you are a student or an alumnus of one of the colleges or universities on their list, you can receive a discounted rate for the instrument.)

LIFESTYLE

In his famous book *Walden,* Henry David Thoreau wrote, "I came to the woods because I wished to live deliberately, to front only the essential facts of life, and see if I could not learn what it had to teach, and not, when I came to die, discover that I had not lived. I did not wish to live what was not life, living is so dear, nor did I wish to practice resignation, unless it was quite necessary. I wanted to live deep and suck out all the marrow of life."

Not many of us would make the lifestyle choice that Thoreau did when he chose to live as a recluse for 2 years in a small cabin at Walden Pond in Concord, Massachusetts. But each of us makes important choices about our lifestyle. It can be thought of as a way of life or living style that reflects the values and attitudes of the person. Lifestyle is something that is frequently discussed today, perhaps more than ever, and is affected by the work people do and the environment in which they do it.

Lifestyle can refer to a person's relationship with a whole range of activities, such as

- The kind of work one does
- The number of hours one works
- The type of people with whom one works
- The kind of town or community one chooses to live in
- The length of one's daily commute
- The degree to which one is involved in the community, society, or environment
- The degree to which one conforms or chooses not to conform to traditions and norms
- The size of one's home
- The number of one's possessions
- The hobbies and activities one chooses to engage in

Career and work are a subset of one's lifestyle. For those who work full time, perhaps no other component of one's life has a greater bearing on lifestyle than one's work. This is true for a number of reasons. First, work (including getting ready for work and commuting to and from work) takes up a large percentage of one's day. An average person might spend two thirds of his or her waking hours in activities related to work on the days he or she is working. Second, the kind of work one does can have a profound bearing on the places one can live. Often jobs are a major factor in considering whether living in a rural environment is feasible, for example (although the connection between work and where one lives is becoming less direct as more and more people use technology to explore alternative work arrangements). Third, the income one derives from working can dictate or at least strongly influence one's lifestyle choices. For example, one may want to work on a part-time basis, but if one's work does not provide sufficient income, this choice may prove infeasible or at least difficult. Finally, one's work can also influence the kind of out-of-work activities one can engage in (e.g., Do work travel demands minimize time for or make community involvement impossible? Does work income allow you to join expensive country clubs?).

On some level, we live in a conflicted time when it comes to lifestyle. Everywhere in suburban America, enormous houses are being built that are far beyond the needs of today's "normal family." The average U.S. family in the year 2000 was only 2.6 people. At the same time, the average floor area of a house in the United States was 2,200 square feet, a 120% increase over the average house in 1950, although families are now smaller. It has been suggested that because of the shrinking size of families and the increasing size of dwellings, each individual now has as much living space as an entire family had 50 years ago. Such houses are expensive to build and maintain, and they add enormous expense in terms of utilities and furnishing. Many people also label commodities as "lifestyle necessities" that were unheard of in the past: third or fourth family cars; second homes; a phone in every room, car, and purse; and multiple computers and television sets. As Juliet Schor (1992) points out in *The Overworked American: The Unexpected Decline of Leisure,*

> We live in what may be the most consumer-oriented society in history. Americans spend three to four times as many hours a year shopping as their counterparts in Western European countries. Once purely a utilitarian chore, shopping has been elevated to the status of a national passion. (p. 107)

Schor goes on to point out that Americans' love affair with spending and their willingness to incur debt has played a major role in creating lifestyles that are increasingly dominated by work. Schor (1992) states, "As people became more accustomed to the materials rewards of prosperity, desires for leisure time were eroded. They increasingly looked to consumption to give satisfaction, even meaning to their lives" (p. 112). This work-and-spend cycle has created a lifestyle in which work must play a more central role in people's lives so that they can finance their "necessities." (It is worth noting here that not everyone agrees with Schor's contentions that Americans are caught up in a consumption trap. Recent works such as Warren and Tyagi's *The Two-Income Trap* (2003) contest this argument. These issues will be discussed later in the book.)

There also appears to be some momentum in the United States for what has been called the simplicity movement, or voluntary simplicity. This grassroots movement encourages people to seek lifestyles that are in contrast to the more consumerist attitudes of many Americans. It preaches a message of "less is more" and seeks to help people find ways to enjoy life without excess spending or material goods. Organizations that promote these approaches include The Center for a New American Dream (http://www.newdream.org) and the Third Path Institute (http://www.thirdpath.org).

Finally, the effect of people's schedules on their lifestyles seems to have changed profoundly in recent years. In large measure because of the increase in the percentage of working parents, both parents and children have seen their lives become more and more scheduled in recent years. Even leisure time isn't leisurely anymore.

LIFESTYLE REPRESENTATION EXERCISE

One of the early MBA courses on career planning was developed in the mid-1970s at Harvard Business School by a team of professors interested in helping MBA students plan their career transitions. The most recent version of the text for that class was published in 1992. In it, Clawson, Kotter, Faux, and McArthur (1992) used an assignment called Creating Life Style Representations to encourage their students to think about and creatively depict their lifestyles. According to the authors, "the assignment is to produce on paper a representation, non-narrative in nature, that will reflect your lifestyle as accurately as you can and provide you with data useful for analysis" (p. 117). Because the world has changed since the writing of Clawson and colleagues' book, we suggest you may also use a paperless approach (potentially a computer slide show or graphic) to convey your lifestyle today, especially if you are artistically challenged. The important thing is to

Not use narrative descriptions to describe your lifestyle

Be creative (e.g., use art, pictures, graphics, charts)

Think about all the elements that make up your lifestyle and their relative importance or place in your life

In the past, students have used a wide range of creative approaches to depict their lifestyles. Some of our favorites have included collages, artistic renderings, mobiles, bulletin boards, life maps, calendars, and custom-made DVDs.

UNDERSTANDING YOUR LIFE GOALS AND PERSONAL VISION

Closely tied to values is an expression of one's life goals. If you are having difficulty clarifying your values, an easy remedy might be to think about your life goals or an ideal future state. When you close your eyes and dream about your ideal life, what does the picture look like? Where are you living? What are you doing for work? Who surrounds you? Somewhere in the image you hold of the utopian future life probably is a strong indicator of your values.

If your life goals sound as if they are moving you out of the fast lane into a slower-paced life that speaks to your values, it may well suggest that fast pace and high earnings are not your highest priorities (unless, of course, you have been able to leave the rat race because you made so much money while you were a "rat"). But if your life goals have you running a major corporation before the age of 40, that also speaks volumes about your values and priorities. Knowing your aspirations and clarifying specifically what they are can help you gain a better sense of what is important to you and why.

In addition to providing clarity, understanding your goals can provide motivation. In *The Fifth Discipline*, Peter Senge (1990) discusses the concept of personal mastery, which he describes as "the discipline of continually clarifying and deepening our personal vision, of focusing our energies, of developing patience, and of seeing reality objectively." He states that "the roots of this discipline lie in both Eastern and Western Spiritual traditions, and in secular traditions as well" (p. 7). Senge states that the essence of personal mastery is learning to generate and maintain creative tension in our lives. Personal mastery embodies two underlying skills and abilities: continually clarifying what is important to us as individuals (i.e., our personal vision) and continually learning how to see current reality more clearly. The distance between one's personal vision and one's current reality is the force that Senge calls creative tension. This tension generates the motivation that drives people to achieve their life's calling and attain their personal vision.

2F LIFE GOALS AND PERSONAL VISION: THE 10-YEARS-OUT EXERCISE

The 10-Years-Out Exercise is intended to give you greater insight into what you hope your work and your career are leading you to. It is perfectly appropriate to be happy and content with your current state (that may be our ultimate aim: to find inner peace). At some point in your career and life, especially in the early years, you will probably find yourself dreaming of something more than or at least something different from your current state. Knowing your aspirations and clarifying specifically what they are will help you gain a better sense of what is important to you and why.

The 10-Years-Out Exercise will help you to achieve the first of Senge's objectives: clarifying what is important to you and articulating your personal vision. Before beginning to answer the questions, create the right environment for this exercise. Find a quiet, comfortable, peaceful place. Consider playing music that will put you in the right state of mind. Read the questions over once, close your eyes for a few moments, and try to create get a mental image (i.e., a personal vision) of your life 10 years from today. If you find that 10 years out is too long a timeframe for you, feel free to call this the 5-Years-Out Exercise and proceed using the same suggested process.

Remember to answer all the following questions as if the date is 10 (or 5) years from today!

10-Years-Out Exercise

1. What is the date today? How old are you?
2. Where and in what kind of environment are you living?
3. What is your family situation?

4. What kind of work are you doing?

5. Describe the institution or organization you work for.

6. What does your workplace look like? What kind of building do you work in? Where is it located? Is the environment urban? Rural?

7. Describe a typical work week or work day.

8. Do you work standard hours, or is your schedule flexible?

9. Describe your lifestyle.

10. Do you have much leisure time, and, if so, how do you spend it?

11. What is your financial situation?

12. Are you as happy as you thought you would be? Why or why not?

SKILL ASSESSMENT

Scottish poet Robert Burns ends his poem "To a Louse" with the hope, "O would some Power the gift to give us to see ourselves as others see us." Understanding your skills is another important element in building your self-assessment and developing your career plan. *Interests* tell you what you like to do, *values* tell you what you want to do, but *skills* tell you what you can do and at what level of proficiency you can do it. Awareness of one's strengths and weaknesses is a critical area in personal development and is elusive. As Warren Bennis (1989), a leading thinker in the field of leadership development, states,

> And [knowing oneself] it is still the most difficult task any of us faces. But until you truly know yourself, strengths and weaknesses, know what you want to do and why you want to do it, you cannot succeed in any but the most superficial sense of the word. The leader never lies to himself, especially about himself knows his flaws as well as his assets, and deals with them directly. (p. 80)

In *High Flyers: Developing the Next Generation of Leaders,* Morgan McCall (1998) stresses the importance of self-awareness as a key to development. He states that effective leaders are self-aware, which reflects what he calls the "ultimate form of self confidence" (p. 205). He goes on to state,

> Knowing one's weaknesses is power, because then something can be done about them; the real danger lies in what one doesn't know. Seeking out feedback, openness to criticism, and learning from

mistakes all distinguish managers considered high potential from those considered solid performers. Lack of awareness, whether through neglect or arrogance, is a major contributor to derailment. (p. 205)

Drucker (1999) makes many of the same points as Bennis and McCall and speaks of three specific implications for action from feedback (what you should do with this information once you have it). First, he says to concentrate on your strengths. Put yourself in work situations where you can maximize or exploit the strengths you have. Second, carefully analyze them to provide further understanding of how to improve on them and how to develop new ones. Finally, discover where your strengths could be. According to Drucker, many people who have great expertise in one area diminish the need to develop skills in other areas. They take pride in areas of ignorance, a trait he calls intellectual arrogance, and that is self-defeating (p. 66).

Although there are tests and assessments that can indicate what you are effective at, there are better sources of data about your strengths and weaknesses. You can probably gather good data from two or three of the sources discussed in this section.

Feedback From Class Experiences

By now you have had a significant amount of formal classroom experience. During your formal education, you have been required to take dozens of classes on a broad range of subjects (e.g., literature, math, business, science). This requirement has served many useful purposes, not the least of which is giving you an opportunity, albeit an academic one, to see what content areas you are good at and which ones you are not. Looking back on old transcripts and report cards probably will refresh your memory about the subject areas where you have displayed mastery and those that were more of a struggle.

Performance Evaluations

A different and perhaps more useful source of skill information from a job perspective might be performance evaluations. Most large organizations (and many smaller ones) have institutionalized some approach for providing formal written feedback to employees. Often, these are used

- To provide employees with a summary of their progress against goals over the past year
- To catalogue individual strengths and weaknesses

- As a basis for determining compensation
- As a basis for determining future development opportunities

Well-written evaluations often include a narrative, with the evaluator providing comments about the employee's performance. In addition, many evaluations are broken down into categories that discuss the individual's abilities in a number of core competency or skill areas. Often these categories include planning, project management, teamwork, customer satisfaction, productivity, quality, and so on.

While receiving a performance evaluation, many people wonder, "What is my overall rating?" or "How will this evaluation affect my salary?" As a result, they may overlook feedback that would be highly useful in planning for their development. Reviewing these evaluations later and for a different purpose (i.e., as data for self-assessment) can help you learn more and gain new insights.

The growing use of 360-degree feedback in recent years as part of the performance evaluation process is a testament to the importance of using feedback to develop strengths and to correct or at least ameliorate problem areas. As McCall (1998) states, "The recent popularity of 360-degree feedback, in which people compare self assessments with data from boss, peers, and subordinates, is a result of the potency of such comparisons. You cannot always be an unbiased observer of yourself, so finding more objective sources if feedback is a crucial component of development" (p. 206).

Feedback From Significant Others

Leveraging from the strengths of a 360-degree feedback exercise, one can also initiate a process of gathering useful feedback from others. Feedback from close work colleagues (including present or former managers, subordinates, and peers) provides one view of your skills, and other sources can also be highly useful. A spouse or significant other may be the best person to provide insights into your strengths and weaknesses and may be in the best position to do so candidly.

The important thing to remember is that although getting feedback is a critical part of knowing yourself, giving feedback can be a threatening activity for others. See the Interview With Significant Others Exercise for some ground rules that might prove useful in efforts to gather good, honest, and constructive feedback. Following these ground rules could dramatically enhance the quality and usefulness of the feedback you receive.

In addition to the insights others can provide, there is ample evidence that significant nonwork-related relationships also provide development. According to Parker (1996),

Theories of adult development, particularly those focused on women's development, have increasingly emphasized the extent to which personal development is driven by close interpersonal relationships at all stages of the life cycle (Gilligan, 1982, Kegan, 1982, Miller, 1991). For example, a parent may learn from his relationship with his child that he cannot be in control and that he may need to let go in order for the child to learn, and then he finds that his approach to subordinates learning has changed also. (p. 181)

As Professor Kathy Kram (1985, 1996), an expert on mentoring, points out, relationships can foster tremendous personal growth that allows the individual to enjoy higher levels of self-esteem and self-awareness that are useful at almost every stage of adult development. Feedback may be the critical link in that development.

INTERVIEW WITH SIGNIFICANT OTHERS

The purpose of this exercise is to get useful feedback about your skills and competencies from those who know you well and can offer useful insights. You can conduct this activity multiple times with people from different spheres of your life, including family members, close friends, work associates, people you work with in a volunteer capacity, and others who have seen you in action.

Before beginning your interviews, you should take the following steps:

1. Decide how many interviews you want to conduct. Be sure there is at least one from your work life and another from your home or personal life.

2. Select people to interview who know you well, have known you for a long time, and have somewhat intimate knowledge of how you operate. When you make arrangements for the session, you might want to mention the guidelines suggested below.

3. Schedule a time that is mutually convenient in a location that is private. Be sure you schedule at least 1 hour to ensure that you have time to get as much feedback as possible.

4. You will want to record the interviewee's comments in some way. You can take notes or, better still, tape record the session (with the permission of the interviewee). Reinforce with the interviewee that the data will be used only by you for the purpose of your own development and will not be shared with others. Prepare a form like the one in Table 2.5 to help you conduct the interview and record the interviewee's responses.

Table 2.5	Interview With Significant Others

1. **When you think about me, what are some adjectives or phrases that come to mind that you feel are good descriptors?**

2. **What do you consider to be my greatest strengths?**

3. **What do you consider to be my greatest weaknesses or areas for improvement?**

4. **Skill Areas**

   Please rate and comment on my skills in the following areas. You may assign a skill rating of "High," "Medium," or "Low." You should also feel free to answer "I don't know enough about you in this area to assign a rating" and then pass on to the next question without commenting. For areas where rating can be provided, comments are extremely useful. Please encourage the interviewees to elaborate as much as possible.

   a) **Analytical, problem-solving skills. Rating:** _____
      Comments:

   b) **Creativity and innovation. Rating:** _____
      Comments:

   c) **Thoroughness and follow-through. Rating:** _____
      Comments:

   d) **Interpersonal skills and teamwork abilities. Rating:** _____
      Comments:

   e) **Leadership abilities. Rating:** _____
      Comments:

(Continued)

(Continued)

f) **Ability to communicate and present ideas (verbally). Rating:** _____
   Comments:

g) **Ability to communicate and present ideas (in writing). Rating:** _____
   Comments:

h) **Ability to listen and convey empathy. Rating:** _____
   Comments:

i) **Drive and motivation. Rating:** _____
   Comments:

j) **Ability to work independently. Rating:** _____
   Comments:

k) **Flexibility and adaptability. Rating:** _____
   Comments:

l) **Planning and organization skills. Rating:** _____
   Comments:

m) **Self-knowledge and self-awareness. Rating:** _____
   Comments:

n) **Ability to maintain work–life balance and perspective. Rating:** _____
   Comments:

5. **If you could suggest three things I could do to improve my professional abilities, what would they be?**

6. **If you could suggest three things I could do to increase my sense of fulfillment in my work or personal life, what would they be?**

Guidelines for Encouraging Candid Feedback

- Let the interviewee (the person you are asking the questions) know that this information is for your own benefit only and will be used as a tool in an important career planning process that you are involved in.

- Communicate that you would welcome balanced feedback that discusses both strengths and weaknesses.

- Display active listening techniques:

  Sit attentively.

  Use nonverbal cues to show you are listening (e.g., head nods, "uh-huhs," occasionally paraphrase answers).

  Do not interrupt the speaker.

  Ask follow-up questions for clarity.

- Do not disagree with or debate the points the speaker makes.

- Do not try to explain your rationale for behaving in a given way.

- Occasionally ask for a concrete example, especially if the point being made is difficult for you to grasp or relate to.

Peer Feedback

Throughout the self-assessment process, we have emphasized that feedback from those who know you can be highly useful. Most often, as is the case in the Interview With Significant Others, this feedback will come from those who know you well. But here we encourage you to seek out someone who can develop a view of you from your data. The peer coaching activity provides the opportunity for someone who knows you mainly through the data you have generated in the self-assessment process to provide you with their feedback, thoughts, and suggestions.

PEER COACHING EXERCISE: GETTING ANOTHER VIEW

The first step in this exercise is to choose someone to be your peer coach. The person should be taking the same career class you are or be someone who might be able to analyze your data and give you useful feedback. The person should be willing to act as your peer coach, and you should feel comfortable sharing your data

(Continued)

(Continued)

with her or him. For the purposes of a class experience, it doesn't matter whether you knew the person before the course; in fact, it may be preferable if he or she has no prior knowledge of you. Either way, it is important that your peer coach focus the feedback on what she or he learns from reviewing your data.

The expectation is that your peer coach will review all your data in detail. This will take a significant amount of time because by now you have generated a lot of information. In addition, strict confidentiality must be maintained. Peer coaches will have access to highly personal data, and they must respect your privacy.

The process is as follows:

1. Provide your peer coach with all the data you have generated. It is important to use a copy of the documents so that your peer coach can mark up the material.

2. The peer coach should review the data in great detail. In reviewing the data, the peer coach should look for patterns or important themes that emerge from your data. About one week should be allowed for the review of data.

3. The peer coach should summarize her observations on a two- to three-page feedback sheet. This feedback should include a list of observations based on a reading of the data. Each observation should be supported by examples of where the observation comes from. For example, if your peer coach suggests that you have a strong inclination toward working in the arts, he or she should cite examples from sources such as your Career Autobiography, Interest Inventory, or 10-Years-Out exercises that validate this observation.

4. You and your coach should arrange a time to meet. The meeting should last at least 1 hour (or 2 hours if you are acting as peer coaches for each other) and should give ample time for reviewing the summary sheets, questions, and reactions from the coach or from each partner in the process. If the coach agrees, you can tape the session for later review.

The Peer Coaching Exercise and the summary sheet your coach provides will become another important source of data for the self-assessment paper you will write later. If it is well done, you may find the peer coaching feedback to be very helpful as you eventually develop your own summary or themes from your self-assessment data.

Summary

This chapter has been light on reading and heavy on doing. We firmly believe that the key to managing one's career is to have a clear sense of oneself. We call this competency identity. If one has a clear sense of identity, it will serve as the foundation for every other step in the career management process.

Identity is best developed through an active quest to generate information about oneself and then to understand that information in a coherent way. In this chapter we have asked you to look at your past experiences, interests, values, lifestyle, skills, and aspirations to better understand the elements that make up identity. In the next chapter we will describe a basic approach for integrating these disparate pieces of data into a more comprehensive picture of yourself. The investment in generating, understanding, and integrating these self-assessment materials will pay off in every subsequent step of the career development process and should help you build an effective basis for a meaningful professional and personal life.

For Further Reading

Boyatzis, R., McKee, A., & Goleman, D. (2002, April). Reawakening your passion for work. *Harvard Business Review, 80*(44), 86–94.

Clawson, J. G. (2003). *Level three leadership: Getting below the surface.* Upper Saddle River, NJ: Prentice Hall.

Drucker, P. F. (2005, January). Managing oneself. *Harvard Business Review, 83*(1), 100–109.

Schor, J. (1992). *The overworked American: The unexpected decline of leisure.* New York: Basic Books.

Sull, D. N., & Houlder, D. (2005, January). Do your commitments match your convictions? *Harvard Business Review, 83*(1), 82–91.

Integrating Your Self-Assessment and Developing Implications 3

A successful life is one that is lived through understanding and pursuing one's own path, not chasing after the dreams of others.

—Chin-Ning Chu

The critical next step in the self-assessment process involves taking all the information you have generated and making sense of it—not an easy task. The process of self-assessment that we have outlined begins with the notion that career satisfaction and career success depend on many factors. These factors include most importantly a clear sense of oneself, and developing this is a complex task. To this point we have asked you to develop information that will provide you with a clearer sense of your identity. This self-awareness is derived through no single source but rather through an understanding of your experiences, values, goals, interests, skills, and motivations. The instruments you have used and the information they have generated now must be integrated into a comprehensive picture.

Integrating Your Self-Assessment

The idea of using career data in a structured fashion to achieve greater self-understanding is hardly new (Bolles, 2007; Clawson, Kotter, Faux, & McArthur, 1992; Hall, 1976). Many writers in the career field have outlined a process of using summarized self-assessment data as a filter or focus for identifying appropriate career options and for managing one's career over time. The process we will use for distilling this self-assessment information into a comprehensive view borrows most heavily from the work that was done at Harvard Business School for the second-year elective course in the MBA program "Self-Assessment and Career Development." This innovative class, first taught at Harvard Business School in the mid-1970s, was developed to help students through the career transitions that many of them were making during their 2 years in business school and in their early careers (Clawson et al., 1992).

You have compiled a lot of detailed information about yourself. How do you pull it all together and make sense of it all? We offer two alternatives. The first and quickest way is a simple summary of the information, drawing implications for what your strengths and weaknesses are and possible actions for development. The second is a more thorough data analysis that will help you find the underlying themes in your self-assessment. The first alternative might be easier to do if you are using this book on your own. The second alternative, thematic analysis, might be done more effectively as part of a formally structured course experience. We describe each alternative in the following sections.

EXERCISES TO ORGANIZE YOUR DATA

Alternative 1: Your Self-Assessment Summary

Now that you have done the hard work of completing the self-assessment instruments and activities, take a few minutes to go over them. Reflect on each one and come up with a few sentences for each that capture what that exercise means for you. What did you learn from it? What strengths did it reveal? What areas for development does it suggest?

To help you pull together all you have learned from these exercises, we have provided a Self-Assessment Summary Sheet (Table 3.1). Please take a few minutes to reflect on the work you have done by completing this sheet. It probably will contain spaces for more activities than most people will be able to do, and we have included some instruments (e.g., the Myers–Briggs Type Indicator), which we did not cover but which many people have taken. Just use the rows for the activities that you were able to complete.

Alternative 2: Developing Self-Assessment Themes

Clawson and his colleagues called for a rigorous inductive reasoning process of developing *life themes*. These themes are grounded in data from a variety of sources and say something significant about the person that can be used for the purposes of career planning and development. In essence, this is no different from the process

Table 3.1   Self-Assessment Summary Sheet

Self-Assessment Tool	My Strengths	My Weaknesses	Possible Developmental Learning
Interview With Others			
Career Autobiography			
Career Values Card Sort			
Strong Interest Inventory or Campbell Interest and Skills Survey			
Identities Exercise			
Lifestyle Representation Exercise			
10-Years-Out Exercise			
Peer Coaching Exercise			
Performance Evaluations			
Peak Experiences Exercise			
Draft Personal Mission Statement			
Learning Tactics Inventory			
Career Leader			
Team 360 Feedback			
Myers–Briggs Type Indicator			
Career Survey			
Learning Log			
Other			

any professional career counselor would use to help a person see how his or her interests and values might suggest a good career fit and help the person choose the right career.

The basic approach followed by the authors includes the following steps (Clawson et al., 1992):

(Continued)

(Continued)

1. *Generate data:* This is done primarily by completing career planning instruments (like those introduced in chapter 2) that cover a wide range of topics and perspectives about the individual.

2. *Understand each data-gathering device:* Once you have used a device or instrument, ground yourself in an understanding of what the device can (and cannot) tell you.

3. *Practice interpretation by following a process of inductive reasoning:* By *inductive* we mean working from the data to develop a theory, not working from a theory to assess findings. Induction sometimes is framed as reasoning about the future from the past, but in its broadest sense it involves reaching conclusions on the basis of what is observed.

4. *Interpret your own data:* To develop the integrated view, we will use a process borrowed from qualitative research. In qualitative research, there is a process that uses inductive reasoning to do theory building. Put simply, the idea is to take various sources of information and mine each source for key pieces of information. The process of interpretation suggested is similar to one used by any qualitative researcher to understand, sort, and analyze data. In effect, one is using an inductive process to build a theory of oneself that is well grounded in facts. The ground rules Clawson and his colleagues suggest for this process are as follows:

   - *Stay close to the data:* State the facts in concrete terms. Do not abstract ideas or make generalizations.
   - *Do not filter:* Use all the data that seem significant. Do not use information selectively to bolster what you already believe to be true. Likewise, do not ignore data that conflict with what you believe.
   - *Avoid use of inference or judgment:* Maintain objectivity when reviewing the data. It is particularly important at the early stages of reviewing data and developing potential themes to avoid making inferences or judgments about what you are reviewing.

Developing Themes From Your Data

To do a thorough thematic analysis, we suggest the following approach. Start by reviewing the data sources and determining what each tells you (or cannot tell you) about yourself. The data sources used thus far include

- The Career Autobiography (CA)
- The Identities Exercise (IE)

- The Career Values Card Sort (CVCS)
- The Campbell Interest and Skills Survey (CISS) or Strong Interest Inventory (SII)
- The 10-Years-Out Exercise (TYO)
- The Lifestyle Representation Exercise (LRE)
- The Interview With Others (IWO)
- The Peer Coaching Exercise (PEER)
- Performance Evaluation Analysis (PEA)

To develop themes, you should follow these steps:

STEP 1: CODING YOUR DATA

Given the richness and depth of information it provides, it makes sense when coding your information to start with the Career Autobiography (CA). Reading through the biography, highlight key pieces of information and code each piece of data. By coding, we mean establishing potential categories of information by identifying data that are similar. It is important at this stage not to get stuck on these as your final themes. They will be a method for you to begin to sort the data. You may need to read through each piece of information a few times to begin to think of how to categorize. These categories might be labeled as follows:

"I have a strong and persistent interest in being in a helping role."

"I am highly motivated to achieve financial success."

"I strive to excel at everything I take on."

"I follow my own instincts rather than path prescribed by others."

"My roots in the South are of great importance to me."

"I have always succeeded in roles that include a significant technical component."

"The importance of family plays a dominant role in my career decision making."

An alternative is to create label codes using letters and numbers. For example, if geographic location surfaces in your data, you might label all data related to this with an *L* (for *location*). Subthemes that emerge could include the area of the country you want to live in (labeled L1), a preference toward living and working in an urban area (L2), and a desire to work in a certain kind of environment (L3). This coding process will allow you to go through your data and quickly assign a code to every important piece of data. One piece of data can support more than one theme. After you've assigned codes, group all data accordingly. **Note: Each time you pull data from its original source (e.g., the Career Autobiography or the 10-Years-Out Exercise), remember to note on each piece of data the original source with the abbreviations listed earlier.** The important thing is to remember that these themes begin as highly tentative. The tentative themes derived from the data serve as a framework for sorting and analyzing the data.

The CA probably will be the richest single source of data for developing these tentative themes. However, when you move to data sources other than the autobiography, it is critical that you dig deeply into them to find and use as much information as possible.

In using the CVCS, for example, it is natural to focus on the "Always Valued" cards because these are areas that you have highlighted as critically important to you. However, it may be equally important to look at cards that appear in other categories, such as "Seldom or Never Valued." The fact that you never value high earnings or profit and gain is extremely important information about you and can have a profound bearing on your career choices. If financial gain does not weigh heavily in your career thinking or your needs, this opens up many options that might be closed to those who are more concerned about financial gains or material possessions.

In using the SII or the CISS, use as much of the rich and detailed data that their reports provide as possible. Look well beyond the most basic information (e.g., "It said I would be a good car salesman") and scan the data from the general themes and orientations, basic interest scales, matches with occupations, and information about your personal style. Dozens of reference points can be drawn from each of the instruments used in the self-assessment process. If you fail to pull out these nuggets, you will develop themes that are not as rich, textured, or robust as they could be. Ultimately, this will decrease the rigor and the quality of your self-assessment process.

STEP 2: GROUPING YOUR DATA

After you have gone through all of your documents and done your coding, cluster each piece of coded data into groups. There are two ways to go about this (assuming you don't have qualitative research software on your computer). One is to write each piece of data on a card or piece of paper, then physically sort and resort the information into groups. The other is to type all data points onto your computer and then sort the information into categories. Unfortunately, both processes are laborious and time consuming. In establishing the groups, lean toward being more discriminating in putting groups together. It is better to have more groups of data that are highly connected. Fewer groups with many data points that are more loosely related will result in less clear themes and will undermine the rigor and usefulness of your themes and your self-assessment.

STEP 3: ASSIGNING TENTATIVE THEMES

Each group already has a tentative label or a code. At this point, the tentative theme should be ratified, modified, or perhaps even changed significantly. If the change is significant, then it is highly likely that some of the data you have clustered under the tentative label should be redistributed. It is important to start by reading all the data in the group and ask yourself, "How would I label this group?" Don't read the tentative theme and ask, "Can I justify this piece of data under this theme?" That approach may lead you to force information into categories that are not appropriate. As stated earlier, an inductive reasoning process goes from the individual facts to build a theory.

STEP 4: CONSTRUCTING THE FINAL THEMES WITH SUPPORTING DATA

It is probably best to create a system with one theme per page. Put the theme title at the top of each page. Then, for each theme, list all the supporting data you have compiled that suggests that the theme is truly an indicator of who you really are. A typical theme should have at least eight pieces of confirming data that suggest the theme's strength. This should include data from multiple sources. Although the CA is a rich source of data, ask yourself, for example,

- Is this theme supported by the values I identified in the CVCS?
- Is this theme supported by my goals as identified in the TYO?
- Do the interest areas identified in my inventory results support this theme?

An important point: In looking for information that builds and supports a theme, it is important not to ignore data that may seem, or in fact be, contradictory. Although they are challenging to work with, contradictory data or even contradictory themes are extremely important to factor into the career equation. Careers often are riddled with contradictions (e.g., "I'd like to help the poor, but don't see how I could live without a summer home in Nantucket."). These contradictions should not be ignored and may hold tremendous value in refining individual themes and understanding and ultimately resolving career conflicts.

SAMPLE THEMES

It might be helpful to helpful to look at one or two sample themes to better understand what your themes will look like. The sample themes presented are merely that; they are not ideal, nor should all themes be like these. It is reasonable and even desirable that some of your themes be highly specific and concrete. You might have themes that state,

I am totally fulfilled in my work in the field of accounting.

I enjoy being part of a very large organization with at least 10,000 employees.

I would not consider a profession in which I could not earn at least $70,000 per year.

Although it is not always possible to be so specific, if your data support a very exacting theme, by all means you should embrace it. The more themes you have that are specific, the easier it will be to focus your job search and to make career decisions.

Theme 1: Location is an important factor in my work and a very significant determinant of career choice and job satisfaction.

Supporting Evidence:

- I was offered an interesting role as worldwide management development manager for HP, a perfect fit for my interests and background with one major drawback: It was based in Palo Alto, California. Despite our lack of interest in relocating, after discussions with the new manager I accepted the position. (CA)
- The company had many opportunities that I did not even consider because they would have required me to leave the Boston area. (CA)
- My motivation to move to Europe was primarily personal. I was looking for an experience that would allow me to live and work in a new culture and travel and learn more about the European continent. (CA)
- I loved my time living and working in Europe and always felt at home there. (CA)
- I was never happy working in California. Not only was I far from home, but I also never felt comfortable with the West Coast as a place to live. (CA)
- My office is in a brick building on campus with a very homey quality. The campus is located in a New England town. (TYO)
- I am living in New England, either in Boston, Portland, Maine, or western Massachusetts. (TYO)
- Location is always valued. (CVCS)
- Lifestyle representation shows home and location as a central theme. (LRE)

- I think that the location and your work environment matter a great deal to you. (IWO)

Contradictory Evidence:

- I accepted an important job in California despite the fact that I could not see myself living there. (CA)

Theme 2: I am very passionate about issues of social justice and value diversity.

Supporting Evidence:

- I had been a long-term member of the business's Diversity Advisory Board. (CA)
- I was asked to act as the executive sponsor for the Gay and Lesbian Employee Network, which I was happy to do. I learned a great deal from working with the officers of this employee group about the prejudices and difficulties they face. (CA)
- "He is a true champion of an inclusive work environment. This stems from his strong personal philosophy and commitment to these issues." (PEA)
- "He was recognized for his work with the disabled and received the Outstanding Citizenship Award from a group that provides employment opportunities for the disabled." (PEA)
- Helping others is always valued. (CVCS)
- Helping society is always valued. (CVCS)
- Diversity is always valued. (CVCS)
- I scored very high on social orientation and basic interest scales, including adult development, counseling, and religious activities. (SII)
- High match with jobs: social worker, counselor, psychologist, religious leader, and rehabilitation counselor. (SII)
- We spend a few weeks every year doing volunteer work with the family. (5YO)
- I took an enormous pay cut in order to work in a role that I felt would have a more direct and positive impact on working people. (CA)
- My sympathies politically have always gone to the poor and disenfranchised. If I had my way, the well off would pay higher taxes, and we would create more social programs to help those in need. (CA)

Contradictory Evidence:

- I sometimes find myself talking about helping others but not acting on it. I get too preoccupied with my own concerns. (CA)
- Most of my career has been spent working in environments that are made up predominantly of affluent white employees with high educational levels. (CA)
- "I know you feel strongly about issues relating to diversity, but that does not always gel with the fact that you live in an upper-class, predominantly white suburb." (IWO)

The question of how many themes one should develop is an interesting one. Although students sometimes are surprised to hear this, about 15 themes is probably a reasonable number to aim for. Some people's first reaction is that 15 themes are too many; there couldn't possibly be that many truths they can derive from the data with conviction. However, it is important to remember that themes do not have to be large, sweeping statements; in fact, it is sometimes better if they are not. A theme does not have to encapsulate your philosophy of life in a single sentence. Instead, they are simply statements you can make about yourself with a high degree of confidence because they reflect a clear pattern of behavior, interests, values, and choices, as is evidenced in your self-assessment data.

The breadth of topics that themes can cover also gives you ample opportunity to develop a large number. Topics probably will include things such as fields you are interested in, the importance of family or friends, things you love doing, places you want to live, and roles you enjoy playing. They might also include such things as the level of your aspirations, the kinds of organizations you like being part of, the importance of certain values in your work (e.g., status, prestige, affluence, helping others), and the importance of values in your life outside work. The following is a sample list of themes:

Sample Themes

1. My career has always involved working in "people" professions, which has been a good fit.

2. I am highly effective process facilitator.

3. When I think about my professional identity, "teacher" or "being an educator" has always been the most central way to describe it.

4. As I get older, family plays an increasingly important part in my identity and is now more important than my career.

5. Living and working in the Boston area is very important to me.

6. My work environment is a very important determinant of job satisfaction.

7. I have a very strong interest in issues of social justice and diversity.

8. I have always enjoyed being in an academic environment.

9. My wife is my best friend and my most trusted advisor.

10. Although I have always been a good saver, I also enjoy having the opportunity to be frivolous (even if I don't act on it).

11. I enjoy working in organizations that have high status and credibility.

12. I deeply dislike traveling on business and being away from my family.

13. I vacillate between being involved too much with others and seeking refuge in isolation.

14. My self-concept wavers from extremely confident to highly self-critical.

15. I no longer have the ambition to climb the hierarchy that I once did.

16. I do not spend enough time smelling the roses and reflecting on my good fortune and success.

17. I take great joy in appreciating the arts, aesthetics, and beauty.

18. I have never lost my connection to growing up in a working-class environment.

19. I enjoy consulting with organizations on complex problems.

Developing Career and Work–Life Implications

Once you have done the hard work of developing your themes, you can now ask the profound question, "So what? Now that I know all this about myself, how can I use this in a way that informs my career decision-making process?" Peter Drucker offers thoughts at this stage of the process that are quite useful. He suggests one should now move to another set of questions:

• Where do I belong? According to Drucker, some people know their calling early on, but many or perhaps most do not know until they are in their mid- to late 20s. This assumes that by that time people understand answers to the more fundamental questions of who they are, what their strengths are, and what they value. Once these questions are answered, people are much more clear about where they belong and where they don't.

• What should I contribute? To answer this question, Drucker suggests three distinct steps: "What does the situation require?" "Given my self-knowledge, how can I make the greatest contribution to what needs to be done?" and "What results need to be achieved to make a difference?" (Drucker, 1999, p. 71).

Drucker's questions move us to a transition process from self-assessment to deriving implications for career choice and development. Referring back to the text originally developed by Kotter and his colleagues at Harvard Business School, then updated by Clawson, this step is called drawing implications from themes. As Clawson and his colleagues state,

The final step in the self-assessment process involves identifying the career and job implications inherent in a set of themes. The ultimate purpose here is to translate the basic assessment into a more useful form. (Clawson et al., 1992, p. 229)

We are indebted for Clawson and his colleagues for developing this process of thematic analysis as a way of summarizing the important elements in a person's career identity. The following approach bridges the gap from self-assessment to career development.

The goal here is to create a list of implications that are derived from your self-assessment themes. In some ways, the implications may sound similar to themes. But rather than stating something about you per se, an implication suggests what your theme means in terms of potential career options. A simple example of the difference between a theme and an implication is as follows:

Theme: I am very committed to living in the Boston area.

Implication: I will focus my job search on positions and employers in the Boston area.

Like themes, implications are rarely derived from one piece of data. Most implications come from combinations of a number of related themes. By combining a number of themes, we can begin to see how these themes spell out implications for one's life and one's work. An example of this is as follows:

Theme: One of my highest priorities in life is to help the poor.

Theme: I am not motivated by the need for high earnings.

Theme: I would like to have a position of leadership in an organization.

Implication: A senior-level position in a social service agency might be an excellent career option to consider.

A process for developing these implications is as follows:

1. Put each theme on a card or piece of paper.

2. Group all themes together that seem to be strongly related.

3. Because each theme probably will relate to more than one group, make duplicate theme cards wherever necessary and have the theme appear in each appropriate group.

4. When the groups are completed, review the themes in each group carefully and come up with an implication that captures the ideas expressed in the collective themes (Clawson et al., 1992, p. 229).

Like themes, implications should be supported by data; in this case, the data are the themes. But as with themes, it is important to remember that contradictions are to be expected. You may find that you have five or six themes that strongly support a given career implication. For example, you might have themes that suggest the implication "I would probably enjoy being a high school teacher in a public school system." However, if you have themes that suggest you are highly motivated by monetary rewards or you value working alone, you cannot ignore this information. These should be listed as contradictory evidence, or perhaps you should develop other implications that ultimately will be incorporated into your career thinking.

An example of a list of implications is provided. Working from the list of sample themes presented in the last section, the following is a list of potential implications and how they could be presented:

Sample Implications

1. I should consider a role in an academic environment, possibly as a college professor. (Supporting themes: 1–8, 11–13, 15, 19)

2. I should focus my job search on careers related to human resource management or workforce management. (Supporting themes: 1–3, 7, 11, 13, 18, 19)

3. I should not seek positions that are or will lead to roles in senior management. (Supporting themes: 4, 8, 12–16, 18. Contradictory themes: 1, 2, 19)

4. I would like a role that keeps me living and working in the Boston area. (Supporting themes: 5, 12, 17)

5. At this stage of my life, my family is more important to me that career success. (Supporting themes: 4, 9, 12, 15, 16)

6. Whatever industry I work in, I should be involved in work that is focused on education, individual development, or organization development. (Supporting themes: 1, 2, 3, 8, 19)

7. I should consider working in high-status not-for-profit organizations that might be focused on issues such as education, social activism, or healthcare. (Supporting themes: 1, 3, 6–8, 11, 12, 15, 17, 18)

You could develop even more implications than the sample ones listed here. The important thing is that you understand the process and apply it rigorously to the development of your implications. This is almost identical to the process you have just used to create your life themes, although it should be much simpler because you are using a much smaller data pool for your implications (i.e., your 15–20 life themes). This activity often benefits from group brainstorming. Working with others who know you, or simply fellow students from a career class you are participating in, can help you to identify implications you may not previously have come up with on your own.

Finally, you might ask, "How specific should an implication be?" They should be as specific as possible. As with themes, don't try to come up with one statement that says it all. It might be possible to look at the sample themes in this chapter and make one sweeping statement that sums them up (e.g., "This person should be a director of education for a high-status university in Boston."). Although an implication such as this is acceptable, at this stage it is premature. We are looking for pointers that give direction, not final answers. Any implication that suggests that there is only one very specific course of action is premature and channels one's focus too narrowly at this stage of the process. Career exploration and information gathering, covered in chapter 4, are the important next steps. Being open to a number of possible options is where most readers should be at this stage of the process.

Summary

At this point you should have an excellent idea of who you are, what is important to you, and what you are looking for from your work. We now have a self-assessment that is grounded in a set of well-developed life themes. We have also begun to think about the implications of this knowledge for your career options, direction, and decision making.

Now it is time to move from your internal world to the exploration of the external world of work. The clarity you have gleaned from the self-assessment phase should help you focus your work as you begin to ponder what work you want to do and in what environment you want to do it.

Finding Ideal Work 4

And both that morning equally lay
In leaves no step had trodden black.
Oh, I kept the first for another day!
Yet knowing how way leads on to way,
I doubted if I should ever be back.
I shall be telling this with a sigh
Somewhere ages and ages hence:
Two roads diverged in a wood, and I—
I took the one less traveled by,
And that has made all the difference

—Robert Frost,
"The Road Not Taken," *Mountain Interval,* 1916

In this new era, a key skill we all need is the ability to identify and secure good career opportunities. The days are long gone when a person would complete school, find her first job, and 20 years later say, "I haven't updated my résumé since I finished college." The facts are clear: People change jobs, employers, and even careers much more often than was the case for most of the 20th century. In fact, according to a recent study, new graduates probably will change jobs five to eight times during their first decade of employment. This short cycle time requires that regardless of our field of work, all of us have one career skill in common: job hunting.

There are three common positions from which most of us are looking for a job. First, you are new to the workforce or reentering the workforce after an extended absence. This is true for new graduates (both of undergraduate and graduate programs) and those who have had an extended period out of the workforce for other reasons (e.g., parents who take an extended break from working to focus on child rearing). Second, you are employed but making a conscious choice to pursue a different position. This could be a role with a new employer or simply a transfer or promotion in your current organization. Third, you have experienced job loss. Whether voluntarily or involuntarily, you often need to begin a job search because your current position has come to an end. Unfortunately, all too often this is a result of job elimination due to reorganization, downsizing, or mergers and acquisitions. Because this phenomenon has become so widespread and at some time touches nearly everyone, we will discuss job loss in some detail. Included in this discussion are its effects on individuals and families and thoughts on how to mitigate its impact. We treat the issue of job loss separately because it raises issues that are complex and different from the other catalysts for initiating a search.

This discussion is followed by an overview of the critical skills you need to market yourself effectively for the right position, whatever the reasons for your job search may be. This process involves more than simply having a good résumé and sending it out aggressively. To find and get the ideal role, it is important to

- *Identify good opportunities that are right for you:* Depending on what your career objectives are, this could range from a large employer to an organization of one (being self-employed). Knowing the market and how to locate job opportunities facilitates the process of exploration that sets the stage for your search.

- *Possess the basic tools of job search:* Despite improvements in technology that have greatly facilitated and perhaps complicated the job search, there are still three basic tools that you will need to master: references, résumés, and cover letters. These three tools, in addition to a summary and synthesis of some of your self-analysis exercises and your professional portfolio, will be your toolbox.

- *Use your network:* It is well documented that most people find jobs through some form of networking. Knowing who is in your network, whom it should include, and how to use your network most effectively will provide a window into a world of job opportunities. Your network can be an excellent source of information about jobs, in both learning what a job entails (through informational interviewing) and finding available opportunities (as a source of job leads).

- *Make effective career decisions:* Once you have generated potential opportunities and created interest, you are faced with the need to make the best choices.

Job Loss

It may seem odd to have a section on job loss begin the chapter about finding your ideal job, but many of us wouldn't be getting this good at job searching if job loss weren't becoming increasingly common. These days, it is the rare person who will not experience an unexpected job loss or unwelcome periods out of work. The goal is to know what to do when such an event or period occurs.

In 1980, William Bridges published a book that has become a classic in the career field—although it is not a career book per se—called *Transitions: Making Sense of Life's Changes.* The loss of a job certainly qualifies as one of these important life changes for many of us (although the pain can certainly be mitigated by a generous severance package). Bridges lays out a three-step process that is helpful for those who are going through such a transition. Ironically, the first step in the process is not called "beginnings," as one might expect, but rather "endings." One of the key points Bridges makes is that every transition begins with an ending, an idea that most of us find quite uncomfortable:

> Considering that we have to deal with endings all our lives, most of us handle them very badly. This is in part because we misunderstand them and take them either too seriously or not seriously enough. . . . Because they scare us we try to avoid them. Endings happen to us in unforeseeable ways that often seem devoid of any meaning—much less any positive meaning. Instead, they are simply events that we try to move beyond as quickly as possible. (Bridges, 1980, pp. 90–91)

Bridges goes on to suggest that our failure to see and deal with endings is a cultural phenomenon not shared by more traditional peoples. The notion that endings, which grow out of periods of disenchantment or disillusionment, are something to be embraced and even celebrated is antithetical to our "let's just move on" approach. But without such endings and the negative feelings that may come with them, moving on is often difficult or even impossible. As Bridges points out,

> Divorces, deaths, job changes, moves, illnesses, and many lesser events disengage us from the contexts in which we have known ourselves. They break up the old cue-system that served to reinforce our roles and to pattern our old behavior. It isn't just the disappearance of the old system [that] forces us to devise a new one. . . . It is rather a breakdown that as long as a system is working, it is very hard for any member of it to imagine an alternative way of life and an alternative

identity. But, with disengagement, an inexorable process of change begins. Clarified, channeled, and supported, that change can lead toward development and renewal. (1980, pp. 95–96)

The following are some tips to consider when beginning a job search after losing your last position. First, avoid rushing into a job search before you are prepared. Despite financial pressures to begin your job search immediately, give yourself time to recover from the shock of job loss. This time can ease the negative emotions that will naturally follow from your job loss. Second, don't see losing your job as a stigma. Movements between jobs and gaps in employment are much more common than they once were. Finally, put your last job (and organization) behind you. Any resentment you feel toward your last employer will not help your efforts to create a new future. Negative responses that come to the surface in an interview will only cast you in a negative light (Gardella, 2000).

As we will continue to point out throughout this book, any change in one's job or career (either positive or negative) affects not only the employee but also his or her spouse or partner and family as a whole. Attaining a new job; getting acclimated to a new employer; receiving a promotion with added responsibilities, stress, and money; and transferring to a new location all have inescapable impacts on the employee's family. Perhaps no change affects the family more profoundly than job loss. In 1996, the Boston College Center for Work & Family partnered with an outplacement firm, Jandl Associates, to study this phenomenon. The result was a paper called "The Displaced Family: Job Loss, Family Supportiveness, and the Role of Outplacement Services."

The study made a number of interesting points that are worth summarizing. Families play two critical roles in job loss situations: *standing beside* and *standing between* the employee and the situation. By *standing beside,* the authors mean that family members suffer along with the displaced worker. They feel the negative effects of job loss, they witness the trials of the displaced person in looking for a new role, and they suffer through the strains in roles, relationships, and economic loss, perhaps as much as the displaced person. *Standing between* refers to how families can serve as a buffer to limit the emotional impact on the individual. They give the displaced person strength and can provide emotional shelter from the dramatic ups and downs one can feel from job loss and during the job search. In most ways the loss of a job is seen as simply a negative experience. However, families can turn the experience into a positive one if it gives a previously work-absorbed parent the opportunity to spend more time with his or her family. That said, the impact of job loss on children can be significant and can include such things as material deprivation, social stigma with peers, emotional instability, anxiety, and a higher incidence of depression.

The study looked at a number of families and, using a scale to assess family environment, identified some specific areas where families showed negative impacts from job loss. These areas included negative impacts on the following characteristics (in italics are the categories that were rated by scales in the study):

- The level of communication (*expressiveness*) lessens during this time.
- Job loss can undermine a sense of *cohesion* among family members.
- The level of *activity* for displaced families decreases. Often vacation plans or family outings are canceled in order to reduce spending to match reduced income levels.
- Job loss alters the sense of *organization* that families have. The structure and schedule that a work role provides, for the worker and the family, are lost. This can create a more amorphous structure within the family as roles and schedules are altered.

Although the families in the study seemed to be okay in other areas, such as conflict, this fact may not be altogether positive. The conflict score suggests that conflict decreases during times of job loss, but this may be the result of a "circling the wagons" phenomenon. Conflict avoidance may mean that healthy levels of conflict are suppressed because family members feel they are in a crisis, and this conflict avoidance may not be positive.

The study concluded that families that can keep activity, communication, and organization levels high during this period would be better off. Some suggestions on how to do this include the following:

Activity: Do not allow lack of funds to cause family activity to decline. Look for activities that do not cost a lot, such as picnics, trips to the beach, and free concerts.

Communication: Spouses and partners want to know about the job search but may be afraid to ask. It is often difficult to have discussions about these issues, but if these discussions occur, they will ultimately have a positive impact. Discuss how the search is going, what you are learning, and what positives have come out of this process.

Organization: Try to maintain and even improve organization during this amorphous time. Don't let schedules and routines diminish. Try to maintain a steady routine throughout.

Keep the family open: Maintain the family's ties with people outside. Do not cut yourselves off from neighbors, extended family and friends, and the community during this period.

Having reviewed the difficult starting point for a job search, we will now discuss the steps involved in finding ideal work. Before commencing job hunting, we recommend a number of information-gathering and career exploration steps. Time invested in these activities can often yield a broader set of potential job opportunities and a more successful outcome.

Assessing the Labor Market

Regardless of whether you are seeking a new job because of job loss or initial entry into the labor market, the process of identifying good job opportunities seems quite straightforward and follows a logical sequence:

1. Gathering data to explore all available options

2. Evaluating each option in terms of one's own utility function (e.g., values, needs, interests)

3. Deciding to pursue the one that fits you best

However, one of the dirty little secrets about careers is that people do not use much information about the job market and its opportunities when making career choices. In fact, most people probably spend more time deciding what kind of car to buy or what their next vacation will be than they do researching the job market.

But if a person does want to look for information to assess the job market, where should she go? There are authoritative sources such as the *Occupational Outlook Handbook* or official government publications, such as the U.S. Department of Labor's monthly reports on employment trends. However, these are not very user friendly and appear to be written more for researchers than for job seekers.

An important part of career management today is an ongoing process of *career exploration*. This encompasses activities directed toward enhancing knowledge of the self (self-exploration) and the external environment (external exploration), which a person engages in to foster progress in career development (Blustein, 1997). In this section we are focusing on the external aspect: scanning the employment market.

Because it is the responsibility of the individual to manage his or her own career, it is also incumbent on each of us to monitor demand for the services we can provide. Staying abreast of the changing dynamics of the labor market is a necessity in today's fast-changing world. Some of the sources of information that we would recommend include the following:

• Read the business press regularly for up-to-date information about the overall state of the economy, your own industry (or other industries that might interest you), and future trends. Good basic sources include *The Wall Street Journal, The Financial Times, The Economist, Business Week, Fortune,* and *The New York Times.* Look for trends in your industry or discipline. Are you entering a period of consolidation and mergers? Are companies outsourcing and exporting jobs? Is there a prediction of a war for talent? Watch for these macroeconomic trends that could affect your organization and your future career opportunities.

• Even if you are not looking for a job, do an occasional scan of the employment listings in your industry publications, newspapers, and relevant employment Web sites (those that focus on your industry or discipline). Believe it or not, employers and job seekers still use the want ads, and they do work.

• Get to know other online resources, such as Monster.com and Craigslist.com. Other sources include The *Wall Street Journal*'s online job search area and recruiters such as Korn Ferry (http://kornferry.com) or Russell Reynolds (http://www.russellreynolds.com). In addition to classified job postings, many of these sites also contain discussion groups on various topics, housing information, personals, services, résumés, and other information from job seekers. For example, the following posting appeared in the résumé section on the Boston page for Craigslist:

Why Should You Hire Me?

1. These are but a few reasons from an almost endless list of my attributes. Enjoy!

2. I am not averse to working long hours with little to no recognition.

3. After working in retail for 7 years and being berated on a daily basis I can put up with anything and can take orders well.

4. Multi-tasking! I really can do 5 (or more) things at once.

5. I am often told that I am a "fast learner."

6. I am highly computer-literate. I can both word process AND make spread sheets!!

7. I have management experience, which means I have no problem telling people what to do.

8. Alternately, I have no problem keeping my mouth shut and letting things go on inefficiently if it is not my job to tell people what to do.

9. I am charming and funny, and that alone should be reason enough to give me a job.

SOURCE: Craigslist.com, retrieved December 16, 2003, 11:08 A.M.

Tim's son Chip, who recently found a job through Craigslist, provided the following assessment of some of the online services:

I know out here (in the Bay Area) that people use something called Craig's List almost religiously (it is where I found my current job before it popped up in the Berkeley/Stanford job boards). It is a list of many things, but the jobs area is well trafficked, and it offers the spectrum of entry-level to VP. The problem is that the quality is hit-or-miss, but it does a really good job of serving local areas (since the locals are the ones who provide the content). Another thing that is just starting to get traction out here are "social networks" like LinkedIn where friends invite you to join online and you are able to electronically play the 6 degrees of separation game and work through buddies to gain new contacts. Check out: https://www .linkedin.com/. For this tool to succeed, it needs to really go national, but for now I know it is getting most of its attention from California (but if network effects kick-in, they should go national fast). . . .

In the end, my points are really analogous to networking in general: it is all about what you know and who you know (and then doing something about it!)

SOURCE: Chip Hall, personal communication, December 17, 2003.

- In addition to information about employers and job openings, a wealth of information about jobs and salaries in general is available. For example, a local tool called BostonWorks.com provides information about jobs and includes the ability to search by industry, location, job title, and level. You can search through hundreds of job descriptions that include responsibilities, qualifications, and salary ranges to get a better understanding not of specific job openings but of a field or industry about which you would like to gather more information.

- Finally, get to know your college or university's career Web site for alumni and use your college network, both undergraduate and graduate. As career networks are becoming more important resources for career development, networks of alumni are increasingly being tapped.

These are just a few of the options for you to use as part of your ongoing career exploration. We encourage you to find additional resources that work well for you. The important thing is to get into the habit of checking in on a regular basis and keeping in touch with the market.

Identifying the Right Opportunities for You

After you scan these sources and come up with some specific possibilities, how do you decide what's right for you? This is where the results of your self-assessment come in. Your preparation for identifying what is right for you is everything that you have been doing up to this point to get to know yourself better. Getting clear on just what you are looking for is the first step in knowing the right opportunity. Your choice may not be right for everybody, and your friends may question your choice (or maybe even your sanity), but if you know yourself, your interests, and preferences very well, you can be confident when you have found the right option for you.

When you are searching for a new job, as opposed to doing general career exploration, your search process becomes more focused. This is the time to use your Self-Assessment Summary Sheet (see Table 3.1) and themes as a personal checklist to evaluate the features of a specific job. For each row in your Self-Assessment Summary Sheet, ask yourself, "How well does this opportunity fit with this aspect of me?"

This is the time to use the relationships you have built around this process. If you are working with a peer coach, a support or learning group, or a career coach, these people, who have come to know you well, can help you think through the pros and cons of various options. In addition to helping you evaluate options, they can also provide the emotional support and encouragement you will probably need during this stressful period.

Here are some of the factors you should think about as you go through the process of identifying the best options for you. They involve different aspects of your life. Some may apply to you, and others may not. We encourage you to add others that are important to you if they are not listed here:

Work Factors (for you and your spouse or partner)

Your professional identity

Professional, career, and business contacts

Job security

Salary

The organization

The nature of the work itself

Your direct supervisor

Opportunities for travel or not

Colleagues

Customers, suppliers, other external stakeholders

The work environment and facilities

Future career opportunities

Lifestyle and Family Factors

Geographic location

Living areas accessible to work, commuting convenience

Types and cost of housing available

Neighborhoods (that you can afford)

Transportation

Schools

Cultural facilities

Recreational facilities

Local social norms, attitudes, subcultures (and how comfortable you feel with them)

Cost of living and unusual expenses

Sports

Local governments and politics

Community organizations

Accessibility or inaccessibility of parents, extended family

Baby-sitters and daycare facilities

Household and other help

Restaurants

Places of worship

Other special facilities or needs

Social relationships, friends

Media and communications

Personal and Individual Factors

Unique personal losses or gains involved in the choice

Giving up old friends

The energy needed to make the move

Emotional costs of readjusting to job changes

Emotional costs of readjusting to new social relationships

Emotional costs of integrating self into new neighborhood

Emotional costs of integrating self into new schools

Emotional costs of changes in family relationships

Anxiety about proving self in new job or environment

Excitement of new opportunities in new location

The Gut Factor

What are your subjective feelings about the choices?

What emotions do the choices elicit in you?

If you had to make the decision right now, what would you decide?

SOURCE: Adapted from Hall and Hall (1979).

Job Search Tools

The ability to find a job is a critical skill for any person. A person who is unskilled in this area is analogous to a company that knows how to design and build a product but has no capacity to market or sell it; such an organization would be out of business in a very short time. But perhaps never before has this skill been in greater demand. This analogy has become all the more clear in recent years as we have seen books published with the titles *You & Co.* and *We Are All Self-Employed.* As Bob Gardella states in *The Harvard Business School Guide to Finding Your Next Job* (2000),

> Searching for a job is one of the most important things that professionals do and they are doing it much more frequently. The changing employer/employee contract, the lack of job security, the increasing pace of change in the workplace, advances in technology, globalization, and even the quest for better work–life balance are all creating significant movement in the marketplace for jobs. (p. xvii)

Gardella goes on to point out that although job search skills are of critical importance, for most professionals they are also "one of the most feared, misunderstood, and mishandled activities, even by otherwise intelligent, accomplished people" (p. xvii). Although this book does not give full treatment to the issue of finding and attaining jobs, it would be an oversight for us not to include a section on this critical step in the career process.

REFERENCES

Although many organizations in the recent past have actively discouraged their managers from giving references on former employees, references continue to be an excellent source of information for hiring companies on applicants. For the applicant, references can also serve as great networking resource. Gardella (2000) suggests several guidelines for selecting references, including the following:

- *Select references carefully.* There is nothing like having a lukewarm reference (not to mention completely negative one) to throw a wet blanket on a job search, particularly one that is so close to being successful (references usually are checked near the end of the process). The key is to select your references carefully and prepare them well beforehand. Do not assume that people will serve as your references until you ask them.

- *Line up your references early, preferably as soon as you begin your job search.* References can be more difficult to line up than you think. Problems can occur if you have been out of the labor market for a long time and have not maintained connections with your former managers or colleagues. Also, if you have been with one employer for a long time and would prefer that no one in that firm know you are looking, you may need to be more creative in identifying references. For these reasons and others, it pays to have references lined up well before a potential employer requests them.

- *Choose three or four people to serve as your references.* These people should know you well and preferably have worked with you. Consider asking former managers, supervisors, peers, direct reports, clients, and vendors. You may also want to include academic references (particularly if you recently graduated from a program or continue to have a strong relationship with a professor) and references from any volunteer activities.

Beyond simply choosing references, it is also important to prepare them, communicate with them regularly, and keep them apprised of your status. The following are some guidelines for preparing references:

- Give your references your current résumé, a list of organizations or positions that you would like to target, and anything else that you think will be helpful to them.

- If you haven't worked with your references for a while, be sure to refresh their memories on the type of work you did, whom you worked with, and so on.

- Talk with your references about what they will say about you. If there are certain characteristics you are trying to highlight by using particular references, this may help you assess the degree to which they will help you in that purpose.

- Communicate with your references in an ongoing manner. Contact references before or soon after you give out their names so they know they may be contacted and for what position. Follow up with references after they've been called to discuss how the conversation went if they were contacted. Keep them updated on your job search status (e.g., whether you were offered the job and whether you accepted). Finally, don't forget to enthusiastically thank your references after you have accepted a job.

If your references aren't kept up to date, it is not easy for them be as helpful as they could be in your job search. Each time you interview for a job, you need to update your reference on what you are applying for and the characteristics you would like to accentuate. That way, your reference can frame her answers in a way that is consistent with your answers and most helpful to the hiring manager (Gardella, 2000).

RÉSUMÉS

Although the world has changed dramatically in the past decade, and many new tools are available for job searching on the Web, the basic tools are much the same. The résumé is still essential. It is a brief way to make clear your areas of interest, summarize your experience and education, and highlight your accomplishments relevant to your aspirations.

Don't think of your résumé as simply a piece of paper or a computer file that you need to update to get your foot in the door for an interview. Instead, think of the creation of your résumé as a valuable process that emotionally and intellectually prepares you for your job search. For these reasons, it is important to write your own résumé and seek feedback rather than relying on someone else to write it for you.

A good résumé clearly and succinctly outlines your skills, education, experience, and accomplishments. Remember that your résumé is not a place to be bashful. Review each of your jobs and be sure to list your main accomplishments for each job in bullet point form. One approach is to outline, perhaps in bullet form, the challenges or problems you encountered, the actions you took to address these challenges, and the results you achieved. Wherever possible, quantify the results you achieved in business terms (e.g., dollars saved, productivity or revenue increase) (Gardella, 2000).

At the same time, you'll want to make sure that your résumé is not overly detailed; hiring managers don't need a play-by-play of all of your jobs. What they need is just enough information to verify that you have the skills and experiences that make you worth their time to screen for what *they* need.

Besides content, the success of your résumé depends on how it looks and reads. Keep your formatting simple by limiting your résumé to two pages or less, and consider organizing your résumé into four or five major sections, listing subcontents in reverse chronological order. Major section headings for your résumé might include

- A *header* (with your name and contact information)
- An *objective* or *summary* section that provides readers with a sense of what you are looking for and what you have to offer
- An *experience or work history* section that cites organizations and job titles, with beginning and end dates, and describes tasks, responsibilities, and accomplishments

- A *formal education* section that lists higher education and degrees earned in reverse chronological order, beginning with most recent degrees

- An *other* section that includes other potentially relevant information (e.g., specific computer skills, foreign language fluency, professional affiliations)

Once you have created your résumé, don't forget to get feedback from a number of different sources. At least one person other than yourself should review your résumé carefully for appearance, grammar, and spelling. Feedback should focus primarily on how the résumé looks and reads.

Finally, if you need to e-mail your résumé or post it online, be sure to check your formatting to ensure that it still looks good. Occasionally you may be asked for a plain text version to cut and paste into a Web site. For samples of effective résumés, go to your university career center or job search Web sites.

A number of cautions with résumés are worth noting. Many people overemphasize the importance of a résumé and put too much stock in it as a tool in their job search. In his classic *What Color Is Your Parachute?* Richard Bolles (2007) offers the following three cautions. First, don't confuse the résumé with yourself. Just because your résumé doesn't work in attaining you a job, don't assume there is something wrong with *you*. Second, résumés can make you feel as if you are aggressively pursuing jobs when in fact they may be lying dormant somewhere. The fact that you posted your résumé doesn't mean it is generating much action. Finally, depending too much on a résumé may cause you to give up, assuming that there simply are no jobs available. If sending out résumés is your entire job search strategy, you are likely to be disappointed.

STARTING A PROFESSIONAL PORTFOLIO

In addition to helping you with your career planning, some of your self-assessment information might be used as part of a *professional portfolio*. A portfolio is a way of summarizing and capturing information that presents you and samples of your professional work to prospective employers or clients. It is a way of documenting who you are and what you can do. Put another way, it is a way of marketing yourself. If you have seen an artist's, architect's, or model's portfolio, then you have an idea of what we are getting at. Portfolios are becoming more common in many fields.

To decide what kind of material from your self-assessment you might want to put into your portfolio, you might anticipate what sorts of questions an employer might ask you in a job interview. And you could select and adapt material for your portfolio that you could pull out and show the interviewer to help answer that question. At the very least, you will become very clear in your interview responses. Some typical job interview questions include the following:

- What kind of work are you passionate about? (Use your Campbell Interest and Skills Survey, Strong Interest Inventory, or Career Leader results.)
- What are your strengths and weaknesses? (Use your Skill Assessment results.)
- Can you describe an experience or a project where you demonstrated
  o Leadership?
  o Distinctive technical contribution?
  o Analytic skills?
  o Strategic analysis?
  o Team leadership? (Use your personal biography for all of these.)
- Where do you see yourself in 5 (or 10) years? (Use your 10-Years-Out Exercise.)
- What are you looking for in an employer? (Use your Career Values Card Sort Exercise.)

To get more a more concrete idea of what a career portfolio looks like, we refer you to the work done at Florida State University. The Web site for their career center shows what a portfolio looks like, with examples of award-winning portfolios, a study analyzing the value of portfolios, and other useful information (see http://www.career.fsu.edu/portfolio/).

COVER LETTERS

Cover letters provide an introduction to your résumé. They accomplish this by stating the reason you are sending the résumé (often in response to a specific opening but not always), highlighting your reasons for being interested in a position, and aspects of your background that are particularly relevant to the position you are seeking. Although it is important to write clear and concise cover letters, it is also important to remember that many cover letters are skimmed or never read. The majority of busy managers or screeners often flip to the résumé first and may read the cover letter later.

The following are some key points that Gardella (2000) believes are important to keep in mind when writing job search letters:

- Personalize your cover letter for each position for which you apply. Do not send blanket letters addressed to "Dear Sir or Madam." It suggests that you have not done a thorough job in researching your potential employer.

- When faxing or e-mailing your cover letter and résumé, consider sending along a hard copy that same day (unless you are clearly instructed not to).

- Keep your cover letters to one page or less, and write each letter in terms of the hiring organization's needs.

- Always include a sentence at the end of your cover letter stating that you will follow up on inquiry if you haven't heard back from them in a few weeks.

- In most cases, you'll want to include a résumé with your cover letter.

- As with your résumé, check your spelling, grammar, and punctuation.

- Over time, develop key phrases and paragraphs that you can reuse in your job search letters.

- Spend time writing a good cover letter, but if it takes more than an hour to write one, you're taking too much time.

You should keep your cover letter to about four paragraphs. The first paragraph explains why you are writing and might include additional information about the job you are applying for and what makes that position or the employing organization of particular interest to you. The second and third paragraphs should highlight areas of your résumé you want to call attention to or discuss specific experiences you have had that are clearly relevant to the position requirements. The final paragraph should be a call to action. Often this paragraph includes a sentence such as, "I will call your office late next week to determine the status of my application" or something to that effect (unless you are instructed not to call). Now, you are ready to launch your job search campaign.

Conducting the Job Search

Planning and pacing your job search campaign is critical. For those who are employed, failure to set aside time and establish milestones could result in a job search that never gets started or falters. For those who are un-employed, too much intensity in the early days can leave people feeling emotionally spent after a short period. For these reasons and others, it is important to develop a strategy for finding a job.

According to Bolles (2007), some of the best ways to execute a job search are to ask for job leads from everyone you know, knock on the door of any organization that interests you whether or not they have an advertised opening, and form or join a job club. Bolles states that some of the worst strategies for finding a job are mailing out résumés, answering ads in newspapers or professional journals, and going to private employment agencies. Ironically, these often are the first strategies job seekers use.

The key to being effective in this phase is to be as organized and professional as you would be at work. Maintaining a set routine around job search activities such as sending thank-you notes, making phone calls, and updating your references on your progress will help you maintain focus and be efficient and ultimately successful.

Networking and the Job Search

By now you have done a rigorous self-assessment and have a fairly clear idea about what you want in a job, a career, and your life. You have gathered information on the labor market and job opportunities and have clarity about where your opportunities for further exploration will be. You have put in place some of the key job search tools—résumé, cover letter, and references—that have helped you begin to launch an effective job campaign. You have also set up a schedule for your job search activities. You are ready for the next phase.

In this phase you will assess some of the key resources you already have available to you: people you already know who might be able to connect you with the right job. Studies have shown that for the majority of successful job searchers the key person that helped them find that job was someone they knew *before* they started their search. Take a moment to consider the meaning of that statement. Someone you already know probably will turn out to be the person who will help you get your next job. All you have to do is figure out who that person is and how she or he can help you.

Your circle of career-related relationships is called your *career network*. It is a set of people you know from various walks of life. It includes family members, friends from school, people in your neighborhood and religious communities, professional associations, clients and customers, current and former co-workers, bosses, and subordinates. This network is important because these people, collectively, hold a vast amount of information about various job opportunities. Moreover, they can also connect you to formal sources of career information. These could include a very broad range of resources including Web sites, employers, people to contact for informational and job interviews, and recruiters. They may also know of people who are about to leave an interesting job or people who have recently moved into a management position and will be hiring new people. In short, any kind of information you might want or need in this stage of the job search might be available from your network.

Monica Higgins, a professor at Harvard Business School, and Professor Kathy Kram, a faculty member at Boston University's School of Management, report that career networks represent the "new mentoring" in today's complex business environment (we will discuss Higgins and Kram's work in greater detail in chapter 5). Rather than the traditional one-on-one junior–senior mentoring relationships, the new kind of interpersonal career assistance is delivered through these larger career networks. And the two most critical qualities of a good career network are *size* and *diversity*. Size matters because the more people you are connected to, the more likely it is that one of these connections will lead to a job. Diversity is important because it connects you to all kinds of different job possibilities. If your network is more homogeneous, you may have many different people all trying to connect you to the same small set of potential jobs. The following activities will help you to analyze your network's size and diversity.

TAPPING THE POTENTIAL OF YOUR NETWORK

The first step in working with your current network is to gain a clearer understanding of whom it includes. Take a few minutes to fill out the network form in Table 4.1 to see who is currently in your network.

Table 4.1　　My Current Network

Where Do I Go for Contacts?	Advantages and Disadvantages of Sources
Friends and relatives	
Faculty and administrators	
Former and current colleagues	
Former and current employers	
Directories of companies and associations	
Fellow or former students	
Networking events	
Community and civic leaders	
Professionals working in my field of interest	
Professional association members	
People in newspapers and magazines	
Alumni of each school I attended	
Government representatives	

The second step is to develop ways to expand your career network. One way to do this is by gaining a better understanding of your interaction style and how you can use it most effectively. For example, if you are an extrovert, getting out to professional gatherings or calling a stranger to request an informational interview might be second nature to you. On the other hand, if you are a strong introvert, these activities would be about as attractive as a root canal. The following activity will help you think about your networking style and how to make the most of it.

NETWORK EXPANSION WORKSHEET

The purpose of this activity is to

- Help you assess and enhance (extend or strengthen) your developmental network relative to major challenges and opportunities you will face in the next 1–3 years

- Help you develop a networking strategy that will work for you

- Help you develop a specific plan to pursue over the next 6 months to 1 year

- Create an accountability mechanism

Assessing Your Network

Research on leadership development has demonstrated that people benefit from a variety of developmental relationships, including short-term and long-term alliances with bosses, peers, senior executives, coaches, subordinates, and family members. The more diversity and depth there is in your developmental network, the better. Depending on our dominant learning tactics, we are more or less likely to pay attention to the quality of our developmental network.

This handout was adapted by Professor Kathy E. Kram from a worksheet developed by Professor Deborah Kolb, Simmons Graduate School of Management. Adapted by permission.

As you think about the major changes that are likely to take place at your place of work in the next few years, what major challenges and opportunities do you foresee that you will need to deal with in the next 1–3 years? List them here.

_____

Given these challenges and opportunities, what type of help are you most likely to need?

a. Help in getting the job done _____
b. Help in advancing my career _____

(Continued)

(Continued)

    c. Emotional support _____
    d. All of the above _____

A. If your major challenge or opportunity is related to your work, how well positioned are you to get information, advice, and resources about new opportunities and possibilities?

    Very well _____

    Okay _____

    Need to expand my network _____

Who can help?

_____

B. If your major challenge or opportunity means making a move into a leadership position, do you have relationships with people who can give you advice and effectively advocate or champion you for important assignments or other developmental activities?

    Yes _____

    No _____

Who can help?

_____

C. If your challenge or opportunity means that you will need emotional support, to what extent do you have people who can give you support?

    I have a strong support network to help me. _____

    I don't have people who can help me through changes I will have to make. _____

Who can help?

_____

_____

D. If your challenge or opportunity means that you will need help in getting the job done, advancing your career, and getting emotional support, do you have people in your network who can fulfill these functions?

Yes _____

No _____

Who can help?

_____

What is your approach to building relationships? How are you at initiating relationships? In what settings are you most comfortable meeting people?

Joint or shared work, projects, and committees _____

One-on-one appointments, with specific agendas _____

Informal "no-agenda" social settings _____

Going for coffee, lunch, or drinks _____

Leisure activities such as golf, tennis, or theater _____

Other _____

What is your preferred style?

Occasional phone calls or e-mails just to ask "how are you?" _____

Phone calls, e-mails, or visits with specific requests or questions _____

Holiday cards and letters _____

Dropping in or calling when you're in the neighborhood _____

Arranging in advance to get together at professional meetings _____

Relying on the chance that your paths will cross _____

Inviting people to join you for lunch, coffee, golf, and so on _____

Contacting people when you find some information, an article, or an opportunity that might interest them _____

Other _____

(Continued)

(Continued)

ACTION PLANNING

What are you going to do, specifically, to get things started? Specify how you will you initiate contact or enhance existing relationships. Where will you start the process? What approaches will you use? Will this be part of your leadership development plan?

Share what you have learned in completing this exercise with your peer coach. Each of you commit to the actions you will take in the next 3–6 months to expand your network in ways that position you to move in the direction you identified above. Set a time for follow-up.

PRODUCING YOUR OWN NETWORKING SNAPSHOT

As you are engaging in networking activities and informational interviews, you will find it helpful to communicate a lot of information about yourself in a concise format. Randi Bussin, a career development specialist, has developed what she calls a networking snapshot that will let members of your network obtain a quick, current picture of you. To give you an idea of what such a snapshot looks like, we have reproduced a copy of Tim's.

Tim Hall

Professional: I am a faculty member in the Organizational Behavior Department in the School of Management at Boston University. My other major role at BU is as director of the Executive Development Roundtable, a School of Management research center that does research on leader development. Last year on my sabbatical I spent the fall semester as a visiting scholar at the Boston College Center for Work & Family and the spring semester as a visiting Erskine fellow at the University of Canterbury in Christchurch, New Zealand (it's 15 degrees in Boston this morning—I wanna go back!!!).

Professional Interests: My research centers on various processes related to career experiences: careers in organizations, executive succession programs, career change, spirituality and careers, and work–life integration. I am interested in learning how people can make protean career adaptations without losing their own calling or path with a heart. My teaching interests include careers, leadership, international management, and organizational behavior. Most of my consulting has dealt with helping large organizations create better processes for helping people do self-assessment and create systemic career management processes.

Past Employers: Before coming to BU I was at the Kellogg School of Management at Northwestern, where I held the Earl Dean Howard Chair in Organizational Behavior and served as department chair. Earlier appointments were at Michigan State, York, and Yale. I also held visiting positions at the U.S. Military Academy at West Point and at the University of Minnesota.

Residence: West Newton, MA

Education: B.S. in engineering, Yale University

S.M. in management, Sloan School, MIT

Ph.D. in management (organization studies), Sloan School, MIT

Family: I am married to Marcy Crary, who is on the management faculty at Bentley College, where she teaches the management of diversity and the freshman seminar. I have three children, Liz, Chip, and Mary Lauran. I also have three grandchildren, Matthew (3) and Megan (1), kids of Liz and her husband, Scott; and Sabrina (2), daughter of Chip and his wife, Christina. Liz and Scott live nearby in Wellesley, and Chip and Christina are in San Francisco. Mary Lauran is a freshman at Newton North High School, where she just made the improv troupe "SponGen," which is staging its annual performance at the end of February. (See me for tickets!)

Hobbies: I dabble in clarinet playing and photography (digital and black-and-white film). We are now building a darkroom in the basement because Marcy and Mary Lauran are also interested in photography. I also enjoy reading and walking our dog, Farley, with Marcy.

How to Contact Me: The best way is e-mail: (office). Telephone: (office number) and (home number). Fax: (office fax number) and (home fax number).

Informational Interviews

One likely result of successful networking (as well as a continuing form of networking) is the informational interview. Informational interviews are exactly what the name implies: structured conversations to gather information. Unlike job interviews, where you are the interviewee (i.e., the one being asked questions in order to provide information), in this instance you are the interviewer gathering information about what is important to you. Informational interviews provide great opportunities to educate yourself on an industry, if not a company itself, and develop a strong relationship with your contact. You may also want to schedule an informational interview to

- Obtain data about a particular career and what it takes to do well in that field

- Receive feedback on and support for your potential to succeed in this career field

- Obtain market-based information on what job opportunities exist in a given field, industry, or market

- Have your résumé evaluated for its selling value to prospective employers

- Practice the art of describing your skills and goals in a nonthreatening situation

Like a job interview, an informational interview can lead to a successful outcome only with the appropriate level of preparation. In the case of an informational interview, most of the time a successful outcome is not a job offer but rather a much clearer sense of what a job entails or what an organization is like to work for and how these match up with your self-assessment, values, and priorities.

GUIDELINES FOR CONDUCTING AN INFORMATIONAL INTERVIEW

In doing informational interviews, it is important to keep in mind a number of guidelines.

- *Have a specific agenda in mind for your meeting.* Your contact is giving you valuable time, so don't waste it. Have one to three clear objectives in mind for the outcome you are looking for. If possible, e-mail these objectives to your contact in advance.

- *Review the results of your self-assessment.* You have already done an extensive self-assessment to better know who you are, what you can do, and why you believe in your potential to succeed. This information will be very helpful as you begin informational interviewing.

- *Be proactive in scheduling an informational interview.* Don't wait for someone else to suggest it. An informational interview may be scheduled when you first contact a person or as a follow-up to an earlier conversation. Along the same lines, always make an appointment. This approach puts the conversation on a more businesslike footing and helps decrease the likelihood of interruptions.

- *Do your homework.* Learn everything you can about the person, the organization, and the field. Know what you want to ask and come prepared with a solid list of 20–30 questions (but don't feel the need to ask all of them in the interview; you can always ask questions in a follow-up e-mail). Two good final questions might be, "Is there anything else you think I should know about this field or this company?" and "Whom else do you think I should contact?"

- *Respect your contact's time.* Don't be apologetic, but do plan a manageable agenda. Do not wear out your welcome.

- *Remember at all times that you are not asking for a job.* You are gathering information on which to base future decisions. Make sure your contact understands this. Also, although it may be appropriate to ask whether the person knows of jobs in your field or what kinds of organizations offer certain kinds of positions, it is not appropriate to shift gears in the interview and ask the person about hiring in his or her specific department or group (unless the person brings it up first).

QUESTIONS TO ASK

Always prepare a list of questions. You are there not only to learn but also to impress.

- What do you do in a typical workday?
- What kinds of problems do you deal with?
- What kinds of decisions do you make?
- How does your job fit into the organization or department?
- What are your major responsibilities?
- How did you enter the field? How long have you been in it?
- How did you reach your current position?
- What skills, education, and experience are required?
- What are typical jobs appropriate for my level of experience in your field?
- What courses or work experience would you recommend?
- What do you find most satisfying or frustrating about the job?
- What are the toughest problems you face?
- What obligations, outside of normal hours, come with the job?
- How many hours do you work during an average week?

- What kinds of changes are occurring in your field?
- What is the career path in your field or organization?
- Can you recommend any publications or associations?
- Any suggestions for how to conduct my job search?
- What is the job market like in your field?
- What industry trends do you foresee over 5 or 10 years?
- What kind of growth or job outlook do you anticipate?
- Whom should I contact for additional information?

SOURCE: Reproduced by permission of the author, Randi Bussin.

- *Recognize that everyone has his or her own attitudes, biases, and feelings that must be evaluated.* Making judgments about a job or an organization based on discussions with one person is premature. Talk to a number of people to flesh out a clear and less biased picture of what you are considering.

- *Ask for referrals.* It's always good to expand your network. Ask for names of people who work in another area of the company, have experiences similar to your own, attended your college or university, belong to a related professional organization, or might just be good contacts. It is not unusual to receive two or three names out of one original contact.

- *Be sure to send a thank-you note* after the informational interview.

- *Keep your contacts informed.* Let them know of job interviews and offers, especially if you believe they have taken an interest in your career or if it is within their organization.

- *Ask your contacts for a business card and keep a record of people you have met.* Maintaining such contacts is an ongoing process that will help you throughout your career.

In conclusion, networking and informational interviewing are processes that grow easier with practice. You will find that the more you engage in intentional networking activities, the more comfortable you will feel doing them. In fact, with time you may come to enjoy them. After all, this is just a process of meeting new friends. Moreover, networking is naturally a *mutual helping process.* That is, as you ask for help from others, think of ways you might help them. And you will want to help them. In this way, you begin to repay specific people for their generosity.

Identifying the Ideal Employer

Like identifying the ideal job, identifying the ideal employer is a task that includes many of the same elements: using your network, conducting informational interviews, doing research through other channels such as business periodicals and company Web sites, and synthesizing the information. The work you have done in your self-assessment should be particularly helpful in identifying the kinds of employers that might be ideal for you.

A number of years ago, IBM ran an advertisement for college recruitment. It suggested that the candidate use a checklist (they provided) to determine who might be an ideal employer for the potential recruit. The questions on the checklist included the following:

Will the employer allow me to work in up-to-date facilities and with state-of-the-art equipment?

Will my co-workers be intelligent and supportive colleagues to work with?

Will the organization invest in ongoing education programs so that I will be continuously learning?

At the end of the checklist, the implication was that if you answered "yes" to most or all of the questions, you should work for that employer, and, of course, that employer happened to sound a lot like IBM. What we need to do now is develop our own checklist for our ideal employer. Rather than using the list in the IBM advertisement, which was effective but biased toward a particular employer, we can use the information gathered up to this point to customize our own checklist.

IDEAL ORGANIZATION EXERCISE

Once you establish what job or function you want to work at, it is at least as important to decide in what environment you want to work. After a short period, many (perhaps most) graduates will find themselves in new jobs or different functional areas. So the organization in which you work may have a greater bearing on your long-term satisfaction.

Write a one-page description or checklist of your ideal organization. In your description, be specific about the characteristics in the following chart. You may also include other characteristics that are important to you. The description or checklist should not exceed one page.

(Continued)

(Continued)

ACTIVITY: IDEAL ORGANIZATION EXERCISE

Products and Services

- What industry or sector is the enterprise involved in?
- What markets does it serve?
- Who are its customers?
- Does it provide products or services?

Structure

- Are you working in an organization or are you self-employed?
- What size is the organization?
- Does it have a single organization or is it made up of multiple sub-organizations (i.e., divisions, business units, etc.)?
- Does the organization operate in a local, national, or global market?
- Is the organization for-profit, not-for-profit, or government?
- If for profit, is it publicly traded or privately held?

Culture

- What is the organization's vision and mission?
- How do they communicate these to employees?
- What is the working atmosphere like?

Management Style

- How do you prefer to be supervised?
- How should management ensure accountability and quality work?
- Is the organization more formal or informal in terms of its ways of operating?

Job Scope

- What do you see yourself doing in the organization?
- What level of responsibility do you have?
- Will you be supervising the work of others?

Values

- How does the organization interact with its employees?
- What does the organization do to interact with the community and the environment?
- What values are important to the organization?
- How would it embody those values?

Evaluation Methods

- How frequently will I be evaluated?
- What methodology will be used?
- Are evaluations by supervisors, peers, both?

Reward Systems

- How does the organization reward its members?
- What are its policies for compensation, promotions, and benefits?
- Will it provide performance-related incentives in the form of raises, bonuses, stock options, etc?

SAMPLE IDEAL ORGANIZATION CHECKLIST

Products and Services

- Would be in the healthcare industry.
- Would serve healthcare providers and patients worldwide with state of the art medical technology.
- Products would be used for diagnosis and treatment.

Structure

- The organization would be quite large (at least 10,000 employees).
- It would have revenues of more than $2 billion per year and would be for-profit.
- There would be multiple business units within the organization.
- Business units would be located in a broad range of markets, with offices in many countries around the world.
- Our products and services would serve a worldwide market.

Culture

- The company's mission and vision would focus on the contribution we are making to improving the quality of patient care and health outcomes for-patients.
- We would have the goal of being a market leader and providing innovative, cost-effective products.
- Our values would reflect the important work we do, and they would include a strong emphasis on quality.

(Continued)

(Continued)

- The organization would hire top-notch people and invest in their ongoing training and development.

Management Style and Values

- The management style would be respectful of employees' needs, and power would be decentralized as much as possible.
- The work environment would be informal, managers would be on a first-name basis, and people would not need to dress in formal business attire on most days.
- Employees at all levels would be aware of strategy and encouraged to give input into the organization's plans and direction.

Job Scope

- The job would involve working on research projects with strategic partners.
- I would supervise a small team of other technical staff members.

Evaluation Methods and Rewards

- I would be evaluated twice a year formally but get regular feedback.
- At least once a year there would be a 360-degree evaluation process.
- Salary would be based on performance and would include some bonuses.
- There would be opportunities to buy stock in the company.

Special Challenges and Tips for International Students Who Want to Work in the United States

It can often seem to international students that there are many legal and cultural intricacies and barriers to working in the United States. However, this process often is not as challenging as people initially think, especially with some good homework and focused attention to the matter.

First, you want to check with your school's career center. It may have a dedicated international counselor who has experience helping international students and who can offer specialized support and advice. Services for international students might include the following:

- Workshops designed to address specific challenges facing international students

- One-on-one coaching on U.S. business practices, hiring procedures, and job search strategies

- Practical strategies for coping with cultural differences in the workplace, keeping you aware of the different attitudes and values that might pose barriers to your job search

A major issue is whether a company will sponsor you in your application for a work visa that will allow you to be employed in the United States. You should do a quick scan of companies that you might be interested in and then see which ones will sponsor international students. Some companies state clearly that they will, and others will not. You should focus your search on the companies that say they are interested in hiring international students. You can also obtain from your career center the names of companies that are known to have hired a number of international students in your field in recent years. The idea here is to go where it's easy. Focus on the companies that are actively seeking people with your international background.

Another great source of help will be your fellow students from your country or region. In this way, you can work on your internal network and gain access to your classmates' networks. Thus, your career network can grow exponentially.

One way to get some U.S. experience is to sign up for courses that include field projects, where you will work on course-related assignments in real companies. This will give you good experience in functioning in a U.S. corporate culture and also help you expand your career network.

Another idea is to look at U.S. or multinational companies that have a strong presence in your country. These companies probably are very interested in hiring local managers in your country who have been educated in the United States, and they will be prime candidates for your search. Network in those companies by contacting managers from your country who are working there now. Try to set up informational interviews with them to get suggestions about how to land a job in the organization.

As you are doing all of this, be aware that business is growing increasingly global and that your international perspective and experience are becoming more valuable all the time. Focus on the advantages that your international identity, experience, and skills bring to an employer, and use that understanding as you market yourself. Do not limit yourself by seeing your citizenship as a barrier. This is where self-confidence can really make a difference, and you want to create a positive self-fulfilling prophecy, not a negative one.

These ideas are summarized in the Box 4.1. Make a copy of this box and keep it next to your computer as you work on your job search.

> ### Box 4.1 Ten Tips for International Students
> ### Who Want to Work in the United States
>
> - Check with your career center. Work with a counselor who has experience working with international students.
>
> - Take any available workshops on job search for international students.
>
> - Use any available one-on-one coaching on U.S. business practices, hiring procedures, and job search strategies.
>
> - Take available cross-cultural or diversity workshops or use any other source that can help you learn about cultural differences between your home country and the United States. Work on developing practical strategies for coping with cultural differences and for helping you become aware of the different attitudes and values that might interfere with your job search.
>
> - Find companies in your field that explicitly say they will sponsor international students for visas. Do not waste time with companies that say they will not consider international students.
>
> - Find the names of companies that have a good history of hiring students from your country or region.
>
> - Get peer coaching from other students from your country or region.
>
> - Take elective courses that have corporate field projects, which will provide you with good experience operating in a U.S. corporate culture.
>
> - Identify companies that have strong operations in your country. Network in those companies by contacting managers from your country who are working for those companies now. Try to get informational interviews with them to get suggestions about how to land a job there.
>
> - Remember that business is growing increasingly global and that your international perspective and experience are becoming more valuable all the time. Focus on the advantages that your international identity, experience, and skills bring to an employer, and use that understanding as you market yourself.

Career Decision Making

You have now done extensive self-exploration, identified suitable employers, and applied and interviewed for positions. Ideally, by now you have some choices to make between jobs. Which one is the best fit for you? Refer back to the exercises you completed earlier when assessing how your personality will fit with a certain job or how your values around family, social background, and socioeconomic factors might influence your choice. Obviously, your life stage is an important factor to consider when sorting through the pros and cons of job alternatives. A role that might seem very attractive to a young, single person who is establishing his or her career identity might seem quite the opposite to someone who has reached greater maturity or has young children at home. Suddenly, the idea of working long hours and taking on extensive travel no longer has the same appeal.

DEVELOPING A CAREER DECISION MATRIX FROM YOUR THEMES

An effective approach to using your self-assessment in career decision making is to use your themes directly to filter career choices by creating a matrix (Table 4.2). On the left-hand side of the matrix is a list of your themes. Across the top of the matrix is a list of jobs or job categories you are considering.

Table 4.2   Sample Career Decision Matrix

	Career Option 1	Career Option 2	Career Option 3	Career Option 4
Theme 1	High	High	Low	Low
Theme 2	High	Medium	High	Medium
Theme 3	High	Medium	Low	High
Theme 4	High	Medium	Medium	High
Theme 5	Medium	Low	Medium	Low
Theme 6	High	High	Low	Medium
Theme 7	High	High	Low	Medium
Theme 8	Medium	Medium	Low	Medium
Summary	High	Medium or high	Low	Medium

In each cell you rank the degree of consistency (high, medium, or low) between your life theme and the job or career you are considering. Clearly not every job will score high on every criterion (e.g., certain roles might maximize earnings but may demand long work days that are contrary to your hopes). However, you might find a number of roles that are good matches for you. Ultimately, the idea is to continue to look for the role that is most consistent with your life themes.

(Continued)

(Continued)

In this example, the job characteristics of Career Option 1 would show a high correlation with the life themes this person has identified. The information you have been collecting during this stage of the process about possible job opportunities will allow you to fill out the matrix with a high degree of confidence that you can assess each option accurately.

Summary

In this chapter we have outlined a process for using your career implications to find a job that meets your needs. We began by outlining ways to assess the labor market and to learn more about jobs and employers that might be of interest. We have discussed the most common job search tools—the résumé, cover letter, and references—and a job search tool that is less common but may be highly useful: the professional portfolio. Having gone through the self-assessment experiences and activities outlined in this book, you have a unique advantage over most job hunters: You have in-depth knowledge about who you are and what you are looking for.

We have noted the importance of having a career network in order to find your next job. Again and again, career experts emphasize that your network will be the major source of your next position. We have also discussed in detail an approach that can both expand your network and give you invaluable insights into careers and employers: the informational interview. When you have completed this extensive data gathering, you have two tools to use to assess your next job move: the Ideal Organization Exercise, which summarizes what you are looking for in your next employer, and a career decision matrix that will allow you to compare how well various options match up with your life themes.

Once you decide on the role you will take, the next step is to articulate a strategy for your own development within the organization. Although many people believe that a career development strategy is simply a career advancement strategy, this is no longer the case. In the next chapter we will discuss a number of different ways to frame your thinking about what career development means for you.

For Further Reading

Bolles, R. (2007). *What color is your parachute? A practical manual for job-hunters and career-changers.* Berkeley, CA: Ten Speed Press.

Gardella, R. S. (2000). *The Harvard Business School guide to finding your next job.* Boston: Harvard Business Reference.

Green, P. C. (1996). *Get hired: Winning strategies to ace the interview.* Austin, TX: Bard.

Career Development 5
Strategies

To laugh often and much;
To win the respect of intelligent people and the affection of children;
To earn the appreciation of honest critics and endure the
    betrayal of false friends;
To appreciate beauty, to find the best in others;
To leave the world a bit better, whether by a healthy child, a
    garden patch or a redeemed social condition;
To know even one life has breathed easier because you have lived.
This is to have succeeded.

—Attributed to Ralph Waldo Emerson[*]

Many in the baby-boom generation were raised with a stereotypical view of work, careers, and success. In the best cases work meant a regular schedule, often 8–5 Monday through Friday. A typical day was spent at the office, commuting to and from the office was a part of the daily regimen, and the commute usually was short or at least manageable. The typical week might include some overtime, occasionally requiring work on weekends, and although getting home from the office in a timely fashion wasn't easy, most people could manage it. Once you were home, work was somewhere else. The physical distance between one's workplace and one's home made the two spheres distinct.

Success was also easy to define. The person who rose to the highest point on the organization chart embodied success. He or she had the most impressive job title, all the desired perks, and the nicest home. (Remember

---

[*]This poem has been widely attributed to Emerson, but an exhaustive search of his work by an Emerson scholar could find no copy of this poem in an anthology by him.

the old joke "He who dies with the most toys wins"?) But even as the world has gotten more hectic and work has become more consuming, people realize, perhaps more than ever before, that no matter what their level of ambition, success is a subjective construct with many dimensions. As Randall Tobias, former chair and CEO of Eli Lilly, said, "We have a clearer perspective when we get a little maturity. . . . When it comes time for someone to write my obituary, I don't want to be defined solely by the boxes I happened to occupy on organization charts. As important as that is to me, I want to be defined as the father of my children, as someone who made my community a better place" (Shellenbarger, 2000, p. 145).

Today, work, careers, and definitions of success are changing rapidly and in many new directions, some of which may be viewed as positive and some not. As travel has become easier and markets more global, some professionals are away from home often and for long periods of time. With advanced technology, late-night teleconferences with international partners and customers often are expected. Feeling secure in a job with a company or organization that takes care of its employees is less common. The pervasiveness of cell phones, personal digital assistants, and access to e-mail have blurred the work and home boundaries. The old image of work as a 9–5 arrangement has changed (for better and for worse).

On the other hand, many organizations are becoming more flexible in how and when work gets done, and more work can be completed at home or in remote locations. Individuals have many more options to shape their work lives to fit with the rest of their lives, especially as their needs change in different life circumstances and stages. Because the lines between work and family have become blurred, we all must be clearer than ever about what we want our lives to look like.

As organizational rules and career paths have changed and the boundaries between work and home become less clear, we need to create our own paths, establish our own priorities, and set our own limits. How we do so will depend, to a great extent, on what we are trying to achieve in our lives and our work. We need to ask ourselves,

> What are the most important drivers of our satisfaction?
>
> Is advancement in an organization the key to our sense of succeeding?
>
> Is balancing work and family our most important task?
>
> Is having time to pursue outside interests or support the community a critical element in our pursuit of a meaningful life?

THE CAREER AND LIFE ORIENTATION INDEX

The following activity will help you determine your need or desire to have flexibility and control in your career or work life—how protean you are. It will provide you with a rating on six different facets of your life and career: self-direction, organizational orientation, value expression, whole life balance focus, family focus, and community involvement.

Career and Life Orientation Index

Please indicate the extent to which the following statements are true for you, using the following response scale. Write the number for your response in the space next to each statement.

1 = To little or no extent	4 = To a considerable extent
2 = To a limited extent	5 = To a great extent
3 = To some extent	

1. I try to shape my career to maximize freedom and autonomy. _____

2. Finding time for myself is important to my overall quality of life. _____

3. My career decisions are made in terms of how they will affect my family.* _____

4. I am in charge of my own career. _____

5. If my current work does not support my values, I'll try to change it. _____

6. It is important to me to have a job that allows me the flexibility to be involved in my community. _____

7. I navigate my own career based on my personal priorities, as opposed to my employer's priorities. _____

8. Having a good fit between my work life and my home life is an important aspect of career success to me. _____

9. My career plans are centered on my present organization. _____

10. Making time to contribute to the well-being of my community is a priority for me. _____

11. Continuous personal development is more important to me than external career rewards such as promotions and income. _____

12. My sense of self, or identity, is focused primarily on my career. _____

13. It is really important to me to consider my family's* needs when making career plans. _____

14. Achieving a high position is an important aspect of career success to me. _____

15. Overall, I have a very independent, self-directed career. _____

(Continued)

(Continued)

16. I would really not want to have a job that did not allow me time to volunteer in my community. _____

17. I believe that I am most effective at work when I am more committed to my own goals than to the organization's goals. _____

18. People who try to do things their own way as opposed to using prescribed procedures are not helpful to the organization's performance. _____

19. Those who work with me are aware of my personal beliefs and principles based on things I do or say. _____

20. If I can't express my values through my work, it's okay, as long as I achieve promotion or financial success. _____

21. My career plans are centered on my family's* needs. _____

22. When a decision comes up that pits life balance against career success, life balance is most important to me. _____

23. When I make a decision about my career, I consider how well the new situation would fit with my personal beliefs and values. _____

24. When I make a decision about my career, I consider how well the new situation would fit with my family's* priorities. _____

25. In the past I have left a job, or strongly considered leaving a job, because it did not allow me to express myself in terms of what is most important to me in life. _____

26. It's important that I find ways to express my own values at work, regardless of whether they match perfectly the organization's values. _____

27. I value being of service to other people in the community where I live. _____

28. Having time for my family* is a driving force in my career decisions. _____

29. When choosing between two career options, I tend to prefer the one that provides the best work–life balance. _____

30. Expressing my values at work is just as important to me as expressing them in other parts of my life. _____

31. Advancement and promotion are very important to me. _____

32. To feel successful in my career, I must have other outlets for expression of my personal interests and talents. _____

33. Following my own path is more important than moving up my organization's career ladder. _____

_____ **Total Score**
_____ **Average Score** (equals Total Score divided by 33)

Scoring

First, add up the numbers for your responses to all of the questions. Enter this total next to "Total Score" above. Then divide this score by 33. This will give your Average Score. Enter this score next to "Average Score" above.

Interpreting Your Average Score

>4.4:   Extremely protean (top 2%)

4.0–4.39:   Highly protean (top 15%)

3.6–3.99:   Moderately protean

3.2–3.59:   Moderately organizational

2.8–3.19:   Highly organizational (top 15%)

<2.8:   Extremely organizational (top 2%)

Hypothesized Life and Career Facets

To compute your Life and Career Facets, add up the scores you assigned to the questions listed in each of the following categories (e.g., for self-direction, add up the scores for questions 1, 4, 7, 12, 15, and 33). Then divide the total by the total number of questions indicated (e.g., to calculate self-direction, divide the sum of your answers by 6).

1. Self-direction $1 + 4 + 7 + 12 + 15 + 33 =$ _____ / 6 = _____
2. Organizational orientation $9 + 14 + 18 + 20 + 31 =$ _____ / 5 = _____
3. Value expression $5 + 17 + 19 + 23 + 25 + 26 + 30 =$ _____ / 7 = _____
4. Whole life balance focus $2 + 11 + 22 + 29 + 32 =$ _____ / 5 = _____
5. Family* focus $3 + 8 + 13 + 21 + 24 + 28 =$ _____ / 6 = _____
6. Community involvement $6 + 10 + 16 + 27 =$ _____ / 4 = _____

Explanation of Terms

- Self-direction: high degree of autonomy
- Organizational orientation: desire to stay with employer
- Value expression: chance to do value-based work
- Whole life balance focus: opportunity to maintain balance
- Family* focus: emphasis on family
- Community involvement: opportunity to work in the community

Developed by Douglas T. Hall, Jon Briscoe, Mary Dean Lee, and Ellen Ernst Kossek. Used with permission

*The term *family* may include your spouse or partner, children, parents, or others with whom you share your life or home.

As you go through this chapter, the Career and Life Orientation Index should serve as a highly useful point of reference. As you think about your personal career plans, you will want to consider how much control you want over your career path, what the major drivers of satisfaction are, what shape development will take, and what kinds of boundaries you want between your home life and your work life. There was a time, not so long ago, when organizations provided clear career paths for all employees. Some organizations still maintain an "up or out" approach to development that suggests that career development equals moving up the hierarchy. But today, people have more license to create their own path. It is now incumbent on each of us to make these decisions and navigate our own unique approach to ongoing development.

Organizational Career Paths

There is good news and bad news about organizational career paths today. The bad news is that many organizations have downsized and delayered, so that there are fewer opportunities for upward mobility than there were 10 or 15 years ago. In short, the old career paths are, for the most part, gone (one meaning of Tim's book title, *The Career Is Dead—Long Live the Career*). The good news is that there is less external pressure for people to move in prescribed career paths. With flatter organizations, the remaining jobs are broader (i.e., have wider scope of responsibilities), and there are far more options for lateral moves.

What remains, though, are some very general directions that people might take in their careers. They include the following:

- *Functional paths.* It is still possible to build your career around a functional specialty, such as finance or marketing, because larger organizations tend to have a hierarchy of positions within these functions. However, in the era of the boundaryless career—a career that is no longer seen in the context of one particular organization— fewer people spend long periods of time in one organization and work their way up a functional path. They might move between organizations while staying within their functional specialty.

- *Industry paths.* Increasingly, people are coming to identify with a broad industry sector rather than a specific organization. Examples include healthcare, information technology, or financial services. We are also seeing professional communities of practice grow up around certain industries, and this reinforces these industry career paths. For example, in the optics industry we have seen the rise of clusters, informal networks of people and companies in the optics industry that are networked for the purpose of information sharing and support.

- *Institutional sector.* Although many people who read this book may be heading toward a career in the business or for-profit sector, many people are oriented more toward the public or nonprofit sectors. In the business school community we are seeing an increased focus on the nonprofit sector as an arena for people with a values-oriented personal mission to pursue their "path with a heart." They are willing to trade a certain amount of financial reward for the chance to pursue a purpose that has greater meaning for them. Although it is certainly possible to cross sector boundaries throughout one's career, people often define their professional identity in terms of the sector in which they work.

FROM CAREER LADDERS TO CAREER LATTICES

Cliff Hakim, the author of *We Are All Self-Employed,* presents us with the following dialogue:

Question: "How does a career ladder fit in flattening organizations?"

Answer: "For the majority, it doesn't." (1994, p. 33)

Hakim explains that as organizations downsize and delayer, more latitude is necessary. People have bigger jobs, with more responsibility and scope. They are empowered, and decisions have to be made where the problems and the customers are and where the work gets done. Organizations can no longer afford hierarchies.

In the past it was the hierarchy that provided the path for career development. Up was the only way for career growth to occur. But now, when organizations work laterally rather than vertically, lateral is the primary way. Thus, as Hakim points out, the new career reality is not the career ladder but the *career lattice.* He describes the career lattice as follows:

A career ladder suggests that there are only three ways to go: up, down, or falling off. Up usually means success; going down or falling off . . . well, most of us try to avoid these.

By contrast, the career lattice is a viable alternative for career mobility and job productivity, for its structure supports different paths, each one involving career choices based on skills, values, interests, competition, workplace and customer needs, and individual and group initiative. A career lattice provides many options that a career ladder cannot. Douglas, for example, worked his way up the ladder to become a partner in a public relations firm. As partner, his role changed from direct consulting with clients to managing workers. But as the marketplace changed, he needed to lay off staff and step off the ladder. Douglas became a consultant again, moving in any direction—that is, using the career lattice—so that customers would be served and the firm would succeed. (1994, p. 34)

As you move from career ladder thinking to career lattice thinking, Hakim suggests that you reframe your career perspective as described in Table 5.1.

Table 5.1   Reframing Your Career Perspective

From Career Ladder Perspective	To Career Lattice Perspective
Moves are limited.	Moves can go in any direction (up, down, across).
Promotions and titles are the main rewards.	What people contribute matters most.
The boss provides answers and direction.	We collaborate ("Let's figure it out.").
Rewards are based on loyalty.	Rewards are based on results.
Employees are dependent on others.	Independence, flexibility, and teamwork are the ways work gets done.

SOURCE: Reprinted with permission of the publisher. From *We are all self-employed: The new social contract for working in a changed world,* copyright © 1994, by Hakim, C., Berrett-Koehler Publishers, Inc., San Francisco, CA. All rights reserved. www.bkconnection.com

What this change means is that the important currency in the career is not advancement but learning. Your current skills are your main form of security in a turbulent business environment, and when you stop learning, your career lifeblood is cut off. Lattice thinking and the mobility and learning that it leads to will keep you on the most promising paths to career development.

One barrier that makes it difficult for people to switch between different career paths is what we call the search for the perfect fit. This mindset is the tendency of employers to look for a job candidate who has done exactly the same job in the past. Thus, they can select someone who has already demonstrated good performance in that job. Although this might appear to be a safe strategy for the employer, it doesn't work for either party. It certainly does not serve a job candidate well who wants to make any kind of career change or a move to a different path.

Even for the organization, this "perfect fit" approach could result in an employee not feeling stimulated and challenged by something new. Even though he or she has the experience and ability to perform well, his or her motivation level might be lower than that of the candidate for whom the job is new. *Career variety* is a powerful source of motivation and adaptability, especially as the person becomes more senior. If an employer selects a person for whom the job represents *low* variety (i.e., a job the person has done before), they are losing out on a good motivational opportunity.

VERTICAL CAREERS AND ORGANIZATIONAL ADVANCEMENT

Despite all that has been said about protean careers and a subjective view of success and all that will be said about alternative career paths, many people still think of careers and career development in more traditional ways. For many, career development and success are equated with how far and how quickly one moves up the hierarchy.

Although we present many alternatives to the traditional view that up is the only way, we recognize that this organizational view of success is both common and, for many, desirable. With that in mind, how does one increase the likelihood of achieving organizational success and moving up the career ladder? A number of tried-and-true approaches to moving ahead in an organizational career are grounded in both conventional wisdom and empirical research.

Linda Hill of Harvard Business School has extensively studied the area of career development and management development in organizations. Hill (1994) offers some sound advice for those looking to be "successful" and to advance within their organizations. She states that managers must take charge of their careers and become self-directed learners willing to invent themselves time and again. They must be prepared to continually learn and grow in response to an ever-changing environment.

Hill outlines what she terms "creating a success syndrome"—the idea that success snowballs and contributions get noticed and build a reputation that garners even higher visibility assignments. How do you do this? According to Hill, one should:

1. *Land stretch assignments.* Find the right balance between assignments where you are learning but also contributing. Learning without contributing or contributing without learning are both recipes for long term problems.

2. *Pay attention to the tangibles but also the intangibles*: Focusing on salary, promotions, and titles is fine but you must also look at other intangible factors that will significantly influence your long-term success. Things to consider: Am I learning? Am I building my support network? Am I building a solid reputation? Am I increasing my self-confidence?

3. *Think strategically*: Don't just think about moving up, think about how lateral moves can broaden and build your skill set.

4. *Think globally:* With the increased emphasis on globalization, the importance of gaining international experience has also increased. The advantages of securing international experience are that you will gain leadership skills, learn new language(s) and cultures, build empathy for other countries, and learn to cope with ambiguity.

As Hill makes clear, even for those who are looking for career advancement in a vertical sense, simply pursuing vertical paths could be a mistake. Especially early in one's career it is important to look for ways to diversify your skills, broaden your understanding of the organization you work for, and build a large support network. While lateral moves and international assignments may not be the fastest ways to advance within an organization, in our experience they increase the likelihood of the long-term attainment of your advancement goals.

MANAGING UP

Like it or not, anyone looking to move up the hierarchy in an organization needs to be skilled in managing up. In 2001, three research organizations— the Families and Work Institute, Catalyst, and the Boston College Center for Work & Family—completed the Global Leaders Study (Box 5.1). This study examined the career development of more than 1,000 senior executives in very large organizations. For the majority of the participants in study, the people most influential in helping them to advance were their direct manager or a manager at a higher level in the organization. When asked, "Who is the one person in your current organization who has helped you most to develop in your career?" nearly 45% of the respondents answered "My manager." Remember, this response is from people at the very highest echelons of major corporations, probably people who enjoy a large and influential network and high visibility in their organizations.

If you are looking to advance through the management ranks, how well you manage your boss is likely to be more important than how well you manage your team or your horizontal relationships. Many senior managers will judge your performance more on how you perform and are perceived than by the way your workgroup operates. Until recently, with the increasing use of 360-degree feedback as a standard part of the evaluation process, few senior managers would solicit feedback on a manager's performance and leadership abilities from that manager's workgroup. Managing your workgroup poorly is a significant impediment to upward mobility, but managing your manager poorly is potentially fatal. Conversely, managing your manager well can be enormously helpful.

A number of years ago professors John Gabarro and John Kotter wrote what has become a classic article in the *Harvard Business Review,*

"Managing Your Boss" (Gabarro & Kotter, 2005). They pointed out that managers can offer a lot to an aspiring junior manager, including sponsorship, resources, coaching, and visibility. They offered some advice for how to manage this most important relationship. It included the following:

- Understand that relationships are always made up of two fallible human beings. It's not enough to be aware of your boss's failings; you also need to think about how to compensate for them.

- Make it a point to know things such as your boss's highest priorities, what his or her boss is expecting from him or her (pressures), your boss's strengths and weaknesses, and how your manager likes to be informed (how often and in what format).

Gabarro and Kotter also offer the following suggestions for managing this relationship:

Be dependable and honest.

Provide a good flow of information.

Make good use of your manager's limited time.

Initiate contact regularly.

Understand mutual expectations (his or hers of you and yours of him or her).

Making your boss a hero or removing a major headache will always be appreciated. Think of your boss as your customer and ask yourself, "What are the two or three things my customer would most want from me?" and "What can I do that would add the most value or eliminate his or her biggest problem?"

**Box 5.1 Organizational Career Advancement:
The Global Leaders Study**

In 2001, three research organizations—the Families and Work Institute, Catalyst, and the Boston College Center for Work & Family—completed the Global Leaders Study. This study was the largest ever done of senior executives in major U.S. global corporations; 1,100 executives in 10 corporations participated. This research focused heavily on women for two primary reasons. First, women play increasingly important roles in business and in the global economy. Second, companies needed to find ways to retain their top female talent. Retaining women in leadership positions had been

(Continued)

(Continued)

(and remains) a serious concern for organizations, where many women find juggling top management positions with family roles to be quite difficult.

Working time for executives in the study averaged about 62 hours a week, with little difference in men's and women's work hours. When they were asked why they work the long hours they do, a few key reasons emerged:

- 76% said, "To meet my own standards for doing good work."
- 66% said, "It takes that long to do the work I need to do."
- Between one third and one half of the participants suggested that they put in the long hours to meet customer needs and to improve the company's bottom line.
- One quarter of the participants said, "To advance at my job."

So although the jobs these people held were indeed demanding, perhaps the greater reason for working the hours they did was an internal standard of quality.

The demographics of the study participants also revealed some clear differences between male and female executives. For example, 91% of the men in the study were married, and 90% had children. By contrast, 72% of the women were married, and only 65% had children. This statistic mirrors a number of other studies of successful women and the high percentage of these women who are childless (e.g., Hewlett, 2002b). Perhaps even more telling, only 11% of the men in the study had a spouse who worked full time, whereas 74% of the women had a spouse or partner working full time.

One of the key areas where gender differences remained clear was in responsibility for child rearing. When participants were asked, "Who takes more responsibility for child care?" 57% of the women and only 1% of the men answered, "I do." In addition to the obvious psychological and physical burden this places on women, it can also affect their ability to fulfill some job requirements. When asked how often overnight business travel was required by their jobs, 38% of participants answered "several times a month." But in this instance there was a significant difference between men's and women's answers. Of those who said this amount of travel was required, 46% were men and 30% were women. These numbers suggest that women might be avoiding jobs that carry a heavy travel requirement due, in some measure, to their family responsibilities. As corporate consolidations increase and long-distance business travel is increasingly becoming part of the landscape for those who seek upward mobility, the still radically unequal distribution of child care responsibilities creates another organizational obstacle to women's advancement into senior-level roles.

Also related to work hours and work demands was the issue of what one puts first, work or personal life. Those who put work ahead of their personal life we called *work-centric*, those who put family first are *family-centric*, and those who try to balance the two evenly are *dual-centric* (Galinsky et al., 2003). As one might imagine, the majority of senior executives are work-centric: 57% stated that they put job ahead of family life often or very often. These executives were more likely to miss family events or work at night and on weekends. This finding was expected. However, an interesting finding was that those who are dual-centric reported higher levels of satisfaction and fulfillment both at home and on the job than those who were work-centric. This suggests that although being work-centric facilitates advancement, having a dual-centric approach to work and life might yield greater feelings of fulfillment.

Key messages from the participants regarding development and the obstacles to advancement included the following:

When asked, "What has your employer done to help you succeed?"

83% said, "Provided opportunities for leadership."

80% said, "Gave me challenging assignments."

50% said, "Provided exposure to senior leaders early in my career."

35% said, "Provided opportunity for international assignments."

21% said, "Provided leadership training."

These responses mirror many of the suggestions from Linda Hill's work on management development. They also support the well-accepted notion that management development occurs primarily on the job, not in the classroom.

When asked, "What factors have been most limiting to you?"

24% said, "A limited number of mentors."

19% said, "Exclusion from important networks" (not surprisingly, the number here was more than twice as high for women as men).

19% said, "Limited role models" (again, this number was twice as high for women).

17% said, "A limited number of sponsors."

17% said, "The need to sacrifice everything for work in our corporate culture."

Finally, the study suggests that if you want to get to a high level in a major organization, this does not occur by accident: 75% of the study participants said that they had planned their career to some or to a great extent.

Alternative Career Paths

If the shift in the employment contract and the struggle for work–life balance has accomplished anything, it has helped many people realize two things:

- Ultimately the true measure of success is determined by one's sense of satisfaction and psychological well-being, not by one's position in an organizational hierarchy. Although it might be argued that this measure of success has always been true, today the illusion that the organization defines success has been stripped away for many of us.

- There are fewer and fewer examples of people following a linear career path up the organization. Today, career paths tend to be more idiosyncratic and more likely to resemble the career lattice mentioned earlier.

Because these trends have now been more widely recognized, there is greater openness to the notion that up is not the only way. Even for those who have chosen and succeeded on a traditional career path, happiness is not assured. In fact, a recent study suggests that CEOs, the consummate organizational advancement role models, may be a rather unhappy lot. A survey conducted at the New York global communication consultancy Burston-Marsteller found that "73 percent of the 369 CEOs surveyed answered yes to the question, 'Do you think about quitting your job?'" ("Survey: CEOs mull quitting their jobs," 2003). In addition, more than four out of five respondents said they are kept awake at night by "company demons," including worries about the competition, how to increase business, and how to keep shareholders happy. More than a third of the executives one rung down from CEO and more than 50% of the women in the survey reported that they would decline a promotion to the top spot if they were offered it. Beyond the pressures that go with the role, the organization that conducted that study further speculated that the rise in corporate scandals had also decreased the desirability of the role of CEO.

Also contributing to the acceptance that moving up the ladder may provide riches but not a rich life is the growing popularity of the simplicity movement, which espouses making a conscious choice to "work to live rather than live to work." This shift has also been influenced by environmentalists, who believe that the consumption trap many Americans are caught in has fueled overwork, created complexity in people's lives, and damaged the environment (Schor, 1992).

But perhaps the most important trend relating to alternative career paths comes about as a result of changing demographics. Recent studies of Generations X and Y indicate that members of these post–baby-boom generations are simply not as interested in upward advancement as their baby-boomer counterparts once were. The voice of these younger people seems to echo the theme that work–life balance and time with family are more important than organizational advancement. As of this writing, a majority of men ages 21–39 (more than 70%) said they want to spend more time with their families than their fathers did and would be willing to sacrifice pay to do so. Furthermore, these men have stated that the most important job characteristic they are seeking is a work schedule that allows them to spend time with their families (Radcliffe Public Policy Center and Harris Interactive, 2000). More evidence of this comes from Families and Work Institute's recent study that found that Generation X fathers spend on average 3.4 hours per day with their children, compared with the 2.2 hours baby-boomer fathers spend with their children of the same age (Families and Work Institute, 2004). And the issue is even more important to women in this group: 83% of women in an earlier study reported that flexible work arrangements are key to career advancement and satisfaction (Catalyst, 2001).

These shifts have led many people to consider alternative career paths. Many of these might fall under the broad umbrella of "downshifting." As Amy Salzman states in her book *Downshifting: Reinventing Success on a Slower Track,*

> Moving ahead on a career track will always be an important part of the success equation for many of us. Work is our anchor—and tells us who we are and whether we measure up financially. But in our quest to conform to a predetermined image of success, we have lost track of our true goals: to lead meaningful and worthwhile lives. We have allowed our careers to control us.
>
> Pulling back will of course, require making sacrifices, the most obvious of which are financial. In terms of pure monetary and lifestyle impact, however, those sacrifices may be surprisingly minimal. Rather than moving backwards economically, the majority of downshifters merely end up plateauing their lifestyles. They learn to live without the remodeled kitchen, a new car every five years, and the bigger dream house they once believed they had to have. Instead they come to appreciate the comforts and sense of belonging that results from staying put. Money, they begin to see matters far less when they are personally and professionally satisfied. (1992, p. 67)

Salzman, a journalist, profiled a number of high-visibility downshifters in her book. She offers five models or prototypes for those who are looking for alternative career paths.

BACKTRACKERS: PEOPLE WHO CHOOSE SELF-DEMOTION TO HAVE MORE TIME AND LESS STRESS

Salzman points out that if there is one given about a stereotypical career it is that we travel up, not down. Moving backwards as a purposeful choice is one that a person might choose only after traveling upward, with an accompanying feeling that one is moving away from where he or she wants to be. As Salzman states,

> Getting over the idea that they will be cast as failures is the greatest challenge facing Backtrackers. For females, for example, who have climbed to a position of authority in male-dominated fields, the

thought of abruptly stepping backward seems to legitimize the stereo-type that women don't have what it takes to make it at the top. . . . In fact, for men and women alike, stepping back is frequently the culmi-nation of a painful personal battle between personal needs and professional expectations. In the competitive world of masculine achievement, backtracking is often viewed as copping out. (1992, p. 97)

For many career climbers the early years of the career are seductive. "Successful" people see changes occurring that are difficult to resist. These changes include increases in power and autonomy, increasingly visible and important assignments, positive feedback from senior management, and often significant increases in earnings. "In the midst of such professional highs, setting limits and saying 'no' seems impossible" (Salzman, 1992, p. 99). Another challenge is that society tells young high achievers that they should feel happy and privileged with the success they have achieved, that "others would kill to be in your shoes."

PLATEAUERS: PEOPLE WHO INTENTIONALLY STAY IN PLACE BY TURNING DOWN PROMOTIONS TO STAY IN CONTROL OF THEIR LIVES

Salzman (1992) states,

Not so long ago the "plateauer" was a kinder, gentler word for "dead-wood." In the corporate world, the plateaued were typically middle managers whose solid but unspectacular performance allowed them to coast comfortably toward retirement while making a minimal con-tribution to the organization. Today, Plateauers are no longer synony-mous with deadwood, and the opportunity to stay in place and avoid political entanglements of the upward track may actually lead to new opportunities for creative and intellectual development. (p. 74)

Salzman goes on to say that confining one's career to an upward or vertical track actually can limit choices, make it difficult to do work one enjoys, and limit the range of skills one can develop. She points out that the delayering of the corporate world actually makes this a very reasonable means of growing and developing while not necessarily seeing manage-ment as the only path to development.

CAREER SHIFTERS: PEOPLE WHO TRANSFER THEIR SKILLS TO LESS PRESSURED FIELDS

Salzman makes a clear distinction between *career shifters* and *career changers*. A career changer is someone who goes from being a doctor to a business executive or a lawyer to a novelist (also known today as *John Grisham syndrome,* fairly common among lawyers). Career changers are not downshifters. They may be going from one high-pressure role to a different one. They are motivated by the desire to do something that they believe is different and more fundamentally aligned with their interests.

By contrast, career shifters are those who still get satisfaction and enjoyment from their professions but feel they have committed to an unnecessarily rigorous course within that profession. Salzman (1992) points out,

> The approach they take is more appropriately labeled career shifting because it involves a refocusing rather than a complete redoing of their professional pursuits. Career changing by contrast often requires returning to school and then reestablishing a whole new set of professional contacts to open doors and help gain a solid footing in a new profession. Such changes can take years and are often a major shock to the ego and the pocketbook. Achieving a more balanced life on a slower track, career shifters realize, will not come from completely dismantling their careers and starting from scratch. (p. 122)

SELF-EMPLOYERS: PEOPLE WHO GO SOLO TO GAIN MORE CONTROL OVER THEIR WORK HOURS AND LOCATION

Somewhat different from the stereotype of a driven entrepreneur, who sinks his or her whole being into a startup business, the self-employer chooses entrepreneurship as a lifestyle. The desire to be one's own boss, set one's own schedule, and avoid corporate bureaucracy is the motivation for this person. In fact, Salzman points to a study of 3,000 new business owners conducted by the National Federation of Independent Businesses. The survey found that "54% said that 'having greater control over their life' was among the most important reasons for choosing entrepreneurship and 32% said that being able to 'live where and how I like' was at the top of their list. By contrast, only 19% said that earning a lot of money and gaining more respect and recognition were primary motivators" (Salzman, 1992, p. 148).

The shift toward self-employment is also a logical response to the growing instability of the corporate world. As Charles Handy postulates in *The Age of Unreason* (1989), corporations are decreasing in overall employment and are creating opportunities for small service companies, contract workers, and consultants to complement or supplement their full-time workforce. Self-employers might see these roles as being more desirable despite their lack of benefits because they create opportunities for greater autonomy and control over one's work life.

URBAN ESCAPEES: PEOPLE WHO OPT FOR MORE HOSPITABLE, LESS STRESSFUL ENVIRONMENTS

Salzman describes this phenomenon as one that has existed for many years: seeking the peace and serenity of the countryside, escaping the pace and lifestyle of the large city in favor of a quieter, simpler life. She suggests that urban escape is gaining momentum for several reasons. The first is the desire to find a greater sense of community and a less expensive way of life. Salzman (1992) states,

> An underlying theme seems to fuel most urban escapees: It is the belief that the high prices, honking horns, and impatient tenor of urban and suburban life have pushed them further and further away from the sense of neighborhood and community found in small-town America. (p. 174)

Additionally, the quest for a less stressful environment in which to pursue careers is compelling. "There is no question that expectations about careers and emphasis on work are much greater in some areas of the country than they are in others. Most notably, the big cities of the East Coast, which attract a large percentage of young professionals, are far more focused on career status and macho workaholism than even comparable cities in the Midwest and on the West Coast" (Salzman, 1992, p. 175). There is little question that Silicon Valley area and other areas of California have joined the East Coast in their reputation for workaholism since the publication of Salzman's book.

Salzman suggests that the transition to urban escapee is not easy. Making a living in a small town is a significant challenge. Salzman uses the example of people who move from an urban environment to open a rural bed & breakfast, a common dream for the urban escapee. Quoting innkeepers' association studies, Salzman states that "the average B&B owner calls it quits after one to two years" and that a study of Colorado B&Bs suggests that "only 14% of establishment owners used them as the sole source of income" (1992, p. 173).

In summary, downshifting may be a desirable career alternative for those who take a more protean rather than organizational view of careers. It also is consistent with Hall's notion of psychological success. As Salzman maintains,

> Creating and following a personal success path means learning to set work patterns that reinforce rather than sabotage our deepest notions about what constitutes a successful life. This is more difficult than it sounds. Even if we know what we want from our careers, the pressures to always strive for more are difficult to resist. More power, more money, more prestige, are the essence of success in our culture. These exaggerated goals push us to accept jobs we don't particularly want and take on more responsibility than we can reasonably handle. (p. 79)

The Portfolio Career

As previously mentioned, in 1989 Charles Handy of the London School of Economics wrote an influential book called *The Age of Unreason*. In this work, Handy put forth a view of the "new organizations" that would no longer directly employ the majority of their staffs. Instead, staffs would be made up of a core group of employees who would be complemented by outsourcing, contractors, and consultants in what Handy called a "shamrock organization." Many of Handy's ideas have come to pass in recent years.

In his book, Handy also raised the notion of the *portfolio* career. He characterized a work portfolio as a way of describing "how the different bits of work fit together in our life in order to form a balanced whole" (1989, p. 183). Handy suggests that to have a portfolio career means that you will no longer be able to answer the question, "What do you do?" with a job title as a response. To understand the portfolio, you must first understand what Handy calls the main categories of work that can make up one's portfolio: wage work, fee work, home work, gift work, and study work. Here's how Handy defines these terms:

- *Wage work* represents time given for money paid. Employees of organizations do wage work and get paid a salary.

- *Fee work* is results delivered for money paid. Consultants or freelancers often do this kind of work, maintaining independence from the organization but getting paid only for the result of their efforts.

- *Home work* includes the whole catalogue of tasks that go on in the home (i.e., domestic tasks and child rearing).

- *Gift work* refers to work done outside the home, typically for free as a volunteer, to support causes and institutions in which one believes.

- *Study work* refers to work you do to maintain or improve your professional abilities.

Handy suggests that seeing work as being made up of these five categories may be a more appropriate way to reframe one's career. Portfolios, he argues, are not new because all small businesses have them in terms of clients. Handy states, "As more people move their paid work outside organizations, or are moved, they are pushed or lured into becoming small independent businesses. They are paid in fees, not wages, and have to develop their own portfolios of customer and activities" (1989, p. 190). If one pursues this logic, it is important to make conscious decisions about what your portfolio should contain. It may mean being conscious about working for a lesser fee or wage work to spend more time in home work with family, for example. By doing this, you are not simply living consistently with your priorities; more importantly, you are saving money that you would spend if you outsourced domestic activities (e.g., daycare or gardening tasks) to a service. In this way you are constructing, rather than accepting in a reactive fashion, the mix of work activities in which you would like to engage.

These career options—organizational, alternative, or portfolio—are not mutually exclusive. It is possible to follow an organizational career path but not look for upward mobility by plateauing or even taking a demotion, for example. Although this was rarely done voluntarily a few years ago, today many women and men take steps "backward" in an organization to make more time for family or other outside interests. It is also possible to have a portfolio career yet still be employed primarily by one organization (your wage work). Many portfolio individuals do this to have a "home base" that provides highly valued benefits such as healthcare insurance but also offer latitude for pursuing other important forms of work.

Ongoing Development

Regardless of what career strategy one pursues, organizational advancement, alternative, or portfolio career, ongoing development is critically important. Even if one is not motivated to climb to the top of the organizational pyramid, it is not a license to stop developing. Almost no job or organization guarantees permanence or security these days, so regardless of your level of ambition, your most important goal is to ensure your ongoing *employability*. And given the number of years we will be working, ongoing development or lifelong learning is a never-ending process.

Certain factors in success cut across all stages; they are always important. These factors include job challenge, relationships, formal training and education, and hardship. First in importance is *job challenge*. The developmental importance of challenge is nothing new (although the organizational research on it is recent). Abigail Adams gave the following advice to her son, John Quincy Adams, who was accompanying his father, John Adams, on what was then a hazardous ocean voyage to their newly independent country:

> These are the times in which a genius would wish to live. It is not in the still calm of life, or the repose of a pacific station, that great characters are formed. The habits of a vigorous mind are formed in contending with difficulties. Great necessities call out great virtues. When a mind is raised, and animated by scenes that engage the heart, then those qualities that would otherwise lay dormant, wake into life and form the character of the hero and the statesman. (McCullough, 2001, p. 226)

Although challenge in the very first job is critical, research at AT&T and the Center for Creative Leadership has shown that challenge continues to be important for learning throughout the career. A challenging job gives you not only important new skills, self-confidence, and resilience but also high exposure and visibility.

Although some people see really difficult assignments as potential career booby traps or setups, not learning challenges, in our experience a challenging assignment is simply that: a challenge that can lead to personal stretching, growth, and the development of character.

How can you tell when a difficult assignment is a true developmental challenge (as opposed to a setup)? Tune in to the signals you are receiving from your manager. If she or he is willing to respond to your questions about the assignment, provides you with good coaching, and expresses confidence in your ability to succeed, then it's probably a genuinely development assignment.

The second critical success element is *relationships*. You do not live and work in a vacuum, and you need the support and help of others to succeed (Hall & Kahn, 2001). The most familiar form of helping relationship is mentoring, which was briefly touched on in chapter 4. Here, we discuss it as an important continuing component of career success (Box 5.2).

Do not expect that any one person will be the perfect mentor; you will be disappointed if that is what you are seeking. Look for different people to help you in different ways, and if one special person emerges to "do it all" for you, consider it a nice surprise.

In a mentoring relationship, the mentor learns at least as much as the protégé and is often flattered by the request, so do not feel shy about initiating contact with people who might be helpful to you. However, keep sight of the reciprocity of the relationship. You may be able to provide him or her with new ideas, new methods, appreciation, recognition, and assistance in meeting his or her job objectives.

Many other kinds of developmental relationships will be available to you in your career, and it will be up to you to notice and cultivate them. A major form of learning will come from your *peer relationships* (peer mentoring), which can be at least as helpful as mentoring by a senior person. Peers often are much closer to you in age and life experience, so in some ways they may be more relevant role models than seniors and may be able to provide more emotional support.

Other help, for example in the form of feedback, can come from subordinates, customers, colleagues in the organization, and family or friends. There is now much emphasis in business on 360-degree feedback, or feedback from all sources in all directions. You never know where or when you might encounter good feedback and learning opportunities. And remember Ken Blanchard's dictum, "Feedback is the breakfast of champions."

You will also be spending a lot of your time in teams, which are excellent sources of developmental relationships. Because teams usually are designed to span many boundaries (e.g., different functions, businesses, geographic locations, ages, genders, ethnicities) so that they include a rich diversity of talents and backgrounds, in turn they present terrific learning opportunities for each member.

Two other kinds of relationships that people are using more in a turbulent environment are personal networks and support groups. In the aftermath of the World Trade Center destruction and related air crashes of September 11, 2001, one important source of hope for the world was the way people came forward so quickly and willingly to help other people. A support group can be any formal or informal group of people who come together to provide help to one another and to others. This can be emotional support (e.g., encouragement, empathy, and acknowledgment), or it can be instrumental (e.g., information, advice, coaching). For example, Tim is part of a men's support group that meets every month or 6 weeks, for a morning, in one member's home. There is no formal agenda, but they start by going around the room for a "check-in" to see what people have brought and then talk about whatever seems most pressing to someone or most common to everyone. They sometimes discuss problems at work, life stage or personal issues, or family issues and occasionally take on one of the problems of the world or discuss some academic issue. The group has been meeting for more than 20 years, and attendance is a high priority for all of us as a support network.

People create similar groups with colleagues at work, in professional organizations, in their local communities, and in other settings. In a career context, they can exist as job search support groups, outplacement assistance groups, and career coaching networks. Employee networks are becoming more common for members who are from a common group or share common challenges at work. Examples include groups based on gender, ethnic or racial groups, groups for gay and lesbian employees, or groups caring for children, older adults, and those with special needs. If none of these exist in your present work environment, you can organize one yourself. You can call it a peer coaching group if no other name comes to mind.

Formal education and training is the third source of learning for success in the career. Surprisingly, this factor is not as important by itself as are job challenge and relationships. But in combination with job challenge and relationships, formal education is a potent success factor. You can best use a seminar or conference for management development when as a result of a job assignment you have a clear need to learn. And if you can get help through a relationship (e.g., from your boss) in deciding when is a good time for training and what is a good job project to work on in the seminar, then you are getting real leverage out of that training. So do not think of training as simply "ticket punching" for getting the next job; think of it as a means of enhancing your learning and performance in your current job, which will, of course, also help you get the next job.

The final factor that is critical to success is *hardship*. This factor has been identified in research by Morgan McCall and his colleagues in which people were studied who had either arrived at the top of their organizations or had derailed along the way (i.e., they had been fired, plateaued, or quit; McCall et al., 1988; McCall, 1998). Surprisingly, the "Arrivers" were just as likely to hit failures or setbacks along the way as were the "Derailers." The big difference was that the "Arrivers" were more likely to learn from their failures. They were more likely to ask others for help, feedback, and ideas on what to do next. The Derailers were more likely to blame someone else, avoid personal feedback, and thus repeat their mistakes. In fact, a study of accelerated development (in which people were promoted very quickly and reached the top of their organizations) found that these fast trackers, though initially successful, were more likely than slower developers to leave their organizations. Why? Because they had moved so fast, they had not experienced hardships or failures along the way and had not developed their resilience and coping skills. They had also not taken the time to develop supportive social networks along the way. In fact, in their rush to the top, they had alienated many people, who were only too happy to see them get tripped up. Therefore, when these fast trackers eventually experienced a setback, they lacked the internal and external resources that would enable them to learn from the failure and to move on (Hall, 1999, pp. 237–239).

You should anticipate that there will be some setbacks along the way in your career. However, you can do your own research, perhaps with information from a mentor or helpful peers, about pitfalls that have hurt other people in your organization, and you can try to avoid those situations. And you can prepare for the inevitable setbacks that will occur by having your network of supporters there, ready to help when you stumble.

Obviously, personal qualities also play a role in career success. In this turbulent environment, personal flexibility, tolerance of uncertainty, and drive are important. Resilience, the ability to bounce from setbacks, is becoming increasingly necessary. Again, these personal qualities become more important in connection with specific experiences that you might encounter in the job environment. Also, note that the three qualities just mentioned can be developed. In other words, effort can make a difference. The most important qualities are not inborn abilities or qualities such as height or eye color. You cannot change your height, but it is not so hard to work on your flexibility, reaction to uncertainty, or motivation if you choose to do so.

Box 5.2 Reconceptualizing Mentoring as Developmental Relationships

Because of its importance, we would like to look at the topic of relationships in greater depth and consider a special kind of relationship, one in which the parties are intentionally working to promote the development of one another. We use terms such as *mentoring* or *developmental relationships* to describe this kind of growth-inducing relationship.

(Continued)

(Continued)

One of the leading thinkers and writers in the field of mentoring is Kathy Kram of Boston University. A traditional mentoring relationship is one in which a senior person working in the protégé's organization assists with the protégé's personal and professional development (Kram, 1985). More recently, Kram and co-author Monica Higgins of Harvard Business School have begun to reframe the notion of mentoring and put it in a new and more contemporary light. In "Reconceptualizing Mentoring at Work: A Developmental Network Perspective" (2001), Higgins and Kram consider the limitation of traditional mentoring practices. The traditional view depended on identifying a particular person who was more senior in one's organization, but this view had many limitations, especially in light of today's workplace realities. The authors include their own observations on this:

- The employment contract between individuals and their employers has changed, and job security is a thing of the past.

- The changing nature of technology has also affected the form and function of careers and career development. Today, organizations put a premium on people who can adapt and learn quickly. This development may bring into question the value of seniority in organizations.

- The changing nature of organizational structures affects the sources from which people receive development assistance. These new organizational configurations may limit the degree to which people look inside one particular organization for development.

- Organizational membership has become increasingly diverse, which affects both the need for and resources available for development (Higgins & Kram, 2001, pp. 265–267).

A contemporary view of mentoring is characterized more as a developmental network where not one but a number of others provide many (perhaps more) of the resources historically derived from a traditional mentoring relationship. (Some writers call this a "Board of Directors" for your career.) One's network might provide different roles at different times. These roles could include providing peer advising and coaching, developing an understanding of a new work situation or culture, providing psychological support, pointing out new opportunities, providing sponsorship for those opportunities, and providing insight into how other areas of an organization operate. When you consider all the roles traditional mentors were expected to play, it is not hard to understand how a network such as the one Kram and others describe could serve this purpose more effectively.

Organizational Career Systems

When you are doing a job search or making a decision involving different job offers, what are some important things to consider in the company's career development process? How can you decide whether the company is doing a good job supporting the career development and ongoing learning of its employees? Beyond the components highlighted earlier, what else are good employers doing to support employee development?

One way to think about organizational career programs is in terms of whom are they aimed at: Are they employee centered or organization centered? The continuum in Figure 5.1 illustrates this approach with some examples. On the left-hand side of the continuum, we find activities that are entirely employee driven (self-directed training) or are company sponsored and run activities that are aimed at helping employees make their own choices and map out their own career plans. Such an orientation is somewhat consistent with the self-directed philosophy we have outlined in the book. However, this approach should not be confused with a sink-or-swim approach. Companies that are skilled at developing their employees may encourage employees to direct their own development, but this does not mean they do not provide resources or support. For example, there is a major difference between an organization that does not offer tuition reimbursement and one that allows the employee to choose how to spend their company-supported after-hours tuition. In the first instance the company is saying, "We do not provide financial support to assist you in your ongoing education efforts." In the second instance the company is offering excellent support to employees but allowing them to choose the direction of their development.

On the other end of the continuum are programs that are more organization centered. Such activities are driven more by the organization, with the aim of directing talent in the company in a way that is consistent with the organization's strategies and needs. For example, this might take the form of highly structured succession planning systems that not only identify employees who are likely candidates for promotion but also stipulate short-term job assignments that will develop the skills those employees need to increase their readiness for promotion. These systems can work fine and can increase organizational investment in training and development, but we offer a few cautions:

• Given the dynamic environment that exists in organizations, predicting who will be available to do what job in 3 to 5 years can be tricky. The instability of organizational life often can render even the best-laid plans useless over time as changes in organizations and key players occur.

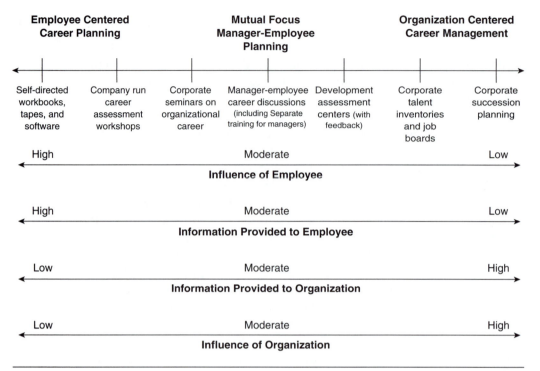

Figure 5.1   The Spectrum of Career Development Activities

SOURCE: Adapted from Hall, D. T. and Associates (1986). The Spectrum of Career Development Activities. In *Career Development in Organizations*. San Francisco: Jossey-Bass.

NOTE: This is a sample of program activities to illustrate different points on the continuum between career planning and career management. This is not a complete list of possible career development activities.

- Such systems can run the risk of creating "crowned princes and princesses" in the eyes of fellow employees. When a subset of employees is designated as "high potentials," if this designation is known to others it may create negative feelings on the part of other employees who have not been afforded this designation. Although it is important for organizations to actively manage performance and development for key human resources, if this creates a culture of haves and have-nots, the consequences may be negative for the organization overall.

- Finally, the organization-centered approach, taken to the extreme, could assume that the organization has more control over individuals' choices than is in fact the case. It may fit an organization's plans to have a high-potential employee take on a challenging 2-year project thousands of miles from home. But with the rise of dual-career couples, single-parent households, and individuals choosing lifestyle over career, such a move may serve the company's interest but not the individual's.

This leads us to the middle ground. This approach suggests a more shared responsibility that ensures that both the employee and the organization are involved in the process, and the needs of both parties are considered. It also ensures that the organization is providing support to the individual, financial and otherwise, in order for the goals of each party to be met.

So in addition to some of the things we have already mentioned (e.g., challenging job assignments, performance feedback, developmental relationships and mentoring), the following are other ways corporations can foster employee development.

Company-sponsored training: Training done on company time that is made available to employees based on need or interest can be very helpful. These offerings can range from brown-bag "lunch and learns" to full-blown graduate degree programs. Especially in jobs with significant change occurring (e.g., technology-related jobs in engineering or computer science), employees may find such learning opportunities not only valuable but necessary.

Tuition assistance: Many progressive companies offer tuition assistance to employees for further education. Specific policies differ somewhat. Some organizations pay for almost anything the employee is interested in. In our experience, most offer to fund education that is related to the employee's present role or to one that they might reasonably attain with their employer. Some organizations approve this education on a course-by-course basis, whereas others support an entire degree program, including courses that are required but may not be (or seem to be) very relevant to the employer's needs. Although tax laws related to the treatment of tuition assistance programs are subject to change, this benefit can be worth a tremendous amount of money to employees. Even more importantly, using these benefits can greatly increase their employability with their present employer and future employers.

Development planning: As a part of or in addition to performance evaluations, a focused development planning activity can be highly useful on at least an annual basis. Such a structured discussion can accomplish a number of things, including making one's manager aware of professional aspirations, planning for attendance at specific courses or conferences, identifying next-step career opportunities, or assigning special projects that might give the employees the skills they need to achieve their career objectives.

Job posting systems and promotion from within: Many employers put a premium on developing and promoting talent from within. This can make good sense for a number of reasons. One is the high level of attrition or failure rates among managers brought in from outside the organization.

According to one expert cited recently in a human resource publication, 40% of executives brought in from outside a company fail within 18 months, and half leave the company (Grossman, 2006, p. 42). Other reasons are the desire to tap into existing talent, reduce recruitment costs, and increase the likelihood of a good cultural fit. Perhaps the best reason for a promote-from-within approach is the extra motivation it gives employees who believe they have the opportunity to develop and advance with their present employer. An effective system of this type often posts all or most jobs internally, gives current employees early news on openings, and gives them preference in the hiring process.

Seminars on career and life planning: Given the focus of this book, this point probably needs little explanation. We believe that many of the ideas and exercises contained here could easily be used in organizational career planning seminars for all employees. There are some limitations to offering in-house programs, however. For example, if one of your preferences is to leave your current employer, this might be difficult or unwise to discuss in an in-house program. On the other hand, an internal program can convey the organization's commitment to developing its people, and it has the added advantage of being tailored to the particulars of the organization with regard to career opportunities and processes for pursuing them.

Although this list is not comprehensive, it does point out some of the things employees or potential employees should look for from their employers. Good employers invest in the skills and development of their people and see this as a primary way to gain and maintain competitive advantage.

International Assignments

At some point, given the unceasing movement toward globalization, you may be offered an opportunity to take on an international assignment. Although some of the merits of such an assignment have already been touched on, you will need to carefully consider what the value of such an assignment would be and what the challenges would be for you.

The value of an international assignment for the organization and the individual is that it is one of the best ways for companies to develop their managerial and executive talent. We have just discussed the value of challenge for career development, and an international position is loaded with challenges. You are exposed to novel situations and great uncertainty. You are in a foreign culture, often surrounded by people speaking a language you don't understand, where the rules seem mysterious. Your standard routines no longer work as they did at home, and no one is motivated to help you learn the new rules. In fact, many of the job factors that have been found to be developmental by researchers at the Center for Creative Leadership (McCall et al., 1988), are reflected in an international assignment:

> Often the international assignment involves a start-up or a turn-around process, which provides wonderful stretching experiences for development. Starting something from scratch produces learning situations, such as identifying what's important, building a team, surviving adversity and realizing the power of leadership. Succeeding in a fix-it assignment helps the person learn to be tough and persuasive and to be tough and instrumental.
>
> And then, in some cases, the international assignment entails a huge jump in scope, going from running a relatively small domestic operation to being head of, say, the company's business in Europe. With a sudden move to a larger operation, the person has no choice but to learn how to depend on other people (she can no longer do it all herself) and to think like an executive. (Hall et al., 2001, p. 335)

In addition to the work challenge, international assignments can also be extremely taxing on a personal level for you, your spouse, and your family. While your adjustment at work may be going smoothly, your family may be feeling lost and depressed. Your kids may resent being dragged away from their friends, and your partner or spouse may be unable to find employment (and may not be able to work under local laws). Because of the new and challenging assignment, you may find yourself working long hours, exacerbating your family's feeling that they are completely on their own. Yet the people from the corporate office expect you to perform at full effectiveness, just as you always have. All in all, it's a very demanding, stressful way of living and working. It usually takes a year before you begin to feel at home.

The challenge and stress usually stimulate a process of self-reflection and experimentation with new behaviors. As a result of these behavior changes, the person comes to see herself in a new way, with greater self-insights and self-awareness. Thus, the international assignment can lead to a *transformed identity*. The manager feels like a different person upon returning home.

For the company, international assignments are part of good management. The most admired *Fortune* companies are twice as likely as other companies to use carefully planned career assignments across countries (Hall et al., 2001).

In addition to these challenges during the international (often called *expatriate*) assignment, there are often even greater difficulties on the return home. Although the manager and her family may have been looking forward to the return for years, with great expectations, they often find that home does not meet those expectations. First, home has changed while they were away, so they may again feel like strangers, but now it's even worse because they are strangers in their own land. And *they* have changed, been transformed, yet no one seems to know or to care. For the manager, often there is not a good back-home assignment. Ironically, for expatriate assignments great care goes into finding an ideal match between the person and the job. But upon return, the person might be put on a special assignment or even into a role very much like the one she had before she left. For these reasons, repatriated managers often leave their companies shortly after they return home. Unless the company and executives who care a lot about the expatriate's career put a lot of work into planning the repatriate assignment, she will probably end up with a poorly fitting job and a negative attitude toward the company.

One of the things the company can do to help ensure success in international assignments is to appoint a senior executive in the home organization to be a mentor for the expatriate. This mentor needs to be in frequent contact with the expatriate, monitoring the person's experiences overseas, running interference with the corporate office back home when the person runs into bureaucratic problems, and helping to plan a good repatriation assignment that leverages the new skills the employee has developed in her time overseas. Attaining a good back-home job may be the most important factor in the retention of repatriated managers.

How do we know when an international assignment has been successful? We need to answer that question from both the individual and the organizational perspective. We also need to consider what success means, both during the expatriate phase and in the repatriation period. During the expatriate phase, success for the individual means good task performance, new skills, learning and growth, and job satisfaction. For the organization it means accomplishing organizational tasks (e.g., successfully opening and operating a new office in that country) and achieving certain objectives (e.g., reaching a certain level of profitability in the new location).

In the repatriation stage, success from the individual's perspective could mean continued development, a promotion, enlargement of one's responsibilities, and the likelihood of attractive future assignments. For the organization, successful repatriation would include the retention of repatriated employees, the use of the person's newly acquired expertise, and the transfer of that expertise to other personnel back home.

Financial Considerations

No book on careers would be complete without a discussion of a major reason we have work careers in the first place: to earn money to support ourselves. This is not to belittle the importance of the sense of meaning, purpose, and fulfillment that we get from working, but most of us have to work for financial reasons. Therefore, good financial planning is a foundation of good career planning.

Financial considerations play an increasingly important role in people's career choices and plans. Married mothers are much more likely to work today than in the 1970s, and one might surmise that, given this additional income, many couples feel they have greater choices about whether only one spouse should be working. However, many dual-career couples find that it is financially necessary for both husband and wife to work full time.

There are different views on why both spouses feel the need to work in families with children. The most obvious reason is simply that things are expensive today, and both spouses need to work in order to meet the family's expenses. A second reason, put forth by Juliet Schor and others, is that the need for both members of a dual-career couple to work is driven by consumption. The thinking goes that we live in a more materialistic time when the need for possessions has created a culture in which parents must work to pay for all their luxuries. This thinking has been contested by others, including Elizabeth Warren and Amelia Warren Tyagi (2003) in *The Two-Income Trap: Why Middle-Class Mothers and Fathers Are Going Broke*. The authors do not believe that overconsumption is at the root of most families' economic problems. Although they concede that families do spend more money on some items—electronic entertainment equipment, computers, and eating out, for example—they reject the notion that Americans are spending more on everything. They argue that Americans actually spend less (inflation adjusted) on many items than they did 30 years ago. They suggest that the impact of globalization has decreased prices for many items, including clothing, groceries, and major appliances.

If Warren and Tyagi are correct, what do they believe accounts for the challenging financial picture experienced by many working families despite the fact that most have two incomes? They outline a few key areas where expenses have spiraled out of control, but not as the result of "greedy consumers." According to Warren and Tyagi, the main problem areas seem to be the following:

The high cost of housing: Without doubt, couples spend far more on housing than was the case a generation ago. At least in part, the rise in housing prices has been the result of the increasing number of dual-earner couples, which has led to bidding wars for many homes. Two factors that make a home in a desirable suburb so expensive, according to the authors, are safety and education. In search of a safe place to raise children and a good school system, parents will pay a premium to live in a particular neighborhood or community.

The price of education: Despite our system of free public schools, the price of education has continued to escalate. Specifically, Warren and Tyagi suggest that it is the cost of preschool and college, which "now account for one-third (or more) of the years a typical middle class kid spends in school, are paid for almost exclusively by the child's family. . . . Today, nearly two-thirds of America's three- and four-year-olds attend pre-school compared with just 4% in the middle 1960s" (2003, p. 39). Furthermore, most Americans now also believe a college degree is a necessity, and the cost of that education is higher than ever. Simply to pay the cost of education (tuition, room, and board) at a public institution, the "average family in the United States would have to commit 17% of its pre-tax income to this one expense" (2003, p. 42). In the meantime, the cost of private colleges and universities has gone beyond the reach of many.

Cars: Families today spend more on cars because the need for a second car is greater. Once a luxury, a second car is now needed in part because both spouses work.

Two other expenses are also costing families more than ever. First, healthcare expenses have gone up dramatically over the past decade. An increasing number of people have lost job security. Given that in the United States healthcare coverage usually is provided by an employer, the burden for worrying about healthcare insurance payments and premiums has fallen more on the individual. Second, much has been written about the aging workforce and the aging population. We live longer in retirement today, and the need for and cost of long-term care are greater than ever. This is happening at the same time that defined-benefit retirement plans are becoming increasingly rare. This adds pressure on working people to save more money whenever possible in individual retirement plans.

So what can working people do to manage the financial aspects of their careers? A good guide to the financial aspects of career planning can be found in John Eckblad and David Kiel's book *If Your Life Were a Business, Would You Invest in It?* (2003). As they point out, if you want to achieve financial independence in your work, you will need three things:

• Knowledge of how much money you need now to live a satisfying life, how much you are likely to need in the future, and when you'll need it.

• Knowledge of how much money you have or can access now and a good estimate of how much you are likely to earn or receive in the future.

• A plan in which you expect to produce the funds you need, when you need them (Eckblad & Kiel, 2003, p. 142).

Eckblad and Kiel also state that the keys to this sort of financial planning process are how you organize the information and the new sense of self-confidence and freedom you feel when you are done. They contend that having worked out your plan, you will stop worrying about money as a constraint on your behavior. You therefore will achieve a level of financial independence (freedom from worry about money), regardless of the actual income you are earning. As they put it, "Enabling you to achieve your chosen Dreams while experiencing independence from your finances is the essential goal of Life Business work" (2003, p. 142).

Eckblad and Kiel have learned from their experience in their career coaching work that people need to be clear on three kinds of budgets.

- *12-month historical budget:* This is a detailed, accurate list of what you have spent, line by line, over the last year. Go back through your financial records from last year and capture, as accurately as possible, every bit of money that you spent on items such as vacations, going out to eat, clothing, food, and entertainment. Your tax records for last year could be a good place to start. And if you use financial planning software, such as Quicken or Microsoft Money, you can use the "Report" tool there to complete this step quickly and easily.

- *12-month look-ahead budget:* This is an extrapolation of next year's expected budget, based on what you spent last year. Think about new or additional expenses that arise. For example, perhaps you just bought a new car, which will mean that your car insurance and auto taxes will be higher next year. Also, think about ways that you might want to reduce your expenses. For example, when Tim and his wife did this exercise, they were astounded to see how much of their money goes to eating out in restaurants. When they thought about it, they realized that they often ended up going out to eat as a default option when they came home late or had no food in the refrigerator. So they started buying frozen prepared foods, and they were able to cut down on their restaurant expenses.

- *12-month plan-ahead budget:* This is an annual budget, based on the line-item funding that would be necessary to implement your life and career plan. This is the budget that will translate your future life and career plan into a financial reality. In your plan-ahead budget there is no space for sources of income. The idea is for you to get clear about what you will need to support what you want to do, without consideration of whether you will have the funding. Eckblad and Kiel's position is that "Dreams drive resourcing, not vice versa" (2003, p. 152). Thus, your plan-ahead budget should focus on your dreams and passions and then indicate how much you will need to support that kind of life.

One of the ironies Eckblad and Kiel find in this approach is that after people do some serious work costing out what they need to live their dreams, they are often surprised to find that they already have the available resources to do so.

Another thing to remember in the financial planning process is that it is often easier to reduce financial stress by cutting your expenses than by increasing your income. For example, one young two-career couple recently was in a financial bind: They had just had their second child when the wife was laid off. Down to one income, with a big mortgage, college loans, daycare, and other big commitments, they were about to make two major commitments that they did not really want to make, but they felt forced to do so for financial reasons. She was about to take a new executive position that would have involved a lot of travel, no flexibility, and a lot of stress, but it paid very well. And they were thinking of selling their house and moving to an adjacent state that they saw as having lower real estate prices and lower taxes.

However, their career advisor encouraged them to avoid making any major decisions right away. Also, he suggested that they go through the life planning and budgeting process we have just discussed. Through this process, they became very clear on their dream for where they wanted to live: They loved their present home and community, and they did not want to move. And she really wanted to use this opportunity to start her own consulting practice. But if they moved to the other state, the taxes on her self-employed business income would be far higher than in the state where they lived. They also realized that they could refinance their mortgage and consolidate their college loans to reduce the rates and take out some cash on their home equity at the same time. By working at home, she was able to keep the baby home for half of the week, enabling them to cut their daycare fees. As a result, they were able to reduce their monthly fixed expenses by more than $4,000 and save themselves the work and stress of selling and buying houses and moving to another state. But it all started by getting clear on how they wanted to live and work and then figuring out just how much money that dream would cost.

Summary

In this chapter we have explored a variety of career development strategies. We have looked at more traditional, organizational career paths and have also discussed alternative options for those who do not see advancement as their primary career path. We have also discussed a new career construct: the portfolio career. The portfolio approach may become more common in the future as more people, out of necessity or choice, work not for an employer but for a set of customers. We have discussed the importance of continuous learning and forming networks as key capabilities in the new career.

In the next chapter, we will look at the issue of work and family. We will discuss how the roles of working parents have changed over the years as fewer families have someone at home to focus on domestic tasks and child rearing. Then, in chapter 7, we will look at the ways leading companies have responded to these challenges by offering family-friendly policies and greater flexibility to their employees.

For Further Reading

Gabarro, J. J., & Kotter, J. P. (2005, January). Managing your boss. *Harvard Business Review, 83*(1), 92–91.

Galinsky, E., Salmond, K., Bond, J. T., Brumit Kropf, M., Moore, M., & Harrington, B. (2003). *Leaders in a global economy: A study of women and men.* Unpublished report.

Hall, D. T., & Associates. (1996). *The career is dead—Long live the career: A relational approach to careers.* San Francisco: Jossey Bass.

Handy, C. (1989). *The age of unreason.* Boston: Harvard Business School Press.

Salzman, A. (1992). *Downshifting: Reinventing success on a slower track.* New York: HarperCollins.

Warren, E., & Tyagi, A. W. (2003). *The two-income trap: Why middle-class mothers and fathers are going broke.* New York: Basic Books.

Work and Family 6

Freud was once asked what he thought a normal person should be able to do well. The questioner probably expected a complicated "deep" answer. But Freud simply said, "Lieben und arbeiten" (to love and to work). It pays to ponder on this simple formula; it grows deeper as you think about it.

—Erik Erikson, *Identity, Youth and Crisis* (1968)

Having gone through a rigorous process of self-assessment and having considered and evaluated job options, you should now better understand your career priorities. Through the process and the related exercises, you have also had the opportunity to think about your work in the context of your relationships at home, at work, and in your community. Activities such as your Career Autobiography, the Identities Exercise, the Lifestyle Representation Exercise, the Interview With Significant Others, and the 10-Years-Out Exercise have all asked you to consider your work from a perspective that includes other important people and priorities in your life and how they bear on your career.

Once you have a spouse, partner, or children, almost no career decision can be made outside that context. What you do to earn a living, who you are employed by and in what geographic location, how much you work, how much you earn, whether you seek or accept promotions, and whether you work from home are just a few of the decisions and actions that will affect your family and your career.

In this chapter we discuss the current issues and dynamics of working couples and dual-career families. We begin with a brief discussion of the differences men and women experience as they confront the issues of work and family. We then discuss some of the challenges faced by dual-career couples (both as couples and as heads of families). We recognize that couples and families clearly have many different configurations today. When we use the term *family*, we embrace the fact that what constitutes a family today can take many forms: a heterosexual single-earner couple with children, a homosexual dual-career couple, or a single-parent household. Whatever form the family takes, we believe that many of the concepts discussed here still apply, but we recognize that special and more intense challenges exist for single-parent households, which represent an increasing number of families these days.

Men and Women, Families and Work

As we begin to discuss the issues of balancing or integrating work and family, it makes sense to touch on the issue of gender and how this affects individuals' realities and perceptions of entering into committed relationships, marriage, and parenthood. With the notable exception of gender bias, men's and women's career experiences may not seem vastly different. But the issues surrounding marriage, other committed relationships, and children make gender and gender expectations particularly important to consider at this point.

It probably goes without saying that most literature over the years has supported the fact that women's careers face greater compromises than men's when marriage and children come into the equation. Even for couples without children, becoming a couple often decreases the male partner's role in domestic tasks, whereas the time spent by the female partner in domestic activities increases. It may seem an oversimplification, but the essence of the gender debate comes down the same basic question for both sexes: How can members of either gender be accepted in their desire to be whole persons? For women, the challenge is to be accepted in their roles as both professional and mother and to not be seen as compromising their primary role in parenting because they also have a career. For men, the challenge is how they can effectively co-parent or even take on the primary caregiving role without being seen as failing in their role as breadwinner. What we would like to see is a situation in which society and organizations accept a wide range of configurations for both genders and for couples in their roles as professionals and family members.

Much has been written and debated recently about whether women can "have it all." One book that raised this controversy to a particularly high level was *Creating a Life: Professional Women and the Quest for Children* by Sylvia Hewlett (2002a). Founder of the National Parenting Association, Hewlett interviewed a number of high-powered professional and executive women who had wanted children but did not have them, favoring their careers instead. She reviews research that shows the risks and difficulties of having children over the age of 40. She concludes that women should strive to get married and have their children early in life, and she provides coping strategies for women and employing organizations that would support younger parenting. Some critics have taken exception to Hewlett's statement aimed at women: "If you go for the brass ring professionally, your chances of having a family life are drastically diminished." Many suggest that Hewlett's book has let men off the hook and provided the fodder for a backlash against the women's movement.

What are the basic points Hewlett makes? In 2001, Hewlett studied successful women, specifically focusing on the top 10% of women from the standpoint of earning power. She defined *high achievers* as women who earned $65,000 per year if over 40 and $55,000 per year if under 40. She also looked at what she called *super achievers,* those earning more than $100,000 per year. Finally, her sample included some high-potential women who had professional degrees and experience but had left the workforce for family reasons.

In her research, Hewlett compared high-achieving women with their male counterparts. She discovered that 79% of men wanted children and that 75% had them. In contrast, only 49% of female high achievers had children, even though a much higher percentage had wanted them. There were also differences between men and women when it came to marriage. For the over-40 age group, 76% of high-achieving men and more than 83% of super-achieving men were married, in contrast to only 60% of high-achieving women. High-achieving men and women also differed in terms of the roles their spouses played. For example, only 39% of high-achieving men were married to women who were employed full time (and of those, 40% earned less than $35,000). In contrast, 9 out of 10 married women in the high-achieving category had husbands who were employed full time.

Gerstel and Gallagher (2001) found that even when men worked fewer hours or had more flexible work schedules, they did not increase the amount of caregiving they did at home. Although there are more dual-earner families than ever before, women are still more likely to accommodate the needs of the family, often by spending less time at work.

Much has been written in recent years about the struggle of working mothers, but until recently much less attention has been accorded to working fathers. The assumption is that fathers have always worked and that the identity of most men is tied closely (or almost entirely) to their career identity. Furthermore, if asked, most people would say that working mothers experience much higher levels of stress than their male counterparts in trying to balance work and family. But is this true?

In *Working Father: New Strategies for Balancing Work and Family* James Levine (1997) suggests that this stereotype is not completely true. Levine cites study after study that shows that fathers have similar levels of stress and anxiety over how well they are balancing the roles of breadwinner and father. He cites one study of the changing workforce done in the mid-1990s that found that 56% of fathers reported "some conflict" or "a lot of conflict" in dealing with their two roles. A Gallup survey in the early 1990s found that 59% of American men derive a greater sense of satisfaction from caring for their families than from a job well done. Levine also cites a 1993 study done by psychologist Joseph Pleck of the University of Illinois that concluded that men now "seek their emotional, personal, and spiritual gratification from the family setting" (Levine, 1997, p. 17). Finally, Levine discusses a study done by Barnett that concluded that fathers experience as much anxiety about parenting as mothers do and that a man's experience as a parent, not as an employee, was the strongest predictor of whether he would have stress-related illness.

What prevents fathers from playing a more active role in parenting? According to Levine, there are a number of key factors. First, as one might expect, most men believe that they are simply not in a position professionally to discuss work–family conflict. Men are more likely to get subtle cues from the workplace that raising these issues could bring into question their commitment to their careers. In addition, role models of outstanding male workers are those who go to heroic lengths to complete projects or resolve a crisis for the company, often without regard to family issues. An employee who travels nonstop for weeks to ensure that a project is implemented well or works countless hours to resolve a customer complaint is seen as a role model. Few ever ask who was watching out for the employee's family during such times, at least if the employee is a man.

Brad's personal experience reflects Levine's theory. At one point in his corporate life, when he had two young children, Brad's job required him to travel from Boston to the West Coast about 10 days a month. When he refused to do additional travel, citing family reasons, Brad felt that he was held up as someone who was "family-centric." However, Brad is convinced that had he been a woman in the same situation, the mere fact that he was 3,000 miles from his young children for 10 days every month would have caused him to be labeled as overly ambitious and a less-than-ideal parent.

Dual-Career Couples

As we have noted, over the last 30 years the complexion of families has changed significantly for many reasons. Perhaps the most significant change is the increase in the number of women who work. Dual-earner couples represented 35% of married couples in 1970, and by 2000 that percentage had reached 59.6% (Jacobs & Gerson, 2004). The number of single-parent families, whether headed by men or women, has also risen dramatically. Dual-earner families and single-parent households share the lack of someone at home to take care of domestic needs (Jacobs & Gerson, 2001).

In recent years the media have written extensively about the "over-worked American," thanks in great measure to the title of the popular book mentioned earlier (Schor, 1992). However, it is not universally accepted that individuals are working longer hours than was the case 30 years ago. In fact, comparing the length of the average work week between 1970 and 1997, Gerson and Jacobs (2004) determined that the length of the average work week remained unchanged. They also say, however, that "the past several decades have witnessed the emergence of a segment of employed couples who are putting in very long work weeks. These couples are especially likely to be concentrated among highly educated workers, who tend to occupy the most prestigious jobs and occupations" (Jacobs & Gerson, 2001, p. 60). They state that in the last few decades there has been not a fundamental shift in how many hours individuals work but rather a large increase in the number of dual-career couples and families. Jacobs and Gerson stress the importance of focusing on the family's work week rather than just the individual's work week. The increase in the amount of time spent at work by dual-earner couples as a unit leaves less time for couples to do domestic tasks and for parents to be with their children. Clearly, couples with or without children today have more challenges in negotiating their roles than in previous years.

Although the issue of overwork and dual-career couples has garnered great media attention in recent years, it has been an area of serious study for many years. Robert and Rhona Rapoport (1971) conducted some of the earliest research on dual-career couples. The Rapoports' research established this topic as a field of study and laid the groundwork for analyzing the issues by separating out the component parts: her career, his career, her family roles, and his family roles. They also identified basic styles in couple members' orientations toward their careers and their relationships. For example, they state that when one member of a couple subordinated his or her career to that of the other, career and family decision making was less stressful than in families where the two careers were both primary and thus in conflict.

The Rapoports also studied the characteristics of happy and less happy two-career couples. They found that four qualities differentiated these two groups. First, the happier couples tended to have a *strategy for coping* with work–family conflicts. Second, the happy couples had *more flexibility* than the less happy group. This flexibility could come in many forms: in their work, in their relationship, and in their individual personal styles. Third, they had a *high level of mutual commitment*. This included strong commitment to each other's careers as well as their own and commitment to the relationship. And fourth, they simply had *high levels of energy*. As one couple in our research reported in an interview, "You just learn how to get by on less sleep!"

Hall and Hall (1979) expanded the notion of couple styles begun by the Rapoports, based on four possible combinations of career and family involvement (Table 6.1). After the descriptions of these combinations, we provide an exercise you can complete with your spouse or partner to determine what kind of couple you are.

Table 6.1   Dual-Career Couple Types

Type	Work Involvement	Home Involvement
Accommodators	Spouse A high Spouse B low	Spouse B low Spouse A high
Adversaries	Both high	Both low (*but* both value a well-ordered home)
Allies	Both low or Both high	Both high or Both low (and both have low value for a well-ordered home)
Acrobats	Both high	Both high

SOURCE: Hall and Hall (1980).

Accommodators are couples who have one partner who is high in career involvement and low in home involvement. The second partner is just the opposite: high in home involvement and low in career involvement. Thus, each accommodates the other. One assumes primary responsibility for home and family roles, and the second partner assumes primary responsibility for career and breadwinning. If both partners are truly involved in their respective roles and value both work and family, then conflicts are minimized.

If both partners are highly involved in their careers and only minimally involved in home or family roles but both value a well-ordered and rich home life, they may be described as *Adversaries*. The identity of each is defined primarily by career. Although home life is important to them, neither takes on the home roles. This is a stressful structure for couples because they are competing over priorities. Major changes such as relocating or having children can be threatening because they represent a difficult change in an uneasy status quo. Each wants to delegate home responsibilities (which could include the responsibility to hire and manage help) to an unwilling mate.

Many couples are highly involved in either career or home, with little identity tied up in the other; these are the *Allies*. As with the Accommodators, their priorities are clearly defined and compatible. If they are both career involved and not home involved, they are not overly concerned with preparing gourmet dinners or entertaining at home frequently; hosting people at a restaurant or eating take-out can work fine for them. The major stress for them is finding enough time to devote to their relationship. For couples who are both primarily home involved, the two incomes provide enough resources for a comfortable life, but they make career choices that minimize spillover from work into the home. One source of stress for family-involved Allies might be an occasional pang of doubt about what would have happened if they had chosen to pursue their careers more aggressively, especially when they compare their careers with those of peers (e.g., at college reunions). Overall, though, Allies have a low level of stress and conflict.

The final type is the subject of popular articles on the idealized two-career couple. That is, those who want high involvement in challenging careers *and* high involvement in a wonderful, full family life. These are the *Acrobats*. They are the couples that want it all, to have their cake and eat it, too. Their identities are not restricted to one particular role; they seek fulfillment in all of them. This is the group that is hypothesized to have the highest degree of stress and conflict.

In fact, there can be two kinds of conflict for the Acrobats. One type is interpersonal conflict between the two partners as they attempt to juggle the overload of role demands. The other type is intrapersonal, the internal conflict of trying to do well in all role areas (e.g., being successful at work, being a loving, supportive spouse, being a caring, involved parent, and providing a comfortable home).

These categories are not static. Couples often move from one type to another as their careers and life stages develop. For example, a young couple might start off as Allies, where both are going flat-out in their careers while they live in a modest, low-maintenance apartment, and they have no children. Their social life may consist primarily of evenings out or pizza dinners at home with other young Ally couples.

Then, as they start a family, and as a well-ordered home becomes more important, they may move to one of the other types. They could become Adversaries if no one assumes responsibility for the home, with constant bickering about who is going to call the baby-sitter or who is going to take care of the sink full of dishes from last night's party. Or if one partner switches to a more flexible work option, they could become Accommodators. Or if they want it all, and neither seems willing to compromise on career or family, they could become Acrobats. The most common switch for young couples is from Allies to Accommodators, perhaps with a stop at Acrobats along the way. This shifting often is caused by financial necessity, and as soon as they can afford it, one partner cuts back on work hours. We will leave it to the reader to guess which gender historically has been more likely to make this accommodation.

WHAT KIND OF COUPLE ARE YOU, AND WHAT CAN YOU DO ABOUT IT?

How would you and your partner describe yourselves as a couple? Take a few minutes and go through this exercise together.

1. Individual ranking. Using the brief descriptions that follow, think about which description best fits the two of you as a couple. Put a 1 next to that description. Put a 2 next to the statement that you feel is the next best description of you, a 3 next to the next best description, and a 4 next to the statement that least well describes you.

_____ **Accommodators:** One of you is high in career involvement and lower in home involvement, whereas the other is low in career involvement and higher in home involvement. You complement each other in your involvements. One assumes primary responsibility for the home, and the other assumes primary responsibility for being the breadwinner (i.e., for doing career work).

_____ **Adversaries:** Both of you are highly involved in your careers, and each of you has minimal involvement in tasks at home. For each of you, your identity is highly defined by your career. Yet having a well-ordered home and a family is important to both of you. You do not want to compromise on the quality of the life that you have at home.

_____ **Allies:** Both of you have your primary identities invested in the same sphere of life, either career or home, and the other sphere is less important to you both. You share the same priorities in life. Either you are both highly career involved and couldn't care less about having a perfect home, or you are both highly involved at home and place far less value on career success. You agree on which aspect of life is most important, and you live your lives accordingly.

_____ **Acrobats:** Both of you are highly invested in both home and career roles. Your identities are not defined primarily by a single role; rather, you achieve fulfillment and satisfaction in both areas. You both give equal weight to home and career roles. You want to have it all.

2. Coming to agreement. Now compare your two rankings. If you disagree on the type that you ranked as 1, ask each other what your thinking was behind your rankings. Through dialogue and good listening, try to come to agreement about your couple type. (If you cannot come to agreement, talk to good friends who know you both as a couple. Describe the couple types to them, and see what they think.)

3. Appreciation of your type. Together, make a list of all of the _good things_ associated with being the type of couple that you are. Do this as a brainstorming activity, which means that you should not be critical of what the other says, and write down each point that is made. When you have finished, take a look at your overall list and share your reflections on what you see there and what those points mean to you.

4. Understanding the challenges of your type. As is true with most things in life, each couple type has its upsides and its downsides. Together, using the same brainstorming technique, write a list of the *challenges* or difficulties associated with being the type of couple that you are. Do not get into a long discussion of each point; just write it down. Then, when you have finished your list, stop and reflect together on what you have written.

5. Action planning. Now do some thinking about two questions:

A. How can you leverage the good things about being your type of couple? What can you do to take more advantage of your couple type?

B. What steps might you take to deal with the challenges of your type? If you know of other couples who share this type, can you see things that they do to deal with these issues?

6. Lessons learned. Individually, reflect on what you have done in the preceding steps. Write down one insight or lesson learned from this assessment activity. Now share your reflections. Together, what have you both learned from this process? Write down this lesson for future use.

Dual-Career Families

One of the realities of going from a single worker to a joint household with two workers to a family with children is that the complexities of how one spends one's time and energy increase dramatically. With every life change, each person in the relationship increases his or her roles; grocery shopping, cooking, cleaning, laundry, the number of hours worked in a day, and travel for work are among the issues that become joint concerns. Add children to the equation, and the demands on your time increase again. Sleep, child care costs, and flexibility become topics for discussion as well as more laundry, more cleaning, and who will leave work to pick up the kids. Add aging parents possibly in need of more attention and you will understand that planning your career for future flexibility can be important. Become involved in church or community organizations or your town, and roles expand once again. The interplay between all of these roles can lead to conflicts requiring significant thought and, ultimately, adjustments to the current system.

There are four major models for explaining the relationship between work and family experiences (Watanabe, Takahashi, & Minami, 1997). One of the earliest (e.g., Dubin, 1956) is the *compensation model*, which argues that individuals attempt to compensate for the lack of satisfaction in one domain by attempting to find it in the other (Evans & Bartolome, 1984). For example, if a lower-wage worker finds no challenge or stimulation at work, she might become highly involved in pursuits such as night courses, tournament chess, or financial investments.

An opposite assumption is found in the *spillover model,* which argues that positive or negative attitudes and energy experienced in one domain spill over and affect the other domain in the same way (Marshall, Chadwick, & Marshall, 1992). Thus, if a person experiences great success and happiness at work, she would bring this happiness home, leading to more satisfaction in this role area.

A third is the *opposition model,* a zero-sum model, which argues that time spent in one role detracts from one's performance in the other (Greenhaus & Beutell, 1985). An example would be a person who has to exert great effort to meet a project deadline at work. Then, when he finally goes home, not only is it late, but he is exhausted and unavailable emotionally to the family.

And the final model is the *segmentation model,* which suggests that work and family are simply two independent domains. This view holds that there is no necessary relationship between work and family. Thus, people who are happy at work are not necessarily happy or unhappy at home, and vice versa. This is the null hypothesis in our theorizing about the relationships between work and family (Zedeck, 1992).

At different points in your career or family life, one or more of these models may apply. Or perhaps, depending on the kind of work you do or your personality type, one of these might match your life better than another. In any case, the interaction between work and home lives can clearly create stress for many people.

SOURCES OF STRESS

There are three common forms of stress among two-career couples as a result of their multiple roles. The first and most common source is *role overload.* The sheer number and intensity of demands on the couple's time cause this type of stress. Overload pressure is especially high for young couples (at a career stage where financial resources are tight) with children. The sheer number of demands on the partners exceeds the time and energy to do them. The sequencing of role loads, when planned, can help lessen this tension. Sekaran and Hall (1989) argue that role overload pressures are more problematic when there is asynchronicity in the work and family roles of each party. That is, each role has a life of its own, with cycles of high and low demand. For the parent role, September is a high-demand time when children have to be outfitted for school, when they are making a difficult transition, and when new activities are getting started. For the work role, this is a time when many people are going back to work after a summer vacation. In the church and community, many organizations are also getting started, needing volunteer assistance, and expecting participation. Thus, many roles are peaking simultaneously, and the effects of the overload are intensified. On the other hand, if one partner can find a way to *reduce* the workload in September (e.g., by taking vacation then, by doing more work at home, or by taking on more during the summer), this can bring the couple's roles in sync. (More detail on the specific ways in which synchronicity can work is found in Sekaran & Hall, 1989.)

The second type of stress for dual-career couples comes from *conflict,* the incompatibility of different role expectations. One type of conflict is interrole conflict, in which one partner's different roles make conflicting demands, as when a person, as an employee, is expected to be out of town next Friday for a client meeting and is also expected, as a parent, to be at his child's school for the fifth-grade play. It is not possible to be in both places at the same time. A second type of conflict is intersender conflict within a role, as when a father is home alone taking care of his daughter, and she wants him to let her stay up past her bedtime to watch a special TV show, but the mother left strict instructions that the daughter should be in bed on time. The third type of conflict is intrapersonal conflict (within the person), in which a person feels torn between two valued activities (going to the son's band concert or to the daughter's softball game).

The third source of stress is *change.* This is certainly not unique to dual-career couples, but with two careers, they are more likely to experience job changes and relocations than one-career families. A relocation can trigger all sorts of other changes: new jobs, new home, new friends, new schools, new community, new culture, and often a more expensive house and the resulting financial stress. The more roles are changing simultaneously, the more the stress is compounded.

ROLE CONFLICT

In most cases, both men and women in dual-career families experience role conflict. Over the years, the words *conflict* and *balance* have often been used in reference to the interaction between work and family. Work–family conflict occurs when pressures from one sphere (work or family) are incompatible with the demands of the other sphere, so fulfilling the expectations from one role interferes with meeting the expectations associated with the other role. However, this does not mean that the types of conflict are the same for men and women. As noted earlier, we often assume that women will have higher levels of work–family conflict, but many studies find similar levels of work–family conflict for men and women (Greenhaus & Parasuraman, 1999). In fact, several studies report more similarities than differences between mothers and fathers with respect to work–family conflict. Greenhaus and Parasuraman (1999) speculate on what they call the surprising lack of gender differences in many role conflict studies. One possibility is that women may self-select into jobs that are less demanding and may provide more accommodations to family needs. Also, the women studied may already have adopted coping strategies, such as reducing their work involvement, which would reduce their role conflict.

Greenhaus and Parasuraman speculate that women may also be better than men at juggling roles and performing the multiple roles needed for combining work and family. Some support for this idea was found earlier in Hall and Gordon's (1973) research, in which the satisfaction of part-time employed women was positively related to the number of role activities they performed. It may be that under some circumstances a high level of activity is satisfying. Such circumstances might include *autonomy* in the job and a high level of *control* over one's work activities. Recent research by Barnett and her colleagues (Barnett & Hall, 2001) finds strong evidence of the positive effects of personal control in mediating the relationship between work and home roles.

The following exercise will help you think about how you cope with role conflicts and how you might better align or balance your multiple roles.

ASSESSING YOUR STRATEGIES FOR COPING WITH ROLE CONFLICTS

How do you cope with the various conflicts between family and work roles? In this exercise we provide a self-assessment tool based on three types of coping. This survey may help you and your partner understand your current strategies and some different ones that you may want to try.

I. Think about the major roles in your life. What conflicts or strains, if any, have you experienced between the various roles in your life? Consider the following examples:

___ Parent vs. partner   ___ One career vs. other career

___ Parent vs. career   ___ Community vs. career

___ Partner vs. career   ___ Insufficient time

II. How do you deal with these conflicts or strains? Use the following 1–5 scale to describe the extent to which you engage in each of the behaviors listed by writing the appropriate number to the left of each behavior.

To little or no extent	To a limited extent	To some extent	To a considerable extent	To a great extent
1	2	3	4	5

___ 1. Decide not to do certain activities that conflict with other activities.

___ 2. Get help from someone outside the family (e.g., home maintenance help, child care, elder care).

___ 3. Get help from a member of the family.

___ 4. Get help from someone at work.

___ 5. Engage in problem solving with family members to resolve conflicts.

___ 6. Engage in problem solving with someone at work.

___ 7. Get moral support from a member of the family.

___ 8. Get moral support from someone at work.

___ 9. Integrate or combine roles (e.g., involve family members in work activity or combine work and family in some way).

___ 10. Attempt to change societal definition of sex roles, work roles, or family roles.

___ 11. Negotiate or plan with someone at work so their expectations of you are more in line with your own needs or expectations.

___ 12. Negotiate or plan with members of your family so their expectations of you are more in line with your own needs or expectations.

___ 13. Establish priorities among your different roles so that you are sure the most important activities are done.

___ 14. Partition and separate your roles. Devote full attention to each role when you are in it.

___ 15. Overlook or relax certain standards for how you do certain activities (e.g., let less important things slide a bit sometimes, such as dusting or lawn care).

___ 16. Modify your attitudes toward certain roles or activities (e.g., coming to the conclusion that the quality of time spent with spouse or children is more important than the quantity of time spent).

___ 17. Eliminate certain roles (e.g., decide to stop working).

___ 18. Rotate attention from one role to another. Handle each role in turn as it comes up.

___ 19. Develop yourself and your own interests (e.g., spend time on leisure or self-development).

___ 20. Plan, schedule, and organize carefully.

___ 21. Work hard to meet all role demands. Devote more time and energy so you can do everything that is expected of you.

___ 22. Do not attempt to cope with role demands and conflicts. Let role conflicts take care of themselves.

(Continued)

(Continued)

III. Computing Your Coping Scores

Role Renegotiation Score:

Sum of responses to items 1–12 = _____ /12 = _____

Personal Role Redefinition Score:

Sum of responses to items 13–17 = _____ /5 = _____

Heroic Role Behavior Score:

Sum of responses to items 18–22 = _____ /5 = _____

Interpreting Your Scores:

4.5–5.0 = Very high

4.0–4.49 = High

3.0–3.99 = Moderate

2.0–2.99 = Low

<2.0 = Very low

SOURCE: This exercise is based on research by Douglas T. Hall and related material reported in D. T. Hall, "A model of coping with role conflict: The role behavior of college educated women." *Administrative Science Quarterly*, December 1972, 471–485, and in Francine S. Hall and Douglas T. Hall, *The Two Career Couple*. Reading, MA: Addison-Wesley, 1972, 75–79.

If your Role Renegotiation score is low, this means that you often let other people's expectations have too much influence on you. And some of these expectations may be unrealistic. You need to negotiate with your role senders to make certain that the things they expect of you are reasonable and compatible with your other responsibilities and interests. Some ideas for action might include the following:

- *Simply let people know that you will not be able to engage in certain activities.* For example, if you have to pick up your kids from a daycare center by 6:00 P.M., let your boss and co-workers know that you will not be able to participate in any meeting that lasts beyond 5 P.M., unless there is enough advance planning so that you can make special arrangements.

- *Get the help of other family members or from hired help to perform certain tasks at home.* Familiar examples include house cleaning, laundry, shopping and cooking, yard work, and child care.

- *Have a "family council" meeting* (parents, children, and any other live-in family member) and discuss the problems of getting home tasks done. Together, work out a good arrangement for getting the work done.

- *Consider integrating your and your partner or spouse's careers* by working with each other or working in related fields so that the two careers bring you together.

These role renegotiation activities have the potential to reduce conflict at the source: the expectations held by the role senders and yourself. If you can make these and other changes in basic expectations, we think you will like the results.

If your Personal Role Redefinition score is low, this suggests that you do not have a clear vision of what is most important to you personally. If you do not have a strong sense of what is reasonable for you to be doing in a particular role, then you are vulnerable to being influenced by others who *do* have a strong sense of what they think you should be doing. You need to reevaluate your attitudes about your various roles and establish clear priorities for yourself. Here are some hints to help with Personal Role Redefinition:

- *Establish priorities.* For example, a child with a fever takes priority over office appointments, whereas a child with a mild cold does not.

- *Divide and establish boundaries between roles.* Devote full attention to a given role when you are in that role, and do not work on tasks related to other roles. For example, leave work at the office, and reserve home time for family and their needs; do not answer the telephone during meals.

- *Try to ignore or overlook less important role expectations.* For example, learn to accept some dust on the floor, and do not expect perfection when children do the dishes and clean the kitchen table after dinner.

- *Rotate attention from one role to another as demands arise.* Let one role slide a bit if another role's demands are more pressing. For example, if your daughter is really stuck on a homework problem and is feeling frustrated, let go of the bills you were paying and take care of them later.

This style of coping means changing yourself and your perspective, or how you frame your roles. Working on this style of coping means working on *yourself* and your own thinking about what are reasonable self-expectations. Before you can change other people's expectations of you, you have to be clear about what you expect of yourself. As the song says, "If you can't please everyone, you've got to please yourself." But we would argue that these two things are not incompatible: If you can be very clear and confident about what is reasonable to do for other people, this will help you be clear and confident and persuasive in renegotiating your role expectations with others.

If your Heroic Role Behavior score is high, you're in very good company because many people suffer from the desire to please everybody. A high score here means that you are not being very discriminating in taking on new commitments or managing old ones. You are trying to take on every role activity that heads your way. You "cope" with conflict by working harder and sleeping less. This style of coping includes the following:

- Planning, organizing, and scheduling better (e.g., by using a personal digital assistant, having an assistant keep your calendar, taking a time management course).

- Working harder to meet all role demands (e.g., staying up late, getting by on less sleep, taking a speed reading course).

- Using no conscious strategy, letting problems take care of themselves. This is reactive behavior, a passive response to role conflict.

(Continued)

(Continued)

It's no wonder, then, that Heroic Role Behavior is linked to high stress and dissatisfaction. It is not a very effective way of solving problems and getting work done. Rather than managing your conflicts, you are letting them manage you. If your goal is to eliminate conflict, then you need to reorient your own perceptions as a first step toward negotiating with others to redesign the roles in your life.

As we conclude this section on two-career couples, let us apply some of the concepts we have just been discussing about identification clarification and using relationships for development. Following is a simple exercise that a couple can use to create a useful dialogue about planning their lives and careers together.

CAREER AND LIFE PLANNING
EXERCISE FOR DUAL-CAREER COUPLES

Step 1. Each member of the couple gathers a summary of all the self-assessment exercises (from earlier parts of this book) they have completed individually so far. In addition to summarizing the exercises, include the list of themes you have identified from your self-assessment.

Step 2. Draw a life map that represents the structure of your life. (The use of the life map here is based on an exercise developed by Marcy Crary, 1981.) Include the different elements that add together to make up your overall sense of identity, your sense of who you are. Some of these elements might include the following:

- Significant relationships
- Activities that are central to your life
- Physical places and spaces
- Organizations and groups of which you are a member

This does not have to be a great work of art. It will probably be a lot simpler than the lifestyle representation you may have done earlier in the book. In your life map, be sure to indicate the following:

- What are the most important elements of your life (you can use size and centrality to indicate importance)?
- What are the relationships, if any, between these elements?

To give you a more concrete example of what a life map might look like, we have reproduced an example in Figure 6.1 (from Crary, 1982, pp. 167 and 170, respectively).

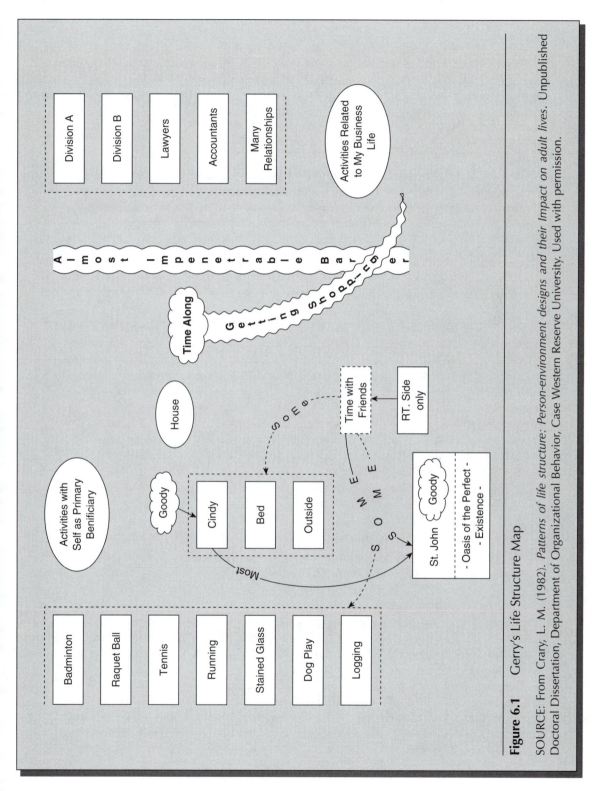

Figure 6.1   Gerry's Life Structure Map

SOURCE: From Crary, L. M. (1982). *Patterns of life structure: Person-environment designs and their Impact on adult lives.* Unpublished Doctoral Dissertation, Department of Organizational Behavior, Case Western Reserve University. Used with permission.

149

(Continued)

Step 3. When you are finished drawing your life map, step back and spend some time reflecting on it. Try to get some detachment from what you have drawn and look at it as a person from Mars would. Or think as if you were an observer of your life, up on a balcony, looking down at the structure of your life. What do you notice as you look at your life map? What stands out for you? As you spend some time gazing at it, what *insights or observations* do you have? Write these insights and observations down.

Step 4. Give the materials from Steps 1–3 to your partner, and receive your partner's materials. Spend some time reviewing and reflecting on your partner's materials. Write down your observations on your partner's materials. More specifically, answer the following two questions:

- What themes do you see in your partner's materials?
- What implications do these themes have for your own career and your life together as a couple (and, if relevant, as a family)?

Step 5. Meet with your partner and have a conversation about these materials and what you have each written in Step 4. Allow at least an hour for this conversation. Follow the rules for dialogue, which include active listening for understanding, asking good questions to clarify and test your understanding, and putting aside your own position on the issue being discussed so that you can be open to true learning from what your partner is saying. Arrange to have this conversation in a quiet, peaceful place where you can relax and where you will not be interrupted. In this conversation do not feel that you have to come up with answers or solutions. The purpose is to have a good dialogue and to understand better what each of you really wants for your careers and your life together.

At the end of your conversation, spend a few minutes in individual reflection. Write down your answers to the following questions:

- What did you learn from this conversation?
- What are the implications of this learning for your own career and your life together with your partner (and, if relevant, as a family)?

Step 6. Develop a couple or family life plan. Using the learnings and implications from Step 5, each partner will brainstorm a list of action steps that might form the basis of a life plan for the couple or family. With each action step, indicate the time frame, the resources needed, who has to be informed and involved, and whose help will be needed for success with the action.

Then meet again with your partner, again in a quiet, peaceful place. Choose a time when you will not feel rushed. Look at the two brainstormed action lists you have produced and discuss them. Decide together which actions make the most sense for you, and come to agreement on a combined couple or family action plan. Use the following form:

Couple or Family Plan

Date: _____

Action Step	Target Date	Lead Person	Resources Needed	Key People Involved
_____	_____	_____	_____	_____
_____	_____	_____	_____	_____
_____	_____	_____	_____	_____

Summary

We would expect that the shorter life cycle of a career would necessarily make for more frequent transitions in dual-career relationships (but not for shorter life cycles of relationships, we hope). Whether the relationship's life cycle is also shortened may depend on the "meta-competency muscle" that is built into it. The ability to create secure bases while facing risk and turbulence is the key to success. Part of the answer is to learn more about managing the psychological role transitions that occur in everyday life. Creating good boundaries in one's life, to separate the secure base from the areas of risk, and then learning to cross those boundaries, can be a way to resolve the paradox.

Success in a dual-career relationship also requires that each partner have a high level of self-awareness and adaptability, two critical career meta-competencies. Self-awareness can be improved by completing some of the self-assessment tools provided in this book. Adaptability involves being able to be flexible and change when appropriate, and some tools, such as the activity in Box 7.1 (which appears in the next chapter) can help you decide when a change might be warranted. Being effective in these career development activities is important and difficult for anyone, but doing it in the context of a dual-career relationship is even more so. Managing two careers and a relationship is not just twice as difficult as managing one career; it is probably at least four times as difficult. But, like most tasks in life, it can be easier with the right tools.

For Further Reading

Barnett, R., & Rivers, C. (2004). *Same difference: How gender myths are hurting our relationships, our children, and our jobs.* New York: Basic Books.

Friedman, S., & Greenhaus, J. (2000). *Work and family: Allies or enemies? What happens when business professionals confront life choices.* New York: Oxford University Press.

Gerson, K., & Jacobs, J. A. (2004). *The time divide: Work, family, and gender inequality.* Cambridge, MA: Harvard University Press.

Workplace Flexibility 7

In response to the dramatic changes in working couples and families and the related issues of dependent care (of children and elder relatives), in the last decade there has been a deluge of information, articles, books, and media coverage on the topic of balancing work and family. Academic research centers have been established at many major universities to explore this complex issue from an interdisciplinary perspective. As Lotte Bailyn and Tom Kochan of the Sloan School and Bob Drago of Penn State University state in their report on this topic,

> The challenges of integrating work and family are part of the everyday reality for the majority of American working families. While the particulars may vary depending on income, occupation, or stage of life, these challenges cut across all socioeconomic levels and are felt directly by both women and men. As families contribute more hours to the paid labor force, problems have intensified, bringing broad recognition that steps are needed to adjust to the changed realities of today's families and work. (Bailyn, Drago, & Kochan, 2001, p. 1)

Regardless of what career strategy people use—organizational or alternative, portfolio or entrepreneur—most individuals or couples will opt to use alternative or flexible arrangements to better balance their work and personal lives at some point in their career. While the rise of dual-career couples and single-parent families has dramatically increased the need for flexibility in modern organizations, the rise of the knowledge worker has increased the range of work options organizations can provide. Today, thanks to the widespread availability of telecommunication devices and computing equipment, work for many has become something you do, not somewhere you go. Beyond technology, many organizations have come to realize that giving workers more control over their work lives and schedules is highly valued. In their longitudinal study of 20 companies, Lee and Kossek (2006) found that many high-level executives and professionals had given up a percentage of their salary to gain greater flexibility in the way their work gets done.

In this chapter, we provide an overview of the current organizational responses to the changing needs of working families. The range of options available today that are particularly helpful for working families is expanding. We explore flexible work arrangements, including flextime, compressed work weeks, part-time work, telecommuting, and leaves and sabbaticals. These new work arrangements have become a necessity in the current work–family climate:

> The problem of family time deficits cannot be solved by chastising parents for working too much. Instead, the time has come to create a more flexible and family-supportive work-place, including more options for reducing working time (Jacobs and Gerson, 1998) commensurate with the family transformation that has already taken place. (Jacobs & Gerson, 2001, p. 61)

In addition, we also review some other forms of family-friendly benefits and programs that do not fall under the heading of flexible work arrangements. We recognize that some of these family-friendly options are not available in all organizations and may not be made available to all types of employees. Often, those in lower-level positions are not offered many of the programs we describe. Surprisingly, those at the other end of the spectrum, high earners, may also have difficulty using flexible work arrangements. Senior executives, doctors, and lawyers often are not afforded much flexibility in their work either, although they often have the advantage of having the financial resources to mitigate the impact of this lack of flexibility that lower-wage workers do not. We suggest that although offering flexible arrangements may be more challenging for some roles than others, creative employers and employees working together can find many ways to incorporate flexibility into all jobs to some degree.

Flexible Work Arrangements

Flexible work arrangements can take many forms, but most involve giving employees greater control over *when and where work gets done* and over *how much time employees choose to work*. This can range from modest arrangements such as allowing employees to telecommute periodically or modified work schedules through flextime to much more dramatic arrangements in which employees almost never work from an office or can take extended periods of time for sabbaticals or leaves of absence.

In 2000, the Boston College Center for Work & Family (CWF) conducted research with more than 1,300 employees and 150 managers in six companies to determine the impact flexible work arrangements were having on both the employees and the organization as a whole. Although not all forms of flexible arrangements were studied, the results were very positive:

- 70% of managers and 87% of employees reported that a flexible work arrangement had a positive or very positive impact on productivity.

- 65% of managers and 87% of employees reported that a flexible work arrangement had a positive or very positive impact on the quality of work.

- 76% of managers and 80% of employees indicated that flexible work arrangements will have a positive impact on employee retention. (Boston College Center for Work & Family, 2000)

In addition to the overall positive outcomes for the companies, the direct managers of employees working flexibly reported favorable results in relation to their own work. Seventy-five percent of managers reported no change in their own workload, and nearly all believed that workgroup productivity and their job performance were the same or better. In the following sections, we will look at some of the most common forms of flexible, or family-friendly, work arrangements in use in organizations today.

FLEXTIME

In the first half of the 20th century, the United States had a manufacturing-based economy, and most employees were paid an hourly rate. Factories in most industries worked on a system of Taylorism (named for Frederick Taylor, the father of scientific management). Taylorism's fundamental tenets were based on the ideals of consistency and conformity to the norm, and the employer established the norm. Many things were prescribed by this system of management, including the times, or shifts, when people worked. Time clocks were used to track employees' hours.

But two changes occurred that began to change this rigid approach. First, in the 1960s, Hewlett-Packard (HP) began experimenting with flexible work hours. The pilot program began in HP's German operations and moved to the Waltham, Massachusetts facility. Although skeptics doubted it could be used successfully in a three-shift manufacturing environment, they were proven wrong. As Dave Packard recounts in his book, HP's flextime program worked beyond the company's expectations and reflected the essence of the company's values:

Perhaps the most widely publicized example of trust at HP is the company's program of flexible work hours. It was initiated in at our plant in Germany in 1967, and we were the first company in the United States to use it. It is now used widely throughout HP and throughout industry. . . . To my mind, flextime is the essence of respect for and trust in the individual. It says we both appreciate that our people have busy personal lives and the we trust them to devise, with their supervisor and work group, a schedule that is personally convenient and yet fair to others. Tolerance for the differing needs of individuals is another element of the HP Way. (Packard, 1995, p. 137)

The second trend was that in the past 15 years, many manufacturing jobs have left the United States and been moved to developing countries where labor costs are lower. This shrinking of the manufacturing workforce is coupled with a corresponding growth in the number of "knowledge workers." In many organizations, manufacturing and others, this has led to the demise of the time clock, although the practice has continued in some sectors such as retailing, service, and hospitality.

As these practices of rigid time schedules fade in prominence, flexible work hours (or flextime) are becoming the norm in many industries. Flextime gives employees greater control of the scheduling of their work days. It has become so pervasive in recent years that some may think it is unnecessary to discuss here. But flextime has more than one variant, and it is important to discuss the pros and cons of this approach.

The 2000 CWF study previously referenced, *Measuring the Impact of Workplace Flexibility,* reviewed flextime and other flexible arrangements. The CWF study outlined two different approaches to flextime: *traditional flextime* and *daily flextime*. Traditional flextime is defined as "a working schedule that has start and end times that the employee has chosen and includes certain 'core hours' that have been determined by the manager or the organization" (p. 1). These core hours typically are based on peak workloads and specify that in the middle of the business day (e.g., from 10 to 3) all employees must be available. Daily flextime is defined as "a working schedule that enables the employee to vary their work hours on a daily basis" (p. 1).

The CWF study assessed the impact of flexible arrangement on productivity, stress, commitment, and loyalty. The study found that employees using *daily* flextime were happiest with their arrangement. They reported that this form of flexibility had a positive impact on productivity, quality of work, and their plans to stay with the company. They also said that they were more satisfied with their jobs, were more satisfied with their lives, and experienced better work–family balance.

COMPRESSED WORK WEEK

Compressed work weeks are used in a broad range of industries, including manufacturing, health care, computer operations, food service, the airline industry, and law enforcement. According to a survey conducted by Hewitt Associates (Hewitt Associates LLC, 2002), one out of five major U.S. companies offered some form of this work arrangement. In compressed work weeks, employees generally work the standard number of hours (e.g., 40) but in a shorter period of time. For example, employees who normally work 40 hours over 5 days would work four 10-hour or three 12- or 13-hour days. There are many variations to compressed work weeks, including a certain number of days on and off (e.g., 4 work days followed by 4 rest days) or a 2-week, 10-day schedule compressed into 9 days.

As with other flexible work options, there are upsides and downsides to this alternative. Employees benefit from compressed schedules by having larger blocks of time for personal business and leisure. Moreover, companies list decreased absenteeism and increased productivity among the gains (Hammer & Barbera, 1997). Sources of problems related to compressed work weeks include fatigue, coverage, scheduling, productivity, supervision, and attention to safety.

Compressed work weeks are particularly attractive to people who have flexible personal schedules that enable them to work longer hours in exchange for more days off between work days. They can be problematic for people who have time-specific responsibilities outside work (e.g., parents who need to pick up their children every day after school at a certain time).

In addition to considering personal responsibilities, it is important to look at the impact longer work hours can have on productivity and job satisfaction. More specifically, people who work monotonous and repetitive jobs may find that longer work hours increase their stress levels and their likelihood of making mistakes over time, particularly toward the end of their work days. Additionally, employees who rely on ever-changing information to perform their jobs may find themselves out of the loop when they return from their days off.

A final potential problem relates to supervision. Employees can run into difficulties when they do not work on the same days as their supervisors and colleagues. Preventive measures such as working overlapping hours and scheduling face-to-face check-ins can reduce potential problems.

On the positive side of the equation, jobs such as piloting, direct service hospitality, or law enforcement patrolling, which have tasks that can be accomplished in discrete windows of time, often work very well under compressed schedules.

PART-TIME AND REDUCED-LOAD WORK

For some, one solution to the frantic pace and the struggle to balance work and family is to simply work less. In *It's About Time,* Phyllis Moen (2003, p. 43) states that three quarters or more of the people in her study say they are working more than they would like to. This observation is consistent with data from the 1997 *Study of the Changing Workforce.* In that study, 63% of the workers expressed the wish to work fewer hours, and this number jumped to more than 80% for those working more than a 50-hour week (Families and Work Institute, 1997). The answer for these people may be to establish work hours that are less than what has been considered a standard work week, typically 40 hours or more. It might be reasonable to assume that working part time is a good solution.

In their study *Making Flexibility Work: What Managers Have Learned About Implementing Reduced-Load Work,* Mary Dean Lee and Ellen Kossek (2006) and their collaborators conducted interviews with 88 managers and executives in 20 U.S. and Canadian companies representing six different business sectors. This was a longitudinal study, conducted over 6 years. Although layoffs and downsizing had happened in more than half of the firms, there was an increase in reduced-load arrangements in 60% of the firms, and this practice gained greater acceptance in 70% of them.

Who works part time? It is clear that women are far more likely than men to work on a part-time basis. Estimates suggest that part-time female workers outnumber part-time male workers by a ratio of about three to one (BPW Foundation, 2004). The majority of the women who work part time (68%) do so voluntarily (Bond, Thompson, Galinsky, & Prottas, 2002). And among women and men who work part time, women who do so are nearly twice as likely as their male counterparts to have a university degree (Comfort, Johnson, & Wallace, 2003).

Reduced-load arrangements work best for the company when the company uses this activity not just to provide a benefit for employees but when it is linked to ongoing strategic change initiatives or effective talent management processes. Thus, this new flexible way of working is integrated into the everyday management of the enterprise.

Why do people seek part-time work? Generally, survey respondents suggest that the move to part-time work is prompted by the desire to spend more time with family or avoid the high stress of working full time. The advantages of working part time for many include the greater attractiveness of part-time hours, greater accessibility to the family, lower levels of stress, and higher levels of life satisfaction (Higgins, Duxbury, & Johnson, 2000; Hill, Vjollca, & Ferris, 2004).

That said, there are often also downsides and barriers to embarking on this strategy. The first and most obvious is that you lose income. If you work 3 days a week, your salary is now 60% of what it was when you were full time (assuming you are not working a compressed work week on the 3 days you are working). Second, there is the possibility of losing benefits. Many organizations do not offer benefits below a certain threshold of hours, and in most cases any benefits that remain are prorated. The typical cutoff for benefits is about 20 hours, Third, economic insecurity that has caused workers to hesitate to ask for reduced hours, fearing that they might be seen as being uncommitted or dispensable. Finally, many employees suggest that working part time limits promotional opportunities. In one recent study of Canadian workplaces, only 17% of part-time employees had received a promotion at any time since being hired by their current employer (Comfort et al., 2003).

Employers might also resist allowing employees to work on reduced schedules. There is often a built-in bias against such arrangements, although the reasons are not always clear. It may in part be the increased pressure for financial performance that many business leaders feel. Also, in many organizations where headcounts are strictly monitored, a head is a head regardless of how many hours that person works. Therefore, when faced with a choice, managers may opt for full-time resources whenever they are allowed to add people. Other factors may influence the degree of support companies give to this option. These can include the economic turbulence an organization is experiencing, whether a merger has occurred, and the state of growth a company is experiencing (Kossek & Lee, 2005). What isn't clear is whether these factors will lead to an increase or decrease in support for reduced workloads. For example, if a firm is growing there are two possible responses that could occur. They might be reluctant to allow people to work part-time when they are so busy. But an organization might respond favorably to such requests in times of growth if they see part-time work arrangements as a means for retaining talent. However, there is some evidence that as flexibility becomes increasingly accepted and contract and contingency work becomes the norm, even professional and managerial roles are being filled with people who are limited to working on a part-time basis.

As a result of all these factors, working part time (or reduced work hours) is less feasible than might seem logical or appropriate. There also seems to be a misconception that many job types simply cannot be done on a part-time basis. According to Barnett and Hall (2001), there is a widely held view that most part-time jobs are not appealing. They are "bad jobs" because they are low paying, have few benefits, and offer little career advancement. Additionally, it is assumed that many people who are working part time are not doing so out of choice. As a result, there is a general perception that part-time work is unappealing. But it is important to distinguish between voluntary and involuntary part-timers. Voluntary part-time workers might be people who have better qualifications and greater control over their career choices than those who are doing so because that is what their employer has decided.

In a study on part-time physicians, Barnett developed three measures for the subjective aspects of reduced work hours. First was the *difficulty of tradeoffs,* the recognition that doctors who reduce their work hours often have to forgo professional activities that might be seen as interesting or developmental. Some physicians found these tradeoffs highly distressing, but others did not. Second were the *rewards and concerns* (i.e., whether workers perceived greater rewards or concerns as a result of their part-time status). Rewards for workers include more time for themselves, their families, and other nonwork activities. Concerns include decreased likelihood of promotions, lower salary, and marginalization at work. Finally, there was the notion of *fit.* Fit is the degree of success people feel in balancing their financial needs and their emotional needs. If their change to part-time status is a good fit, it should yield a higher quality of life (Barnett & Hall, 2001, p. 198). The strength of Barnett's approach is that it provides much greater specificity and clarity regarding the ways in which reducing work hours either improves or does not improve the quality of one's life.

Management is one role that some may think cannot be done on a less than full-time basis. A study done in the 1990s by Lee, MacDermid, and Buck of 47 managers and 36 professionals seems to refute this commonly held notion. The researchers looked at the impact of reduced hours from a comprehensive perspective, including interviews with many key stakeholders: the manager, his or her boss, a co-worker, a human resource professional, and the employee's spouse. According to the respondents, 93% rated the arrangements a moderate or high success (two thirds were in the "high" category). Senior managers (i.e., the participants' managers) reported that work performance was maintained or improved, and "91% of the employees said they were happier with their work–home balance as a result of the reduced-load work arrangement" (Barnett & Hall, 2001, p. 197).

Despite the concerns that have been outlined, there is ample evidence that organizations will benefit from making part-time work more readily available. According to Rosalind Barnett (2003), there is a growing consensus among researchers that reduced-hours workers are at least as productive as their full-time counterparts (Committee on Part-Time Careers in Clinical and Investigative Medicine, 2000; Olmsted & Smith, 1994). Barnett cites a 1998 study by Catalyst of 2,000 managers and their supervisors in four companies (i.e., a Fortune 100 pharmaceutical company, a Fortune 100 technology company, a leading law firm, and a major consulting firm). The majority of the part-time workers and their supervisors reported that their work arrangement either improved or didn't affect the employee's productivity. In fact, 46% agreed that people working part-time realized productivity gains. Barnett cites other studies that suggest absenteeism and turnover are lower among reduced-hours employees than among full-time employees (Blank, 1990) and that part-time workers tend to take fewer breaks and less personal time while on the job (Epstein, Seron, Oglensky, & Saute, 1999). Increased organizational commitment and increased likelihood of returning to one's job after leaves of absence have been associated with reduced-hours schedules (Barnett, 2003).

Our own experience supports Barnett's observations. We have observed and spoken to many part-time employees who have managed to get their jobs done in a highly efficient fashion. Their short time at work forces them to focus on their most important priorities and avoid distractions. In addition, many part-time workers, especially parents, are so appreciative of the opportunity to work part time that their sense of commitment and loyalty to their employers is extremely high.

One final perspective on reduced work arrangements is that part-time work can be measured in a work year rather than work week. Most people who work three-quarter time probably work 30 hours a week over the course of the full year, but *part-year* jobs would offer another version of three-quarter time. In such an arrangement, a person might work a standard work week for 9 months a year but not work at all for three months. This arrangement may work particularly well for parents whose children are out of school for the summer. It may also mesh well with the needs of organizations whose work is seasonal and whose needs for employees at some times of the year are greater than others (e.g., school systems, accounting firms).

JOB SHARING

Job sharing is just a particular form of part-time work from the employee's perspective. Generally in this situation, employees' salaries and benefits are prorated. Job sharing tends to work particularly well for positions that require more than 40 hours per week and that cannot be divided into distinct part-time positions. From the organization's perspective, however, job sharing is not part time. The organization has a full-time job that must be done, but they use more than one employee to do it.

According to a 2001 survey conducted by CCH Human Resources Group, only one third of the organizations surveyed had job sharing in place. One reason job sharing is not more popular may be because it can cost companies more in benefits and training to have two people share the responsibilities of one position. Additionally, some managers assume that having two people share a job can more easily lead to communication breakdowns, increase the need for coordination, and lead to confusion between the job share participants and with managers, subordinates, customers, and suppliers.

For those who are considering switching from a full-time to a part-time schedule, job sharing has a number of advantages over traditional part-time work. First, a job share may allow you to continue in a job at a high level of responsibility because it counters the argument that a high-responsibility cannot be done on a part-time basis. Second, it may allow the employee to trade time with his or her co-worker to accommodate unexpected personal or family situations. A third advantage (for both the employee and the employer) is that you may share a position with someone who has complementary skills and knowledge. As the old saying goes, two heads are better than one. In this case, having the opportunity to share responsibilities based on your work styles and strengths can make your job more appealing and actually increase the productivity of the role from the company's perspective.

Job sharing also has several challenges. There is the obvious downside of earning less income than in a full-time job, but if you have already assessed your priorities and decided working full time is not possible, this is one that is easily anticipated. More problematic can be issues pertaining to job movement. As with other reduced-hour employees, there is some evidence that employees who share jobs may have fewer opportunities for promotion than their full-time counterparts. In many instances, even to apply for an opportunity to job share, you must identify your job share partner before applying for the position. For job sharing to run smoothly, you and your job sharing partner will need to be excellent communicators and team players. Finally, job sharing entails greater coordination and effort on your part. For these reasons, it is important to educate your manager on the uniqueness of the position. Because communication, teamwork, and coordination are prerequisites of success, these areas should be identified in your performance evaluations.

Once you have a person in mind, you can start the job proposal, which should include your definition of job sharing, how it will benefit your work, reasons why your company should consider restructuring the position, and the specifics of your proposed work schedule and plan.

IS PART TIME FOR YOU?

The decision to work reduced hours often is made by couples as a unit. Couples assess their economic and emotional needs and their individual preferences and develop a work–family strategy. These strategies can vary widely from couple to couple. For example, one partner might decide to work full time, the other part time, or both may decide to work part time, and so forth. After developing a strategy, the couple tries to optimize it in the marketplace.

Fit is the degree of success they achieve. Those who create a good match are said to have achieved a good fit and should experience low distress and high quality of life (QOL). Those who fail to find a good match are said to have low fit and should experience high distress and low QOL. Thus, fit mediates the relationship between number of work hours and distress and QOL outcomes.

To assess fit, Rosalind Barnett developed a measure asking respondents how well the number and distribution of their work hours and the flexibility of their work schedule met their needs and how well their own and their partner's schedules met their own, their partner's, and their children's needs (Box 7.1). Thus, fit represents a subjective assessment of the degree to which each spouse has optimized her or his work schedule.

Box 7.1 Fit Items

_____ 1. Taking into account the number of hours you would ideally like to work and the number of hours you are currently working, which of the following applies?

    a. You are working too few hours.

    b. You are working roughly the right number of hours.

    c. You are working too many hours.

Please choose from the following response categories to answer the next several questions.

Extremely poorly	Mostly poorly	Slightly poorly	Neither well nor poorly
1	2	3	4

Slightly well	Mostly well	Extremely well
5	6	7

_____ 2. How well does your current work _day_ schedule meet your needs (e.g., you may work Monday through Friday or you may work weekends)?

_____ 3. On the days that you work, how well does your schedule of work _hours_ meet your needs (e.g., you may work 9 to 5 or you may work 8 to 3)?

_____ 4. How well does the overall flexibility of your current work schedule meet your needs?

_____ 5. Taking into account your current work hours and schedule, how well is your work arrangement working for you?

_____ 6. Taking into account your current work hours and schedule, how well is your work arrangement working for your spouse or partner?

_____ 7. Taking into account your current work hours and schedule, how well is your work arrangement working for your children, if any?

_____ 8. Taking into account your current work hours and schedule, how well is your work arrangement working for your elderly dependents, if any?

_____ 9. Taking into account your spouse's current work hours and schedule, how well is his or her work arrangement working for you?

_____ 10. Taking into account your spouse's work hours and schedule, how well is his or her work arrangement working for him or her?

(Continued)

(Continued)

____ 11. Taking into account your spouse's current work hours and schedule, how well is his or her work arrangement working for your children, if any?

____ 12. Taking into account your spouse's current work hours and schedule, how well is his or her work arrangement working for your elderly dependents, if any?

Scoring Instructions:

Step 1. Add up responses to items 2–12. Do not use item 1 in computing the fit score.

Step 2. Divide total from Step 1 by the number of items answered (excluding any questions that do not apply). This is your fit score. Total fit scores range from 1 (low) to 7 (high).

SOURCE: Fit Items © by Rosalind Barnett.

TELECOMMUTING

Telecommuting (as it is called in the United States), *teleworking* (as it is called in Europe), *home-working, working-at-a-distance, off-site workers,* and *remote workers* are all terms used to reinforce the idea that work is something you do, not someplace you go (Baruch, 2002). In CWF's study *Measuring the Impact of Workplace Flexibility,* we define telecommuting as "a schedule in which employees conduct their work off-site for some portion of their core working hours" (p. 1). The location of work may be the employee's home, a satellite office, or some other location outside the traditional office space (e.g., while on the road or from a client site).

Telecommuting is one of the most popular yet complex of all flexible work arrangements. There are many types of arrangements, and each brings with it a unique set of issues and challenges. Telecommuting has also become quite pervasive for many organizations that believe in virtual teams and in allowing employees to work from their present locations rather than move to take on new roles. Although this flexibility is desirable, it can bring with it a fresh set of problems. At a recent meeting Brad attended, one IBM employee quipped that "IBM used to stand for 'I've been moved'; now it stands for 'I'm by myself,'" referring to the isolation some virtual employees feel.

Telecommuting first gained prominence in the late 1980s and early 1990s with the advent of home computers and sophisticated telecommunication technologies. In 1996 the federal government introduced a national telecommuting initiative. For the federal and state governments, the primary motivators were environmental considerations, congestion mitigation, and compliance with the Clean Air Act of 1990. By contrast, for private sector corporations the implementation of telework initiatives was driven primarily by financial and human resource objectives (Van Horn & Storen, 2000).

According to a survey conducted by the International Telework Association & Council (Fetto & Gardyn, 2002), an estimated 28.8 million Americans, one fifth of the adult working population, worked from home, on the road, in a telecenter, or in a satellite office at least one day per week in 2001. Despite this high number, telecommuting has yet to revolutionize the American workforce as originally expected. Early predictions were that there would be 55 million telecommuters in the United States by the beginning of the 21st century (Wells, 2001).

Although organizations are offering telecommuting programs in greater numbers than ever before, acceptance and use of these programs are still limited by a number of factors. These factors include manager reliance on line-of-sight management practices, lack of telecommuting training within an organization, misperceptions of and discomfort with flexible workplace programs, and a lack of information about the effects of telecommuting on an organization's bottom line (Wells, 2001). Despite these limitations, at the beginning of the 21st century, a new "anytime, anywhere" work culture is emerging (Van Horn & Storen, 2000). Continuing advances in information technology, the proliferation of a global workforce, and increased desire to balance work and family are only three of the many factors that will erode the current barriers to telecommuting as a dominant workforce development. With implications for organizational cost savings, especially with regard to lower facility costs, increased employee flexibility, and productivity, telecommuting is increasingly of interest to many organizations.

Telecommuting Arrangements

Telecommuting programs can be full or part time, formal or informal, and employee or company initiated. Although the frequency with which telecommuting is supported or used varies by organization, findings from the CWF study indicate that the optimal telecommuting arrangement allows employees to telecommute no more than 3 days per week. It can also be desirable to limit the number of consecutive days an employee is out of the office, thereby preventing individuals from feeling isolated from their work teams. It also allows the scheduling of meetings and interactions with clients, co-workers, and managers.

Formal telecommuting programs are characterized by a contract between the employee and employer that outlines the specifications of the arrangement. This contract could include information such as the specific days that the employee will work off-site; hours the employee will be available to clients, customers, and colleagues; frequency with which the employee will respond to voice mails and e-mails, and objectives and deadlines for the completion of work tasks. Informal programs usually are not supported by a contract and may be structured to include only one scheduled day per week or month or may be unstructured, with the flexibility to work remotely as the need arises.

Employee-initiated telecommuting typically stems from the desire to reduce commute time, reduce the disturbances to work encountered in an office setting, or more efficiently manage and balance the demands of work and family. Anecdotal evidence suggests that many roles can be done more productively with this type of arrangement. This is especially true for positions with a high percentage of reading, writing, or other work activities that entail extended periods of focused concentration. Company-initiated telecommuting arrangements are aimed at reducing overhead costs or retaining highly talented personnel who would not be able to work for the organization in a traditional work arrangement.

Jobs and Individuals Suited to Telecommuting

Telecommuters are concentrated primarily in professions that rely heavily on telephones, computers, and other information technology devices (Van Horn & Storen, 2000). Specific roles most conducive to telecommuting are those that are information-based and portable, require a high level of concentration, and can be done with a high degree of autonomy. In addition, it is helpful if the work can be planned in advance and if the work itself can be done at varying times. Roles that require minimum instruction and limited physical access to fixed resources also lend themselves to telecommuting arrangements (Doherty, Andrey, & Johnson, 2000; Gil Gordon Associates, 2000; Nilles, 1998; Weijers, Meijer, & Spoelman, 1992).

Telecommuting is not a performance- or satisfaction-enhancing work arrangement for all individuals, however. Care must be taken to select employees whose personal and working characteristics are best suited for such a highly autonomous work arrangement. Those best suited for telecommuting demonstrate the characteristics listed in Table 7.1.

Some managers may also be better suited than others to supervising employees who telecommute. The most effective managers of these employees are skilled communicators and listeners who trust employees and empower them to take responsibility, make decisions, and be accountable for their own

Table 7.1   Characteristics of an Ideal Telecommuter

- *Self-motivation:* Telecommuters should be self-motivated and skilled at setting routines and meeting deadlines.

- *High level of job knowledge and skills:* Telecommuters should have sufficient knowledge of their positions to facilitate working and solving problems independently.

- *High performance:* Telecommuters should be high performers, although it may be important for some top performers to remain in the office setting to serve as mentors to co-workers.

- *Independence and confidence:* Telecommuters are less exposed to supervision and feedback and therefore must be able to make independent decisions. It is beneficial for new hires who will telecommute to work in the office environment initially to facilitate organizational assimilation and develop relationships with co-workers.

- *Comfort with solitude:* Telecommuting can arouse feelings of isolation, so people with a low need for social interactions are better suited for telecommuting arrangements.

- *Time management and organizational skills:* With limited daily demands or check-ups placed on employees by their managers, telecommuters must possess the ability to schedule and organize their work to meet deadlines.

- *Concentration:* Telecommuters must be very focused and able to handle home distractions.

- *Strong communication skills:* Telecommuters must make greater efforts to stay in touch with managers and co-workers, providing them with necessary information and updates while working away from the office.

- *Trustworthiness and reliability:* Telecommuters must be held accountable for getting the job done to the same extent as if they were being supervised in the office setting.

SOURCE: Adapted from Shilling (1999).

actions. These types of managers tend to use a more hands-off, participative management style and focus on results, not appearances (Wells, 2001).

Benefits and Costs of Telecommuting

Telecommuting presents advantages and challenges for both the organization and the employee. From the employee's perspective, perhaps the greatest advantage of a telecommuting work arrangement is the increased autonomy and flexibility of the work schedule. Although employees often must be available to clients and co-workers during typical business hours, working remotely allows employees to focus on work when they feel most energized and efficient. It also provides flexibility to attend to outside issues and family needs, such as a doctor's appointment or a child's school activity, without reducing work time or productivity.

Although this autonomy and flexibility in managing work can increase productivity and satisfaction among employees, they also present some key challenges, including difficulty in segregating work and home lives and feelings of social isolation. Employees who work from home may find it difficult to create clear demarcations between work time and personal time, which can lead to role confusion (Ashforth, Kreiner, & Fugate, 2000). Because the home also serves as a workplace, telecommuters can sometimes find themselves working overtime late into the evenings, on weekends, even on vacation. According to the CWF study, 46% of telecommuters worked while on vacation, compared with 34% of traditional office workers. In addition, only 24% of telecommuters rated their work–life balance as good or very good, compared with 26% of traditional workers and 38% of those using daily flextime.

The lack of face-to-face interaction with co-workers can also leave many telecommuters feeling socially isolated and out of the loop. This feeling can manifest itself in many ways. The telecommuter misses informal learning that takes place daily in the cafeteria or around the water cooler. One reason that part-time telecommuting, or working remotely only part of the week, is considered optimal is that it reduces such feelings of social isolation and allows for the benefits of teamwork and learning. Finally, telecommuters may worry about their development and career progression. There is the possibility that employees who are less visible in the organization will not be considered for higher-level positions. "Out of sight, out of mind" is a very real phenomenon that can affect the number of opportunities one is asked to consider.

Telecommuting also offers many advantages to organizations that implement this work option. A telecommuting arrangement can improve employee productivity because people who work remotely are unaffected by typical office environment distractions. This can facilitate a greater focus on work for more concentrated periods of time. When telecommuting is offered as an option, geographic distances become less significant or potentially irrelevant in the consideration of employment. Finally, telecommuting can reduce the organization's overhead and facility costs. With increasing numbers of employees working from home or in other remote locations, organizations can reduce their investments and expenditures in office buildings, parking lots, and other physical capital.

Despite its advantages for organizations, telecommuting also presents some challenges. The most obvious for many is the perceived difficulty in monitoring employee performance and measuring employee productivity. How does a manager know what his or her employee is doing if the employee cannot be seen? Organizations that implement telecommuting arrangements must be committed to trusting employees, empowering individuals to make decisions, and measuring work by outcomes, not face time. Another challenge presented by telecommuting concerns developing synergy and teamwork between telecommuters and their co-workers. It is often difficult to establish a mutually trusting and supportive relationship between individuals who seldom interact face to face. For goals such as developing working relationships, combining telecommuting with on-site work is more effective than a full-time telecommuting work arrangement (Kurland & Bailey, 1999; McNerney, 1995; Telecommute Connecticut, 2002; "Time to Take Another Look at Telecommuting," 2002).

The employee and organizational advantages and challenges of telecommuting are summarized in Tables 7.2 and 7.3.

Many employees assert that they would agree to a slightly lower salary if they could have greater workplace flexibility and the opportunity to telecommute on an occasional or consistent basis. As the convenience and acceptance of working "anyplace, anytime" grows, companies that are unable to provide the most competitive salaries may still attract and retain the best people by offering flexibility through work arrangements such as telecommuting.

Table 7.2   An Employee's Perspective on Telecommuting

Advantages	Challenges
Autonomy and flexibility in work schedule	Difficulty distinguishing between work and home time
Elimination or reduction of commute time	Feeling of isolation form workplace social network
Less money spent on commuting, parking, work attire	Inadequate equipment or lack of technical support
Higher morale and job satisfaction	Implications of limited interaction with manager for career
Avoidance of office politics	Feelings of hostility or resentment from co-workers

Table 7.3   An Organization's Perspective on Telecommuting

Advantages	Challenges
Improved employee productivity	Difficulty in monitoring employee performance
Lower employee absenteeism	Difficulty in measuring employee productivity
Increased employee retention	Change forces organization outside comfort zone
Larger talent pool from which to recruit and select	Possible negative effects on workplace social network
Reduction in overhead facility costs	Difficulty in fostering team synergy

The issue of real importance to organizations is whether high quality work gets done on time, regardless of where work is done or whether it is completed during the 8-hour window called "the work day." Companies involved in the development of telecommunication technologies that make telecommuting possible and companies that are strongly committed to work–life balance often are the types of progressive organizations that understand the value of telecommuting work arrangements.

LEAVES

There are times when for personal, medical, military service, or educational purposes, employees need to interrupt their careers with a leave of absence. Leaves of absence are paid or unpaid employer-approved absences from work due to circumstances such as childbirth, dependent care, elderly care, illness, and education. They differ from career gaps because people continue to be employed by their companies even though they have stopped working there for a mutually agreed-upon time.

In general, leaves of absence tend to be less detrimental to wages than career gaps. According to research conducted on wage losses due to career gaps, women who reentered the workforce after a career interruption earned on average 30% less than before the career gap. Moreover, even after these women had been employed continuously for 20 years, they still earned about 5% less than their counterparts without career gaps (Jacobsen & Levin, 1995, as cited in Judiesch & Lyness, 1999).

Yet even if leave taking is less detrimental in terms of salary, it does have its downside. Judiesch and Lyness (1999) examined the career consequences associated with leave taking among more than 11,000 managers in a financial service organization. The results demonstrated that leaves of absence were associated with significantly fewer promotions and smaller salary increases. Additionally, leaves tended to have a significant negative impact on performance ratings during the year in which the leave was taken.

There are some encouraging signs that these negative consequences are beginning to change. In a recent U.S. census, the percentage of new mothers who worked declined for the first time in many years (from 59% in 1998 to 55% in 2000). As a result, according to an article in the *Wall Street Journal* (Chaker, 2003), companies are devising new ways to lure mothers who have taken leaves and decided not to return to work back into their organizations. According to Chaker, traditionally many employers did not take seriously women who decided to leave work to stay at home with their children. Today, many organizations are creating new strategies to retain working mothers or those who hope to become mothers. There are even some organizations that will allow leaves up to 5 years. This is occurring despite the fact that the economy is on an upward trend. Chaker cited companies such as KPMG, Deloitte & Touche, and Citigroup as exploring these programs and IBM as an organization that for many years has had leaves as long as 3 years.

Once you decide to take a leave, you need to determine your company's policies regarding leave taking and the amount of time that you will be allowed to take. If your organization has at least 50 employees, it is required to follow the Family Medical Leave Act (FMLA) of 1993. This act states that organizations with 50 or more employees must provide up to 12 weeks of unpaid leave and continued health coverage in connection with childbirth, adoption, and medical illness per 12-month period.

Since FMLA has been introduced, the results seem mixed. Overall, median leave time for all leave takers has been 10 days. Approximately three quarters of leave takers took fewer than 35 days, far less time than the 12 weeks allowed, and half of the leave takers returned to work early because they could not afford to take more time off. Thus, for half of the workers who took leave, the amount of leave was constrained by financial reasons. Similarly, among the employees who qualified for and needed to take a leave but chose not to, two thirds reported that they could not afford to take unpaid leave.

A number of larger companies offer more generous leave-taking policies than provided under the FMLA. In these cases, the amount of time an employee is allowed to take off depends on a number of factors (e.g., your company's overall leave-taking policies, the culture and workflow of the specific department you work in, and, of particular importance, your manager's views on leave taking). To illustrate, in *Taking Time* (1998) author Mindy Fried examined family leave-taking practices at a respected financial services institution that offered a generous family leave policy of up to 1 year. Fried discovered that middle managers acted as the key decision makers for leave taking and that the length of leave granted depended on several factors, including managers' perceptions of the temporary loss on the department, their own ideologies regarding leave taking, and the trust that they felt toward their employees. Thus, when one nonmanagerial professional that Fried followed asked for time off after the birth of her first child, her manager granted her a 1-year leave. However, when the same employee became pregnant again she had a new manager, and this person was willing to grant her only a 6-month leave. This example from Fried's study illustrates the important role managers play in determining leaves within the same employing organization.

SABBATICALS

An increasing but still small number of employers are offering sabbaticals to long-term employees to allow them to spend more time with their families, enroll in courses, and pursue personal hobbies. Sabbaticals are short leaves of absence that typically last from 4 to 8 weeks. Employers generally offer sabbaticals to their full-time, long-term employees who have been employed at least 4 years. For example, Intel offers 8 weeks of paid leave to its employees every 7 years.

There are several types of sabbaticals, including unpaid leaves of absence (employee funded), paid leaves of absence (employer funded), and self-funded leaves. Private companies fund the majority of paid leaves, whereas self-funded leaves tend to be more common in the public sector. With self-funded leaves, employees elect to have a portion of their income withheld over a period of several years. This income is subsequently paid to the employee when he or she becomes eligible to take a sabbatical.

Employees who are interested in taking a sabbatical should review their employers' sabbatical policies early because many companies require that interested employees submit detailed plans within a year or two before their actual leave of absence. Even if your company lacks a formal sabbatical policy, it still may be reasonable to pursue one. New corporate policies often come about as a result of creative employees who are willing to ask for what they want and package their proposals in ways that make sense for the employer and the employee. If you take this route, be sure that you do your homework beforehand. Make a case for why you believe you need a sabbatical and how it will help you to become a better employee.

Other Elements of the Family-Friendly Workplace

In addition to flexible work arrangements, employers offer a wide range of policies, programs, and services that can greatly support working families (Pitt-Catsouphes, 2002). These offerings often are packaged under the label of work–life or family-friendly workplace programs. They might include the following:

Conventional benefits. The provision of certain benefits can be of enormous assistance to working families. Once they were the norm from many employers, but today there are no givens in what employers will provide and to whom they will provide it. One of the most basic of these benefits is health insurance, which in recent years has become an increasingly large expenditure for employers and employees alike. The percentage of total compensation represented by wages and salaries declined significantly between 1950 (95%) and 2004 (81%). Whereas salaries have grown very little in the past 5 years, the amount employers have paid in health care benefits grew from $596.8 billion in 2000 to $859 billion in 2004 (EBRI, 2005). Employers have attempted to control these costs by raising deductibles, increasing copayments, and raising the premiums employees pay for insurance. Good benefit plans can also include the availability of life insurance, dental insurance, and, increasingly, long-term care insurance.

Newer forms of benefits aimed at enhancing work life. In additional to conventional benefits, many employers provide other benefits aimed at improving the quality of or simplifying employees' work lives. Examples include health and wellness programs. Effective workplace health and wellness programs can cover a broad range of activities, from building awareness about disease prevention and healthy lifestyles to helping individuals cope with specific issues related to health and well-being. The most successful programs are integrated into the business and comprise multiple components including benefits, health promotion, disability management, health screening, counseling, and employee education efforts. Such programs can yield quantifiable benefits to companies by boosting productivity, reducing absenteeism, and cutting healthcare and worker compensation costs (Business for Social Responsibility, 2004).

Some organizations also provide on-site fitness centers (or discounts at area gyms) and concierge services that can offer anything from dry cleaning pickup and dropoff to fully prepared meals. These conveniences are aimed at simplifying the lives of busy working people.

Dependent care support. Perhaps the most important benefits for working parents and family members include those targeted at dependent care. These can include dependent care supports such as

- Information, referral, or the provision of daycare services for preschool-age children.

- Increasingly, companies are offering benefits for parents who decide on adoption. Although specific policies vary widely, the most common forms of assistance include resource and referral services, payments to help cover adoption expenses (which generally range between $3,000 and $10,000 for a domestic adoption), and provisions for paid or unpaid parental or family leave that meet or exceed the levels required by the FMLA (adoption.com, n.d.).

- Information and referral for after-school programs. It has been estimated that approximately 39% of children in kindergarten through third grade receive some type of before- or after-school care on a weekly basis from someone other than their parents. This translates to more than 6.1 million primary school children (Brimhall, Reaney, & West, 1999). Concern about the care of school-age children after school (before parents return from work) has been called parental after-school stress (PASS). Researchers suggest that the risk of having high PASS is decreased by half when there is workplace access to information or referrals to local after-school programs (Barnett & Gareis, 2004).

- Increasingly, support for elder care is valued by employees who are facing the difficulty of coordinating or directly offering care for aging parents and other relatives. Elder care can encompass a wide variety of issues and services, including information, resources, and referrals on caring for an aging parent, finding appropriate healthcare and adult day-care services, and making difficult decisions about moving an older adult person from the home environment to a residential care setting or hospice (University of Utah Health Sciences Center, 2003).

Family-Friendly Workplace Culture

Most successful organizations have long understood the importance of attracting, engaging, and developing a committed, creative, and productive workforce. They have seen that innovative human resource practices and work–life strategies are an important factor in recruiting and keeping talent. Increasingly, such organizations have implemented aggressive steps toward a comprehensive flexibility strategy.

Although there has been a great deal of progress in the work–life field, there is still a feeling on the part of many organizations and leaders that work–life programs are the exception rather than the rule. If it is generally understood that a balance between work and family is good and desired by most people, why have changing human resource policies had limited impact? Why do many managers still view these benefits as a special accommodation, primarily for female employees, rather than a main-stream innovation for workforce management? Why do we still have so far to go in order to gain universal support for this approach?

In his recent book on leadership, Jack Welch states, "Bosses know that the work–life policies in the company brochures are mainly used for recruiting purposes and that real work–life arrangements are negotiated one on one in the context of a supportive culture" (Welch & Welch, 2005, p. 149). Unfortunately, too often what is espoused in company literature or even corporate policies does not mirror the company's actions when it comes to work–life balance and flexible work arrangements. The key to this disconnect between espoused theory and theory for action seems to be in the underlying assumptions that are part of the culture of the organization (Schein, 1988). The underlying assumption held by some organizational leaders seems to be that "work–life = work less," and in these competitive times, employees working less cannot enhance competitiveness. If this is the case, then the human resource field needs to do a better job of assessing and influencing the *culture* of organizations, not just the policies and programs (Harrington & James, 2005).

In 2001 Kathy Lynch and other staff members of the CWF worked in conjunction with some of its leading corporate partners in order to address this issue. This team of human resource practitioners and academics devoted significant time and attention to ways to address the disconnect between organizations' stated work-life policies and corporate culture. Early in their work, the team realized that one of the difficult challenges in implementing work–life programs is that of measuring progress on such initiatives and connecting that progress with business impact. The team believed that the business adage that "what gets measured gets done" is particularly true for human resource programs whose connection to the bottom line is not direct (i.e., "If I spend x dollars here then sales will increase by $3x$ dollars.").

The team decided that the starting point for this type of evaluation and measurement might be a set of *standards* that provide the framework and tools for measuring the existence of an effective work–life culture within organizations. Such standards would offer organizations guidance on how to implement and maintain an effective work–life culture that promotes productive, committed, and engaged employees at all levels. The team defined and established as the national norm for measuring work–life culture *The Standards of Excellence for Work–Life Integration* (or *Standards*).

At the core of the Standards framework is a set of guiding principles: core values that state the importance of understanding the reciprocal impact of work and life and the shared responsibility of both employer and employee to manage the issue. The Standards provide companies with the tools they need to achieve competitive advantage: a set of guidelines, assessment and planning tools, and metrics for companies striving to create a work environment that maximizes both individual and organizational effectiveness. The Standards do not assess the effectiveness of individual work–life programs or policies but rather look at organizational elements that suggest that work–life balance is imbedded in the corporate consciousness. These include the following:

- *Leadership:* Organizational leaders recognize the complementary importance of work and life priorities for the success of the business and integrate this approach to build a supportive work environment.

- *Strategy:* The work–life strategic plan supports the vision, goals, and priorities of the organization and its employees.

- *Infrastructure:* The organization actively supports work–life strategies through a systemic (proactive, integrated, and ongoing) rather than programmatic approach.

- *Relationship building:* The organization promotes a culture built on relationships of respect and mutual prosperity with its employees and community partners.

- *Communication:* The organization's work–life strategy and resources are consistently and effectively promoted in communications, both internal and external.

- *Measurement:* The organization strives for continuous improvement of work–life integration through ongoing measurement of its work–life strategies, including evaluation, assessment, feedback, and response.

For each of these elements, the Standards outline a set of performance indicators that would provide evidence that the organization is not simply talking about providing a family-friendly culture but is in fact "walking the talk." The Standards are available to organizations that want to undertake an intensive assessment of their company's progress in creating a supportive work environment where work–life policies and core business strategies are aligned. They provide guidance to organizations about how to implement and maintain an effective work–life culture that promotes productive, committed, and engaged employees at all levels.

From an individual perspective, it might be useful to review the Standards in order to assess the current reality in your own organization. A complete list of the performance indicators reviewed by the Standards is available in the appendix of this book (or at the CWF Web site: http://www.bc.edu/cwf). Although it would be difficult for a person not directly involved in your organization's work–life integration efforts to assess all the indicators listed, many may prove useful in assessing the depth of commitment to work–life balance in your present organization.

The Dark Side of Flexible Work Arrangements

Although flexible career strategies and family-friendly work arrangements can offer employees many benefits, including meaningful work situations, increased feelings of psychological success, and greater work–life balance, these options come with some risks and potential compromises. As we have already discussed, although many organizations see the value in these approaches, these arrangements can also be perceived negatively in a number of ways, including the following:

- Employers may question whether the employee is truly committed to his or her role and to the organization. Managers and other employees might see employees who ask for nontraditional work arrangements as uncommitted to their work. Although many organizations espouse the importance of family and work–life balance publicly, not all support these practices in reality.

- At times of organizational downsizing, employees who have chosen nontraditional work arrangements can run the risk of becoming what one of Brad's former corporate bosses called WCRT's (walking cost reduction targets). When headcount is being reduced, managers may opt for traditional, full-time workers to staff their increasingly lean organizations.

- Employees who take time off for family, work reduced schedules, or do not work regularly in the office might be overlooked for promotion, especially into management positions. This could be the result, in part, of the reduced visibility they have in the organization but could also indicate a reluctance to position such employees as role models.

- Many flexible work arrangements ease the conflict between work and home roles, but some flexible work arrangements might actually cause more conflict between the work and family domains by blurring the boundaries between the two.

Although we strongly believe that new career paths and flexible work arrangements are appropriate in light of the realities of today's world of work, that does not mean that no negative repercussions will result from taking these roads less traveled. Many progressive organizations fully embrace nontraditional flexible work approaches, but others do not. It is important that as you enter into a flexible arrangement, you do so understanding that it is not without risks, and you should understand those risks up front. Which path you choose to follow will depend on your personal priorities. The key is to choose consciously and to feel comfortable with your decision and the path you have chosen.

Summary

Perhaps nothing illustrates the connection between one's work and one's personal life more clearly than issues concerning one's family. Almost every career or work change, whether positive (e.g., a promotion, an exciting new project, a transfer to a new location) or negative (e.g., forced overtime, a major project deadline, a demotion, or a job loss), has a significant impact on family. In a similar way, family experiences and transitions (e.g., marriage, divorce, birth, serious illness, or death in the family) all affect how we feel about work at any given time, sometimes in a very profound way.

In this chapter we have discussed different ways in which couples and families might deal with life challenges and changes. We have covered a range of approaches being used by leading employers to help working family members. One thing that is certain about work and family life in our contemporary society is that things are not static in either sphere.

In the final chapter, we will discuss how careers and work change not because of changes in family status but rather because of transitions between developmental stages. We will discuss the concept of adult development and how stages of life can profoundly affect one's thinking about careers and their importance at any given time.

For Further Reading

Jacobs, J. A., & Gerson, K. (2004). *The time divide: Work, family, and gender inequality.* Cambridge, MA: Harvard University Press.

Kossek, E. E., & Lambert, S. J. (Eds.). (2005). *Work and life integration: Organizational, cultural and individual perspectives.* Mahwah, NJ: Erlbaum.

Pitt-Catsouphes, M., Kossek, E. E., & Sweet, S. (Eds.). (2005). *The work and family handbook: Multi-disciplinary perspectives and approaches.* Mahwah, NJ: Erlbaum.

Career Development Over the Lifespan 8

Even when you think you have your life all mapped out, things happen that shape your destiny in ways you might never have imagined.

—Deepak Chopra

Given the idiosyncratic nature of careers today, it is a challenge to discuss general trends in careers over the lifespan. One need look no further than the lifespan of a typical baby boomer to see how much career patterns have changed in only the past 20–30 years. The advice given to baby boomers when they were graduating from college in the 1960s and 1970s ("Find a good, secure company and stick with it") seems dated and contradicts the advice one would give to new graduates today.

People are now far more likely to have multiple careers over their lifespan. Therefore, much of the study of lifespan development that was done in the past is difficult to apply today. In the past, stages of adult development and stages of career development often closely paralleled one another. Today, however, career stages may be quite short, and a person in late midlife, for example, might nonetheless be in the earliest stages of his or her latest career endeavor. However, to help you anticipate the dynamics of your career journey, we discuss the stages of adult development in this chapter and offer some indications of how these stages affect careers.

Finally, we bring this book to a conclusion by summarizing the key points, suggesting other actions you can take, and offering some final thoughts.

Lifespan Development: Are Career and Life Stages Still Relevant Today?

First, let's consider whether the basic premise that life and career stages go hand in hand is still relevant in this era of complexity and rapid change. Maybe the concept of regular, predictable stages or phases is an anachronism. Our answer to this question is clear and definitive: yes and no.

When we say "yes," we mean that adult development, like career development, is not as easy to characterize in a predictable way as it was 25 years ago. If career or life stages still exist, they are not as well defined as they once were. We now have a new way of looking at careers over time: careers as learning stages. As discussed later, the career is a process of continuous learning. Over a lifetime of work a person passes through many career role transitions. Each role transition entails a sequence that looks like a miniature version of the more traditional career stages: exploration of the new role, establishment in the new role, mastery, exploration of different roles, and finally exit into something new. These mini-stages often are superimposed over longer, more traditional phases or seasons in a person's life and career, as Daniel Levinson (1986) calls them. So, yes, there is a new way of looking at career and life stages.

However, we have not lost the experience of regular, predictable changes in our roles, expectations, concerns, and self-images that come packaged as life and career stages. We are still adults who go through a regular series of life experiences and tasks that lead to phases of adult development. During our adult careers, even though we may make more shifts in occupational, organizational, and institutional contexts and moves from performer to learner and back, these careers still have a beginning and an ending (even if that ending occurs at a much later age). Also, if the careers have beginnings and endings, by definition this means that they have middles—points at which we become aware of being more senior and of seeing the end coming closer. Thus, we can still talk about early adult life and early career, midlife and mid-career, and later life and late career.

One factor that makes these life and career stages appear so different today is the greater asynchronicity between various life and work roles. That is, the stages of our career and our life stages do not line up together as neatly as they did in the past. It was once the case, with the one-life, one-career imperative, that early adulthood and the early stage of a lifelong career occurred at the same time. Today, however, a person is almost as likely to be starting a new career at age 35, 45, or 55 as at age 18, 20, or 25. Also, because the cycles of work and life stages interact in different ways now, the experiences often feel different. Thus, our life stages and our career stages often feel out of sync with each other. To summarize, we assert that career and life stages are still relevant to modern careers, but they have more complex interactions and overlays.

Adult Life Stages

Unlike the life stages of childhood and youth, which are well defined by age and institutional role transitions (e.g., the start of grade school, driving age, high school graduation, voting age, college graduation), the important changes in adulthood are more difficult to delineate. The fuzziness of adult life stages has increased in recent years, as life's boundaries have become more permeable in contemporary society (Sheehy, 1996). Marriage and parenthood often are the last institutionalized status passages experienced before retirement; thus, a person tends to pace his own life cycle in terms of the life cycle of his children and the total family. In fact, a person's social behavior probably is related more to his stage in the family life cycle than to his age (Levinson, 1986). As Tim has found through personal experience, being the father of a teenage daughter evokes similar feelings and challenges, regardless of whether the father is in his 60s or his 30s.

The person's stage in his or her career is another factor that can strongly affect (and is likewise affected by) social behavior and attitudes; this variable may not be closely tied to age either. A lawyer or manager on the first permanent job after professional training (law school or business school) probably will be concerned about establishing a reputation among colleagues and advancement, whether he or she is 25 or 45 years old. (A 45-year-old who started a career in that occupation at 25 probably will have quite a different set of concerns, which are described later.)

From a historical perspective, the field of adult development is new. Psychologist Eric Erikson was one of the first to identify discrete stages for adults in his book *Childhood and Society* (1963). The idea of adult stages became more widely accepted and understood in the 1970s with the publication of two popular books: Gail Sheehy's *Passages: Predictable Crises of Adult Life* (1976) and Daniel Levinson's *The Seasons of a Man's Life* (1978). In 1997 Levinson also published *The Seasons of a Woman's Life,* in which he attempted to identify stages of women's adult development.

Levinson and his colleagues assert that in two longitudinal studies they found that "the life structure evolves through a relatively orderly sequence during the adult years" (Levinson, 1978, p. 49). A life stage is composed of a series of stable, structure-building periods called *stages,* separated by a series of structure-changing periods called *transitions.* A transition serves a dual purpose: terminating the existing life structure and introducing the new one. Thus, a transition is a bridge or boundary zone between two time periods of greater stability. For example, the midlife transition is the bridge between two major eras in life: early adulthood and middle adulthood.

Levinson and his colleagues (1978, 1996) claim that the ages they use to demarcate life stages are accurate to within approximately two years. Ages 17 to 22 are called the *early adult transition,* during which childhood and adolescence end and *early adulthood* begins. From ages 22 to 28, one is entering the adult world, which is the initial creation of an adult life structure. This might be the initial job, the first committed love relationship, one's first home away from parents, and so on. The person is exploring a range of new possibilities as an adult and creating a stable life structure. Finding a balance between these two tasks is not easy because they represent opposites, expanding out versus settling down. Managing these polarities or paradoxes is a major way in which development occurs.

In recent years, more has been written about a stage that has been called emerging adulthood (Arnett, 2004). Changes in patterns have been identified in young people in Generations X and Y since the time of Levinson's work. Marriage age is an example of these changes. In 1970, the average age of women at marriage was 21, but by the year 2000 this had climbed to age 25. For men, the average age at marriage has climbed from 23 to 27 over the same 30-year period. Although factors such as rising education levels have contributed to this change, Arnett believes that it is the result of an increase in the desire of young people to delay the obligations of adulthood. In addition, emerging adults increasingly are experiencing an extended period of exploration and instability in their career development. But Arnett suggests that this exploration is different from the exploration we have described thus far:

> Often it is not as systematic, organized and focused as exploration implies. *Meandering* might be a more accurate word, or maybe drifting or even floundering. For many emerging adults, working simply means finding a job, often a McJob that will pay the bills until something better comes along. This is especially true for emerging adults who don't have an idea where their interests and abilities lie. (Arnett, 2004, pp. 149–150)

This exploration is also important for the growth of the person's *identity* and clarity of self-concept in these more turbulent and less predictable career times. This notion of an extended period of searching in one's 20s has also garnered attention as a result of the bestseller *The Quarterlife Crisis: The Unique Challenge of Life in Your Twenties* (Robbins & Wilner, 2001). Its authors make many of the same points Arnett does about the extended periods of floundering young adults are experiencing in light of the new career models. Referring to the quarter-life crisis, the authors state:

> [It] can be just as, if not more devastating than the mid-life crisis. It may be the single most concentrated period during which individuals relentlessly question their future. It is what we call the quarterlife crisis. . . . [It] occurs precisely because there is none of the predictable stability that once existed. After 20 years in a school setting, goals were clear and ways to achieve them mapped out distinctly. But after

graduation, the pathways blur. . . . What once was a solid line has now disintegrated into millions of different options. (Robbins & Wilner, 2001, p. 2)

Levinson calls ages 28 to 33 the age-30 transition. At this point, the person reexamines the choices made in the 20s and has the feeling that if he or she wants to make a change, it should be done soon. Otherwise, it seems as if it would be too late. The result of this transition is that the person could either make a renewed commitment to the initial life structure or make a significant change of structure. Then, during ages 33 to 40, the person forms a second adult life structure, which is called the settling-down stage. During this period, the person tries to establish a niche in society and to achieve success.

Then, from ages 40 to 45 there is another questioning of the previous structure, the midlife transition. This is a serious reexamination of previous choices, with a stronger sense of time urgency than in the 30s. Parts of the self that had been neglected earlier are now seeking to be expressed. In this way, the person becomes "more himself or more herself" as time goes by. This transition marks the move to the next great era in adult life, middle adulthood. Then, ages 60 to 65 represent the late adult transition, which begins the move into late adulthood, which is the third great adult era.

Although Levinson calls life after age 65 "late adulthood," as with other stages of development, a more refined look at the post-age-65 years is in order. Moreover, this age group may be the one, currently and in the future, where the greatest changes will occur in career and life patterns. This stage has been called the third age. According to Laslett (1991), this period is not age bound but rather a period of personal fulfillment reached by those in the period after work and active parenting. In our readings, though, the third age often is designated as the period from 65 to 79, when people are no longer as active in work and yet are still likely to be in good health. An excellent examination of personal stories of people in this third age of life is found in Abigail Trafford's book *My Time: Making the Most of the Rest of Your Life* (2004).

The research director of the Boston College Center for Work & Family, Jacquelyn James, has recently co-edited an interdisciplinary book on this new stage of life. What's new about this stage is not that people are reaching this age (that has been the case for many years) but rather that they are more likely to live through and beyond it. As a result, it makes sense to talk about this as a new life phase characterized by good health, low mortality, and the opportunity for new or extended career endeavors (Sorensen, 2007).

James and her co-editor, Professor Paul Wink of Wellesley College, make some interesting observations about this stage of life:

- It is a period of generally good health and vitality. Although small health declines occur, more than two thirds of the population still report being in good health at age 79. One exception is the increasing rate of obesity for those in this age group, which is now nearly twice what it was in 1984.

- The economic status of the current generation in the third age is better than that of past generations, although there is greater variability. There are clearly more rich and more poor individuals than there once were.

- Given the level of financial and psychological well-being for many, those in this age group are more likely to work or actively volunteer past the age of 65, and such trends have yielded positive outcomes in overall well-being (James, 2005).

In summary, an interesting feature of the Levinson model becomes apparent if we add the years spent in each of these types of periods, stages, and transitions. Before age 65, traditionally considered the normal retirement age in North American culture, the total time spent in transitions is 24 years, and the total time spent in adult life stages is 27 years. Thus, almost half of an adult worker's lifetime according to Levinson is spent in a period of change. This is in contrast to the view many young people hold that once they become adults, their lives will settle down and they will feel grown up. In fact, we spend our adult lives doing the work of growing up. Growth is a process, not a destination, and in these turbulent times it seems that growth experiences are both plentiful and lifelong.

Gender and Life Stages

There has been much debate throughout the years about whether Levinson's life stage developmental model, which was developed from his male sample, adequately describes the lives of women. Levinson's much-awaited book, *Seasons of a Woman's Life* (1996), found that that it does for his sample of 45 women academics, homemakers, and business professionals. All were in the in the 35 to 45 age range, and the same age-related stages fit their life experiences (although this is a very small sample on which to base any conclusions). However, he did report that women had to deal with more conflicts regarding the way they enacted their life roles. Also, it appears that the age-30 transition relates to choices about life roles more for women than for men, whereas these choices about life roles assume more importance for men in the midlife transition. In a similar vein, Roberts and Newton (1987) report that the age-30 transition for women involves choices about switching from a career focus to a family focus or vice versa.

It also appears that women are more likely than men to have "split dreams," as Roberts and Newton (1987) call them. That is, their dreams are more likely to involve combinations of or balance between different life roles, as opposed to a desire to develop within a particular role domain, such as career or family. Perhaps a better term to describe this pattern for women is *integrated dreams. Split* implies that the life focus contains two incomplete entities, whereas *integrated* implies a positive, holistic orientation. For example, in her comparison of male and female entrepreneurs, Candida Brush (1992, 1999) found that women had an integrated orientation, in which their business and their family were interconnected. Men's focus was much more single-minded, focused on the business.

Differences in the ways women and men make developmental progress in their lives are also highlighted by researchers. Going back to the pioneering work of Jean Baker-Miller (1991), we know that men tend to learn in childhood how to deal with problems related to independent mastery (Fletcher & Ragins, 2007). Women, on the other hand, learn in childhood how to grow in connection (i.e., through their relationships with others). Thus, women come to view development more as a mutual, interdependent process than do men. These relational ideas have also been applied to adult and career development by Joyce Fletcher (1999; Fletcher & Ragins, 2007). Fletcher's research has found that the following features characterize growth-fostering relational interactions:

- *Interdependence:* Both parties believe that interdependence, which includes vulnerability, need, and inadequacy, is the ideal state in which to grow and develop.

- *Mutuality:* Both parties approach the relationship expecting that each will grow and benefit from it.

- *Reciprocity:* It is expected that both parties will have the skills to use this two-directional model of growth and will be motivated to use them.

We suggest that these relational qualities have become critical factors in facilitating development for all people, not just women (Hall & Associates, 1996). Indeed, as organizational resources become more limited and less available to individuals for career development, relational resources are becoming increasingly important (Kram, 1996).

A New Model for Middle and Later Years: Learning Cycles

One of the keys to understanding the new contract is the fact that the employee's needs and career concerns change during the course of the career, in a much more dynamic way than in the past. Continuous learning is needed for continued success. An issue for women and men in midlife and later is how to learn continuously and be adaptable after establishing an initial life structure that works and yields psychological success. Early adult success can reinforce a stable routine of behavior and lifestyle, which can put the person at risk later in her or his career of being closed to necessary new learning. Although success breeds success, the subsequent overuse of skills can lead to later career derailment as the person tries to repeat the use of skills that created success in the past but are no longer relevant to current challenges.

The same meta-competencies discussed earlier, identity and adaptability, seem to be the keys to career success at all stages in light of the new career realities (Hall, 1986b; London, 1998). If the older person has the ability to self-reflect, to continue assessing and learning about herself or himself, and to change behaviors and attitudes, the chances are much better for successful career transitions at any stage and a good fit with the new work environment.

Career routines in one's middle or later career can be interrupted by various triggers in the person and in the environment, leading to conscious exploration of alternative ways of being, "routine busting," and new cycles of learning. If this exploration leads to experimental changes in behavior that lead to success, they are likely to be integrated into the identity and may encourage future explorations and adaptations.

Because of the greatly increased variety and complexity in the work environment (Handy, 1989, 1994), there is an equally great potential variety in the range of individual responses to changes in this environment. What we are seeing now, instead of one set of career stages, is a series of many shorter *learning cycles* over the span of a person's work life (Hall & Mirvis, 1995). Careers will be increasingly driven by the core competencies of the fields in which a person works. As the life cycle of technologies and products has shortened, so have personal mastery cycles. As a result, people's careers will increasingly become a succession of mini-stages (or short-cycle learning stages) of exploration, trial, mastery, and exit, as they move in and out of various product areas, technologies, functions, organizations, and other work environments. The key issue determining a learning stage will be not chronological age (in which the 40s and 50s were considered "mid-career") but career age, where perhaps 5 years in a given specialty may be "midlife" for that area. Thus, the length of a career stage would be driven by the half-life of the competency field of that career work. This model is shown in Figure 8.1.

This model of career learning mini-stages provides a more specific view of the functioning of the protean career as the person grows older. As the person acquires career experience, his or her protean qualities usually are not random or capricious changes. They are not something negative, and proteanism should not be confused with indecision. It is a process of doing

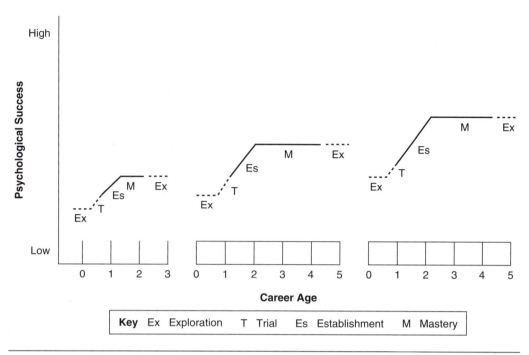

Figure 8.1   A Model of the Career as a Series of Learning Cycles

identity exploration and development, becoming more complex and mature, as one learns from experience.

This point is especially crucial in understanding the rich possibilities for later career stages that Jackie James describes. The more psychologically mature the person is (and most developmental models posit that maturity increases with age), the freer the person is to be a protean self-learner. If we can remove the sources of insecurity that plague older workers (e.g., job insecurity, health insecurity, and physical insecurity), we can free up these positive self-direction and growth drives and tap into a rich supply of experienced human talent.

Interestingly, this focus on lifelong learning for the older employee can produce a gender benefit as well. The more we come to view continuous learning as part of the new career contract and not just as a type of career pattern for a certain type of person, the more we can value both female and male patterns of development. By this we mean that the protean form involves more horizontal growth, expanding one's ways of connecting and collaborating with other people, as opposed to the more traditional model of individual mastery (upward mobility). As we described earlier, in the protean form of growth, the goal is learning, psychological success, and expansion of the identity. In the more traditional vertical form, the goal was advancement, success and esteem in the eyes of others, and power.

Thus, the protean form can embrace both mastery and relational growth—that is, both of what are sometimes labeled male and female ways of developing (Fletcher, 1999; Miller, 1991).

What this means is that careers unfold erratically over time. They move in fits and starts. They take sudden turns. They are not nearly as orderly as our traditional theories of career and adult development stages suggest. In fact, contemporary careers might be viewed as a series of learning cycles over the person's life. Thus, the new career is not likely to be one long cycle containing stages (e.g., exploration, trial, and establishment), as we described careers in an earlier era (Hall, 1976). Careers today are composed of many short cycles or episodes lasting perhaps as little as 2 years, during which the person learns about and masters a new area of work. Each episode might have an exploratory phase, a trial or testing period, and a period of getting established or mastering the work. Then, whether for external reasons, such as new technology and market changes, or for internal reasons, such as personal or family needs and values, the person might begin to explore some new terrain. For example, when dot-coms boomed, many people explored this new business model. With the dot-com bust, information technology professionals jumped back to traditional companies.

The Second (or Third or Fourth) Career

Given all we have discussed thus far, to discuss the notion of a second career seems a bit tame. We have described a new protean career, the end of the employer–employee contract, and many types of alternative career paths. But it is important to point out that for many people, pursuing a second (or even third or fourth) career is something that holds great appeal, especially at midlife. Earlier, we cited the late Peter Drucker's article "Managing Oneself" in reference to the importance of self-awareness and the self-assessment process. But Drucker adds one other important reason for knowing oneself: the second half of your life.

Drucker states that people will work for a long time in the 21st century, perhaps 50 years or more. (Drucker, who died in late 2005 at the age of 94, was a great example of the potential of the third phase of life. He continued to be enormously active and productive with his work nearly to his last days.) Despite the long careers many of us will have, Drucker postulated that most of us would begin to peak professionally halfway through our career (which he suggested was around age 40) (Drucker, 2005). This presents two choices for the individual:

- "Hang in there for many years," trying to survive in an organization without dying of boredom before retirement. Obviously, given the length of time we will work and the new employment contract, Drucker implies this is a highly dubious strategy.

- Start a serious second (or third, or fourth) career.

Drucker suggested that age 45 is about the time many make the move into a second career. This is the period Levinson called the midlife transition, one where career (and life) transitions are particularly common. According to Levinson, this is a time when many people ask, "What have I done with my life?"

More recent work on multiple careers updates and modifies Drucker's thinking. There is little question that interest in multiple careers has grown in recent years. All the forces we have outlined in this text create not only the possibility but the likelihood of multiple careers for individuals. Although the instability and anxiety that this turbulence creates may appear problematic, there are reasons to see this as a positive trend as well. Career changing opens up new possibilities, keeps people stimulated in their work, and allows couples to make changes that reflect where they are in terms of family demands.

Daniel Feldman has written about this phenomenon in an article called "Second Careers and Multiple Careers" (2002). Feldman begins by defining a career change to differentiate it from a job change, organization change, or other less significant transitions. Feldman describes a career change as "entry into a new occupation which requires fundamentally different skills, daily routines, and work environment from the present one" (2002, p. 76). In contrast to Drucker's point of view that most career change occurs at mid-career, Feldman suggests that there is little empirical evidence to support this and that switching careers is more prevalent among young adults.

Feldman points out that there is always some uncertainty associated with career change, but there are factors that motivate people to opt for career change despite the risks. These factors differ depending on the age or stage of the individual but include the following:

- *Education:* The more one has invested in one's career education and the more vocationally specific that training has been, the less likely one is to switch careers, at least in the early career stages.

- *Degree of change in occupation:* In later adult stages, those who have seen a great deal of change in their occupations over time are more likely to seek a career change. Occupations that have seen radical changes in recent years, including roles as diverse as medicine and manufacturing, are likely to engender a career change orientation among their members.

- *Changes in family situation:* As one might imagine, the financial and time issues that go hand in hand with having a family influence the likelihood that one will seek a career change. If the nest is getting emptier in mid-career, this creates greater options for the primary wage earner to consider changing careers, even if it will mean a decrease in earnings. On the other hand, the secondary wage earner (still often the wife in two-career couples) may seek more demanding work as his or her child-rearing responsibilities diminish. By contrast, couples or single parents in the heart of the child-rearing years are less likely to seek a career change unless they are moving to better-paying jobs that will help them pay their children's college expenses.

- *In the case of older workers or those in the late-career stage, health, wealth, interest and involvement, and organizational tenure* all affect one's ability or interest in pursuing a career change. As one would expect, good health and some wealth increase the likelihood that one will be interested in and willing to pursue a change. Likewise, those who have serious interests outside their work might seek opportunities to turn that interest into a work-related pursuit. Those who have particularly long tenure in a position or a particular organization may be less likely to pursue a change. One of the primary factors inhibiting career transitions has been the loss of salary or benefits that has historically accompanied long tenure in an organization, although this may continue to change as fewer companies offer incentives (e.g., defined pension plans) for long-service employees.

What determines the likelihood of success in making a career change? Feldman suggests that two primary character traits facilitate effective career transitions: extroversion and openness to new experience. Making transitions often entails a high level of initiative, seeking out of new information, and networking with others. Extroversion makes it easier to break in and settle in to new careers. In addition, major career changes come with uncertainty, ambiguity, and feelings of ambivalence. According to Feldman, "The greater an individual's openness to new experience, the more likely he/she will be able to cope effectively with change, master new environments, and persevere in the face of adversity" (Cooper & Burke, 2002, p. 89).

Protean Careers and Older Workers

What does a protean career look like for an older worker? There are several advantages of *flexibility and autonomy* in the protean career concept for older workers, related to the current work environment. First, flexibility provides new ways to think about *time* over the course of the career. Rather than following the more traditional concept of the career as a linear progression of upward moves or as a fairly predictable series of discrete stages (e.g., Dalton, Thompson, & Price, 1977) or even as a regular pattern that might be unique to each individual (Driver, 1994), the protean concept encompasses a more flexible, mobile career course. Rather than focusing on an ideal generalized career path, the protean career is unique to each person—one's own "career fingerprint."

Flexibility and autonomy seem tailor-made for the older worker. At this point in life, many of the external constraints (e.g., children's education) and internal drives (e.g., advancement) that may have imposed a more linear, externally defined career path on the person have receded. As long as healthcare and other basic needs are met, the older person is freer to pursue more flexible career options than her or his younger peer.

A second kind of flexibility provided by the protean career is the *enlargement of career space.* The literature on careers has tended to associate careers with paid work and with what goes on within the boundaries of a formal organization. In the discussion of work and family issues, there is an assumption of a clear boundary between those two domains (Hall & Richter, 1990; Kossek & Lobel, 1996). In contrast, "a more elastic concept, however, acknowledges that work and non-work roles overlap and shape jointly a person's identity and sense of self . . . under the rubric of attaining psychological success" (Hall & Mirvis, 1994a, p. 369).

Unfortunately, though, the outlook for older workers is not totally sunny. For older employees, flexibility of space means recognizing that there are more paths to psychological success than just those associated with paid employment and that there are now options for combining paid work with work related to personal interests. The boundaries between paid work and life can be more permeable (or nonexistent) for the older worker. In fact, learning how to deal with this increased freedom of choice may be one of the more difficult challenges facing the older worker.

Another increasingly popular form of space flexibility is working out of the home, done by many people either informally, as independent contractors, or as part of an organization's formal home work program. (This option is discussed in great detail in chapter 7.) This option may not be as attractive to older workers as it is to younger employees. The older person may be looking for an opportunity to get out into a structured social situation. For the older employee looking for social interaction, the more traditional organization-based workplace may be more satisfying.

Perhaps most fundamentally, the protean career concept provides a different way of thinking about the relationship between the organization and the employee. Whereas most of our previous literature on the organizational career has had the organization as the figural element, with the individual as background, in the protean career the person is the figure and the organization is the background. Organizations provide a context, a medium in which individuals pursue their personal aspirations. This model is analogous to the free agent in sports or the arts. Both parties have freedom to end the relationship, but it is possible that the relationship may become a long-term, highly valued one. This model is something other than simply a relational or a transactional contract. It is the free person pursuing her or his own "path with a heart," as Herbert Shepard (1984) describes it.

As we have mentioned, this freedom from the organization has its downside, and this may be especially evident for the older worker. In a world where personal identities sometimes are tied to formal organizational work roles, there can be problems of self-definition and possible normlessness when one is working independently (Mirvis, 1995). As mentioned in chapter 7, research on telecommuting shows that people who are not working within the physical boundaries of an organization need to find other ways to meet their social needs and need for identification (Christensen, 1988; Hall, 1989).

For the worker at mid-career and beyond, the prospect of being forced to pursue a more protean career may be even more daunting. Having spent 20 or more years developing a work identity tied to an organization and a group of co-workers, being suddenly on one's own, totally responsible for oneself, could be terrifying, as we know from research on job loss (Brockner, 1988; Kaufman, 1982). After years of psychological success based on a certain set of job skills, to be told that new skills must be developed is a tremendous blow to one's self-esteem and confidence, calling for major identity development work (Hall, 1986b).

The prospect of the older employee's moving from a full-time job in the core of an organization to contract or contingent status (Handy, 1989) can be daunting. The lack of benefits, especially health insurance, and a very short-term commitment, at a time in life when one's healthcare needs may be higher than ever, can make the protean career appear highly unattractive. In fact, increasing attention is being focused on the problems of stress and fairness for the contingent worker (Christensen, 1995; Shellenbarger, 1995).

Finally, to make these new approaches work successfully, stereotypes that currently limit options for older workers need to be overcome. These include the following problems:

- *The perception that it is too costly to continue to invest in developing older employees:* In most organizations the more senior employees are at higher pay levels and therefore often are more at risk for layoffs and job elimination than their younger counterparts, despite the legal proscriptions that apply. Many firms prefer to lay off older workers and develop younger ones. This is ironic in view of the fact that the older worker may possess superior basic skills and already represents a significant level of developmental investment.

- *The belief that the older worker is too inflexible and difficult to train:* This idea persists despite the fact that a survey of employers shows that they give high marks to the older worker's performance, loyalty, attendance, and job skills (American Association of Retired Persons,

1989). There is also much research disputing stereotypes about older workers' adaptability and learning potential (Branco & Williamson, 1982). A problem here is that even though we know that most of a person's career development comes from actual job experiences, the lessons of experience are hard to document and frame as learning (in contrast to formal education, which often goes on the résumé).

- *A perception that retraining for older workers represents too much effort for a small group of employees that may not work for much longer:* However, the fact is that by the year 2020, the percentage of workers over age 55 will increase to 39%. In actual numbers, this change will be an increase from 51 million older workers in 1990 to more than 93 million in 2020 (Barth, McNaught, & Rizzi, 1993). And these figures represent only workers over age 55; they do not include those in earlier midlife years. Thus it seems clear that no society can afford to ignore the developmental needs of this skilled, experienced population (Hall & Mirvis, 1993, 1994b).

Despite all these negative stereotypes about the older worker, there are many competitive advantages for workers in this age group. Organizations that stress continuous learning will find that their older workers will continue to provide a competitive advantage for many years.

As one concrete way of providing more protean options for older employees, we need to recognize that there are great individual differences—both between people and over time for one individual—in what people are looking for in a job. For some people, or for one person at one point in her or his life, the "path with a heart" may be one full of challenge and stimulation (including perhaps stress and overload), with high intrinsic rewards. Those people, at that point in their lives, might opt for what might be called a *high-involvement path* (Hall & Rabinowitz, 1988).

However, some employees in later career stages may be more oriented toward balance in their lives and want less demanding work with steady pay, good benefits, and congenial working conditions. This work option could be called a *low-involvement path,* which could be a feasible, low-stress alternative to always being on the fast track. Providing employees with sabbaticals, leaves of absence, or early retirement to pursue personal goals are also examples of movement in and out of the high-involvement work path.

In addition, an increasing number of companies are offering phased retirement. This may involve a shift from higher- to lower-involvement work roles. According to a recent study, more than 80% of white-collar workers are employed in an organization that permits some form of phased retirement (Hutchens & Chen, 2004). It appears that healthcare, education, and manufacturing are the leading sectors offering this approach and that two thirds of workers over 50 hope to phase into retirement at some point (Watson Wyatt Worldwide, 2004).

More accepted use of this individualized approach to career development would aid employees as they age within career cycles and could provide rich protean opportunities for older workers. However, using this
option requires a *strategy of continuous learning* for older employees.

How Do We Tap the Potential of Older Workers?

If an employer is convinced that there is a need for and a value in continuing the employment and the development of workers into the third phase
of life, what can the organization do to tap the career potential of the older
worker? What specific steps would be necessary to promote an environment of continuous learning? We see four straightforward, high-impact
areas of great potential: relationships, new and varied job experiences,
better job–person brokering, and information technology (Table 8.1). Let
us consider each source of later career development in turn.

Table 8.1   New Sources of Continuous Learning for Older Workers

Relationships (co-learning, not mentoring)

Varied experience (the Mae West rule)

Key facilitator: better brokering ("selection is development")

Use of information technology for

   Self-assessment

   Opportunity information

   Recruiting, staffing

   Learning (e.g., human resource software, online career services, nets)

USE DEVELOPMENTAL RELATIONSHIPS

As we have often stated, a key source of ongoing development is relationships with other people (Hall, 1993; Higgins & Kram, 2001; Kram &
Hall, 1995). We see that *developmental networks* are becoming the best
form of relational development (recall that a developmental network is
the set of people you know, in your personal and your professional life,
who take an interest in your development). No one person may provide
for all of your developmental needs, but taken together the entire network of your relationships can have a powerful impact on your career.

Professional associations, team structures, coaching, and other relational activities also are important promoters of growth. Like workers at other career stages, older workers can benefit greatly from these positive developmental relationships. In time, these workers can also contribute in numerous and sometimes unexpected ways to others in their network.

OPT FOR NEW AND VARIED JOB EXPERIENCE

The best way for experienced employees to maintain their adaptability is to get varied experience (Hall, 2002). The simplest, cheapest way to provide continuous stimulation and challenge is to keep moving through different assignments that demand different skills. Tim calls this the Mae West rule. Mae West was a sex symbol in the early film era who said in one of her roles, "When choosing between two evils, I prefer the one I haven't tried yet." The opportunity for varied experience is one resource that is in abundant supply in the otherwise lean, turbulent organization.

IMPROVE PERSON–JOB BROKERING

To enable this mobility and varied experience, it is necessary to improve brokering of people and assignments. In the human resource function, selection and development traditionally are viewed as quite distinct functions. However, in today's 3F (i.e., fast, flexible, and focused) organizations, because the major source of development is a challenging new assignment (McCall, 1998), selection is in fact development. Staffing will become an increasingly important part of the human resource department's role as developers of employees.

Older workers might be particularly amenable to trying new assignments and roles. Some might question this premise because of the challenges inherent in learning and developing new skills (the stereotype that "you can't teach an old dog new tricks"). We fundamentally disagree with this view. In addition, older workers may be less fettered by financial need or role status demands than their younger colleagues. This could lead to a greater openness to trying new roles in order to improve the person–job fit. Fit in this case could refer to both job content and job design. It seems clear as studies of older workers are emerging that flexibility is something older workers value highly.

An important factor in helping older workers participate in fast and flexible organizations would be the provision of career seminars to help them plan for and make their transitions. Such classes would follow much of the same content and flow we have described up to this point. The sessions would help older workers identify what they want to do with their late career and "retirement" stage. Such seminars seem to be on the rise. A recent special issue of *BusinessWeek* (July 24, 2006) dedicated to older workers and retirement featured an article called "A Course in What Next?" suggesting that such seminars targeted at older workers are increasing rapidly (Hoffman, 2006, p. 66).

USE INFORMATION TECHNOLOGY

To make better use of real-time learning resources such as job variety and developmental relationships, information technology is a critical enabler. For the human resource brokering function, the use of technology is essential. Excellent software exists for functions such as self-assessment, posting information about opportunities, staffing, and facilitating interactive learning (groupware). Also, numerous online job and career services (such as Craigslist and Monster.com) are a rich venue of resources for people who use the Internet.

Countless other steps might be taken for the career growth of older workers. However, these four are the most available and highest-impact factors in the current business environment. Organizations that focus on these four sources will enjoy a huge competitive advantage in attracting and retaining older workers. We have already seen this in the case of companies such as Home Depot, CVS, and McDonald's.

The American Association of Retired Persons (AARP) compiles an annual list recognizing the "best companies for workers over 50." These include corporations, universities, and hospitals. The factors that AARP sees as providing such a positive work environment for older workers include the following:

- Recruiting practices

- Opportunities for training, education, and career development

- Workplace accommodations

- Alternative work options, such as flexible scheduling, job sharing, and phased retirement

- Employee health and pension benefits

- Retiree benefits

More detail on these company rankings and other information about employment and career issues for older workers can be found on the AARP Web site (http://www.aarp.org).

Retirement

In March 2004, an article appeared in *Harvard Business Review* with the captivating title "It's Time to Retire Retirement." As the title suggests, the authors argue that our old notion of retirement, not unlike our framing of careers, is going through a fundamental change. They list many reasons for the changes, including longevity, the potential of labor shortages and the brain drain caused by exodus of baby boomers, the financial needs of the aging population, and the desires of baby boomers to continue working (Dychtwald, Erikson, & Morrison, 2004). This article and accompanying research indicate that as careers come to be more of a series of ongoing learning cycles rather than a single cycle of discrete stages, the notion of retirement has been undergoing a fundamental transformation. There are several reasons fewer people will completely stop paid employment and take up a life of full-time leisure:

- With employers' pensions and contributions to employees' retirement savings accounts decreasing, most people will not be able to afford to stop working completely. Recently, many employers have eliminated defined benefit pensions for their employees. In late 2005, Verizon joined other technology companies including IBM, Hewlett-Packard, and Motorola in stating that it would freeze the guaranteed pension plan that covered 50,000 of its managers. Although the company will pay the workers the benefits they have already earned, these managers will not build additional benefits. Instead, they will expand their 401(k) plan. "This restructuring reflects the realties of our changing world," said Verizon chief executive Ivan G. Seidenberg. "Companies today, including many we compete with, are not implementing defined benefit plans or subsidized retiree medical benefits" (Belson & Ritchel, 2005, p. C1).

- With some people retiring from their primary occupations in their early 60s, somewhat longer lifespans, and the fact that many of us will have better health, people will have a longer "third phase" (what we called the third age) of life. During this time, from the early 60s to perhaps the 80s, people will be more likely to be healthy, capable, and motivated to engage in productive, paid employment.

- With the baby boomers now in their 50s and 60s, the populations in the United States and other developed countries, most notably Japan and parts of Europe, are aging at a dramatic rate. The result is that there will be a smaller base of younger, employed workers to support these older segments of the population, and this may not be viable.

- From a macroeconomic perspective, it may be necessary for older people to continue working, although this is a topic of some debate. Given the changes in technology and the push toward globalization, it is not clear whether there will be a labor shortage in the United States in the years ahead. Over the past two decades, corporations have demonstrated the readiness and capacity to shift the work to where they can find the labor, especially low-cost labor.

Ironically, as the prospect for traditional full retirement looks dimmer, we are also seeing a trend toward slowing down, achieving greater balance, and perhaps even entering a state of semiretirement at an early age (in one's 40s and 50s). Earlier we mentioned the phenomenon of downshifting, and this is at least part of that phenomenon. But many people see the life transformation they want as more than just downshifting; they want to cut back to working part time, and they want to be free of the control of an organization so that they can be their own boss.

The result of these different trends is that there will be much greater variation in the career patterns people seek as they get older (middle age and beyond). Some people will want to slow down early, and others will want to keep going full speed into old age. For each of us as individuals, then, this means we will have to answer two questions for ourselves:

- What do I most want to do with my work and life right now?
- In view of my financial resources, what can I afford to do now?

Let us offer some suggestions to help you address both of these questions.

HOW DO I WANT TO DESIGN MY LIFE FOR THE THIRD PHASE?

The short answer to this question is that you could use almost all the self-assessment exercises we have presented so far to help decide what you want your life to look like at any life stage. A few that are particularly relevant include the following:

- *The Career Values Card Sort:* Whereas many of your values tend to be enduring, others may be more influenced by situation, context, or life stage. Things that you always valued in your 20s and 30s may be lower in your priorities in your 50s and 60s. At any stage of your life, revisiting and reprioritizing your values periodically is time well spent. You may find that a life or career change is in order or at least more possible given your present circumstances.

- *The 10-Years-Out Exercise:* Especially as we approach midlife or tradi-tional retirement age, it is very useful to once again ask, "What are my dreams today?" "What are my hopes and plans for the future?" The 10-Years-Out Exercise is very useful as a planning exercise that takes you outside the traditional territory of financial planning for your later years and may reignite a dream that persists but is still unfulfilled.

- *The Interview With Significant Others:* If your values and goals sug-gest that a change might be in order or is at least worth considering, knowing your skills (especially your transferable ones) is extremely important. Taking the time to meet with others who know you well to get their feedback on your skills and plans may be an invaluable step in your transition process.

Finally, one of the ways to explore new options for retirement or semi-retirement is to simply try doing some new activities, without a lot of fanfare, and see whether you enjoy them. For example, sign up for some community volunteer work. Talk with some friends who are volunteering and ask to go with them, read your local newspaper to identify active orga-nizations, check the Web pages of organizations in your area that do good work, or check your local house of worship. Just put your toe in the water and give it a try. As Herminia Ibarra (2003) found, this is how people make large changes in their lives by starting with small, tentative experiments.

FINANCIAL PLANNING AND CAREERS IN LATER LIFE

Given our increasing lifespan and the demise of defined-benefit retire-ment programs, a key ingredient of maintaining control of one's career in later life will be effective financial planning. Because we discussed the importance of finances earlier (and we are not experts in this area), this will not be a complex financial analysis but rather a straightforward dis-cussion of practical ideas. We will highlight the commonality of ideas pre-sented by three major financial service institutions: TIAA-CREF, Fidelity Investments, and the U.S. Social Security Administration.

One of the authors recently attended a retirement planning seminar at his university where each of these firms gave a presentation. The advice of each presenter was the same: Because your retirement funds will need to last longer than those of your predecessors, because of longer lifespans and better healthcare technology, if you are happy in your work, keep working as long as possible. For each additional year you work, your retirement fund will be that much larger, and it will need to last 1 year less. These experts made a similar argument about part-time employment. If you still enjoy your work but would like a little more time to yourself, continue doing it at a reduced level. Each additional year of part-time work also makes a net contribution to your retirement fund and 1 year from the time that money will need to last. Of course, it is also important to calculate what your retirement resources are, both current and projected, and what your financial needs will be when you do plan to stop working. Here we are referring to paid employment but realize there are many other forms of working that older citizens participate in. For some of the tips that one organization, TIAA-CREF, offers for people thinking ahead to retirement, check out its retirement planning Web site at http://www.tiaa-cref.org.

In addition, organizations such as TIAA-CREF, Fidelity Investments, and the Social Security Administration all provide good tools for helping you assess your goals for retirement, your financial resources, and your anticipated budget needs. For Fidelity, see http://personal.fidelity.com, and for the Social Security Administration, see http://www.sec.gov.

When you reach the point where you are considering retirement possibilities, this is a good time to revisit the ideas of Daniel Levinson and his colleagues (Levinson, 1978) regarding what they call "the dream." The dream is that notion we have about what would be an ideal life outcome or way of living (this should sound familiar from the 10-Years-Out Exercise). Our awareness of the dream often ebbs and flows at different stages of our lives. It may start when we are children, and it may be salient in early career, when we are making our first choices and plans for our lives. And then, as we become involved in a particular type of work and get caught up in striving and enjoying, we become so absorbed in the present that we do not think about our fondest hopes for an ideal life and career. The dream may reassert itself as we go through the midlife transition, forcing us to confront the gap between our career realities and our ideals. And then, as we make it through this midlife transition, the dream recedes.

But as we get further along in life to the point where we can consider new, creative options, we may again think about the dream. At this point, the dream can help us to calibrate where we are and to explore some new options. Unlike in earlier life stages, at this point we might have more freedom (in terms of financial needs and family responsibilities) to consider wider options than might have been possible in midlife. For example, a 45- or 50-year-old might be helping to care for and support aging and ailing parents, or she might have children approaching college age. These realities often demand a high level of income. But when these responsibilities are not present, and if there are fewer children at home, the options increase for how you will be able to live and what it will cost.

A major lesson from the retirement financial planning process is that for every dollar less that you spend supporting your basic lifestyle, you need one dollar less in income. (Actually, considering taxes, you are saving significantly more than one dollar in income.) If you can trim your lifestyle and your budget, you reduce your financial burdens and your overall life stress.

Summarizing Careers Over the Lifespan

To recap, we have argued that under the new career contract between employee and employer, we all still go through life stages, but our career stages have become much shorter. These changes in the career life cycle can be more challenging for the older worker than for her or his younger colleagues. Along with the negative stereotypes that hinder the older worker, the complex issues of career identity in the new protean career can be especially difficult for the employee at midlife and beyond. For example, moving from a position as a manager or executive to one as an individual contributor many take away some prestige, status, and access to information that comes with these roles. In addition, the unique attributes (e.g., varied experience, relational skills) of the older worker often are not recognized. These are not just career issues. They get to the core of what Shepard (1984) describes as "a life worth living" for the person and to the heart of successful restructuring for the organization.

We need to understand more about how to provide work environments that not only develop people through continuous learning (a key element of the new career contract) but also *provide caring for people* (Kahn, 1994) throughout their careers. Organizations that provide a valued mission and challenging, meaningful work combined with an environment of fairness, good pay and benefits, support, and caring for employees will not only meet the needs of the whole person but will also engage that person (Kahn, 1990) and thus profit from a vast supply of untapped human potential.

Book Summary

In this book, we have endeavored to present a contemporary view of careers that has been profoundly influenced by the fundamental changes in work and in families and has become the new career reality for many of us. Changes in the global marketplace, the tumultuous life in contemporary organizations, and the enormous changes in and pervasiveness of technology have created a new "career contract" for most people and organizations. At the same time, dramatic changes in the nature and structure of families coupled with the increasing number of working women, single-parent households, and dual-career couples have also made it clear that old work patterns and career models simply don't apply to most workers today.

We believe that the combination of changes that have occurred in society, the economy, organizations, and family life call for a new way of conceptualizing careers and success. Tim has labeled this new career orientation the protean career. Although there are many ways we have described this model, there are a few key points to remember. First, the protean career is managed and navigated by the individual in accordance with his or her own view of success. This means that it is critical for each of us to understand who we are, what we are good at, and what matters most to us. Because this is of such importance and is an individual undertaking, we dedicated a significant portion of this work especially in Chapter 2 to helping you understand and practice the art of self-assessment. We encourage you to reflect in structured ways on your interests, values, lifestyle, skills, aspirations, and life goals through the instruments we provided or recommended or through other methods. However you get there, the key is to develop a clear sense of identity in order to ensure that *you* are driving your career strategy. Second, we encourage you to always view your career goals in the context of your life goals overall. It makes little sense to discuss career advancement or success as if it were unrelated to the quality of your life as a whole.

In chapter 3, we provided an approach to integrating your self-assessment data into a coherent whole. One of the approaches, developing life themes, is rigorous and time consuming. But we believe the investment will pay dividends. Life themes lead naturally to the next logical step: developing career implications. It is critical to know who you are and what matters most to you. But it is equally critical to take these insights and to consider, "What are the implications of this self-awareness to my career decision making?" It is easy to be influenced in managing one's career by others' standards, expectations, and timeframes. Turning life themes or self-awareness into a conscious template for how you will make important decisions is a critical step in the process of managing a healthy career and living a healthy life.

In chapter 4, we turned our attention to finding ideal work. We argued that the churning that is occurring in the labor market and in organizations has made the process of career exploration and job search a critical competency for all of us. We reviewed the basic tools of job search but also discussed the importance of understanding and actively managing one's network. Your career network is critical at almost every stage of the career management process (e.g., finding work, assimilating into new roles, advancing in your career). But at no stage is this in greater evidence than in job exploration and job search. The facts are clear: Most of us will find a job through our career network. We suggested ways to evaluate, expand, and use your network in your search for the best career fit.

In chapter 5, we discussed career development strategies. In keeping with our view that a career should be designed and managed by the individual, we reviewed different models of career development. Although we hold true to our notion that the protean career is becoming more and more the norm, this does not discount an organizational career as a viable option. Advancement up an organizational career ladder remains a highly sought-after strategy and outcome for many working professionals. Our goal is to encourage you to think more broadly about ways to frame your concept of career advancement. We want you to see development as occurring in many different ways. We discussed the importance of alternative career paths, career lattices, and portfolio careers. These are but a few ways to think about career development. We also discussed the importance of ongoing development as a lifelong endeavor and the benefits of working for an employer that offers tangible support for your career pursuits.

Chapters 6 and 7 were aimed at helping you better understand the interplay between work and personal life. We gave particular attention to the issues of work and family, which for many of us are the most basic and important spheres in our lives. We discussed in great detail the myriad policies, programs, and initiatives that some employers are using to help employees deal with this difficult juggling act. We fully recognize that not all employers offer such progressive programs, but awareness of them is critical. Remember, even large progressive employers often began their work–life initiatives as the direct result of a few courageous employees who asked to work in a new and different ways. Eventually, these small experiments led to programs and options that today are offered to thousands of employees.

In the final chapter, we discussed the concept of lifespan development. It is important to recognize that life stage and life situation have a profound effect on how we look at careers and how much time and energy we have to invest in them. Although career stages today may not be as predictable as they once were, the stage of life and the life and family circumstances we find ourselves in will be of great importance as we think about the marathon we are all running called our careers.

In summary, we return to the meta-competencies that we articulated in the opening chapter: *identity* and *adaptability*. Our belief is that in these fast-changing times, when fewer clear career milestones and markers exist, it is important to understand that a clear sense of identity coupled with the ability to adapt to changes in the workplace, your family, or your life situation will be the keys to success in your career. As changes in the external environment call for a continuous rethinking of outdated formulas, one's sense of self becomes the ultimate arbiter for what it means to do meaningful work in the context of a meaningful life. Good luck on your journey!

For Further Reading

Bridges, W. (2004). *Transitions: Strategies for coping with the difficult, painful, and confusing times in your life* (2nd ed.). Reading, MA: Addison-Wesley.

Hall, D. T., & Richter, J. (1990). Career gridlock: Baby boomers hit the wall. *Academy of Management Executive, 4*, 7–22.

Levinson, D. J., with Levinson, J. (1997). *The seasons of a woman's life*. New York: Knopf.

Levinson, D. J., Darrow, C. N., Klein, E. B., Levinson, M. H., & McKee, B. (1978). *The seasons of a man's life.* New York: Knopf.

Sheehy, G. (1976). *Passages: Predictable crises in adult life.* New York: Dutton.

Sheehy, G. (1995). *New passages: Mapping your life across time.* New York: Random House.

Trafford, A. (2004). *My time: Making the most of the rest of your life.* New York: Basic Books.

Appendix

Standards of Excellence Index

LEADERSHIP

1.1 Leaders are working to build a culture where work–life integration is valued.

1.2 Leaders communicate the importance of work–life for the organization to other managers and employees.

1.3 Leaders communicate the importance of work–life to other organizations by promoting its "best practices."

1.4 Leaders reward those within the organization who support work–life needs and initiatives.

1.5 Through their behaviors (e.g., role modeling, sharing their own work–life experiences, listening, showing empathy), leaders create an environment conducive to work–life integration.

1.6 Leaders support work–life strategies and programs as a means of enhancing work productivity and effectiveness.

1.7 Leaders include work–life in an organizational recruitment and retention plan.

1.8 Leaders represent diverse groups, including those from different ethnic and gender groups.

1.9 Leaders include those who work a variety of schedules.

1.10 Leaders consider employee workloads in making business decisions.

1.11 The leadership development process considers both organizational and individual needs.

1.12 Leaders trust and respect their employees as the foundation for an effective organization.

1.13 Managers discuss the integration between career and life goals with employees.

1.14 Managers evaluate employee performance on results, regardless of work schedule or work location (e.g., telecommuting).

1.15 Managers are empowered to use work–life policies and programs to meet both organizational and individual needs.

1.16 Managers are rewarded for using work–life policies and programs to meet both organizational and individual needs.

STRATEGY

2.1 The organization has a separate work–life vision and mission.

2.2 The organization has a separate work–life strategic plan.

2.3 The business case for work–life is included in the organization's vision and mission.

2.4 Organization identifies important work–life issues for the business, the employees, and the communities in which it operates.

2.5 Work–life strategies are applied throughout the organization (regardless of geographic location or section of the organization, if applicable).

2.6 Organization's work–life strategy is directed at the broadest spectrum of employees possible.

2.7 Strategic plans take into account changing workforce needs (e.g., societal demographic trends, business trends, other changes).

2.8 Organization creates long-term strategies to address the work–life needs of the next generation of workers.

2.9 The organization uses its understanding of community resources to develop its own work–life benefits (e.g., day care centers, after-school programs, etc.).

2.10 Organization uses its resources (financial, human, etc.) to have a positive impact on the community where it is located.

2.11 The overall culture of the organization is consistent with work–life practices.

2.12 Strategies are designed to create or sustain an organizational culture that supports work–life integration.

2.13 Work–life strategy contains the elements of a good strategic plan (i.e., makes the business case, addresses potential barriers, has measurable goals, etc.).

2.14 Work–life strategies and programs are developed using appropriate data sources (e.g., employee surveys, external benchmarking, research).

INFRASTRUCTURE

3.1 New work–life initiatives (programs, policies, and services) are integrated with existing programs and policies (as appropriate).

3.2 Sufficient resources are allocated to work–life programs (either budget or time or staff).

3.3 Managers receive training about work–life strategies.

3.4 Managers are trained to help employees work through work–life issues and conflicts.

3.5 Employees are educated about the availability of work–life programs and benefits.

3.6 Policies and guidelines to support work–life strategies are developed (as needed).

3.7 The organization has a set of programs and policies tailored to the needs of its employees.

3.8 The organization provides tools and opportunities (e.g., education, training, interpretation) for departments to implement work–life programs and policies.

ACCOUNTABILITY

4.1 Leaders are held accountable for balancing business goals with work–life initiatives.

4.2 Leaders encourage employees to use a range of work–life programs, services, and policies to achieve better work–life integration and meet business goals.

4.3 Managers are held accountable for implementing work–life programs and policies (consistent with organizational goals).

4.4 Managers and employees are responsible for working together to achieve work–life integration (consistent with organizational objectives).

4.5 Employees in the organization understand that some jobs, opportunities, and assignments are less conducive to better work–life integration.

4.6 The performance management system for managers is linked to work–life efforts and effectiveness.

4.7 The informal systems at the organization support work–life integration (e.g., promotions, new opportunities, etc.).

RELATIONSHIP BUILDING

5.1 Work–life professionals work with those in other departments to integrate the work–life function into the culture of the organization.

5.2 Organization collaborates with external organizations to provide effective work–life solutions (e.g., child care, elder care, after-school programs).

5.3 Organization contributes to the work–life field through collaboration and support for professional organizations (e.g., work–life associations, research organizations, etc.).

5.4 Organization communicates the importance of employee involvement in communities.

5.5 Organization establishes programs to facilitate employee involvement in communities.

5.6 Organization works with public policy makers to strengthen policies that benefit both employers and individuals.

COMMUNICATION

6.1 The business case for work–life has been clearly communicated throughout the organization.

6.2 Employees receive regular communications about work–life strategies.

6.3 Employees feel free to openly discuss work–life issues in the workplace.

6.4 Direct communication with work–life professionals is available to employees throughout the organization.

6.5 The organization shares its work–life policies, programs, and strategy with other organizations.

6.6 The organization acts as an advocate for work–life issues (e.g., serving on community boards, etc.).

6.7 The organization communicates with other practitioners through professional work–life organizations.

6.8 Managers communicate and listen to their employees regarding work–life issues.

6.9 Work–life is publicly communicated as one component of organizational identity.

MEASUREMENT

7.1 Work–life strategy has measurable goals and objectives.

7.2 The organization collects work–life information (e.g., demographics, future trends, etc.) from its employees on a regular basis.

7.3 The organization uses the information collected from its employees to plan new programs and policies.

7.4 The organization measures the work–life needs of its employees.

7.5 The organization tracks the utilization of its work–life initiatives.

7.6 The organization tracks the effectiveness of its work–life initiatives.

7.7 The organization tracks satisfaction as part of its work–life efforts.

7.8 The organization tracks information related to the workload of its employees.

7.9 The organization examines the relationship between work–life programs and outcome measures (e.g., productivity, quality of work, etc.).

7.10 Cost–benefit ratios or other "return-on-investment" analyses are conducted to examine the impact of work–life programs.

7.11 Measurement data are used to identify obstacles to implementing work–life programs and policies.

7.12 Research findings are used to develop and improve work–life programs.

7.13 Regular benchmarking is conducted to compare the organization's work–life practices with other organizations.

SOURCE: © 2003 The Trustees of Boston College. Permission granted by the Center for Work & Family.

Bibliography

Adoption.com. (n.d.). *Employer adoption benefit package.* Retrieved August 16, 2005, from http://glossary.adoption.com/employer-adoption-benefit-package.html

American Association of Retired Persons. (1989). *Business and older workers: Current perceptions and new directions for the 1990s.* Washington, DC: Author.

American heritage dictionary of the English language (3rd ed.). (1996). Boston: Houghton Mifflin.

Argyris, C., & Schon, D. A. (1978). *Organizational learning: A Theory of action perspective.* Reading, MA: Addison-Wesley.

Argyris, C., & Schon, D. A. (1995). *Organizational learning II: Theory, method, and practice,* Reading, MA: Addison-Wesley.

Arnett, J. J. (2004). *Emerging adulthood: The winding road from late teens through the twenties.* Oxford: Oxford University Press.

Ashforth, B. E., Kreiner, G. E., & Fugate, M. (2000). All in a day's work: Boundaries and micro role transitions. *Academy of Management Review, 25*(3), 472–491.

Bailyn, L. (1993). *Breaking the mold: Women, men and time in the new corporate world.* New York: Free Press.

Bailyn, L., Drago, R., & Kochan, T. (2001). *Integrating work and family: A holistic approach.* Cambridge: MIT Sloan Work–Family Policy Network.

Baker-Miller, J. (1986). *Toward a new psychology of women.* Boston: Beacon.

Bardwick, J. (1980). The seasons of a woman's life. In D. G. McGuigan (Ed.), *Women's lives: New theory, research and policy* (pp. 35–55). Ann Arbor: University of Michigan, Center for Continuing Education of Women.

Barley, J., & Sorensen, D. (1997). Work and family: In search of a relevant research agenda. In C. L. Cooper & S. E. Jackson (Eds.), *Creating tomorrow's organizations* (pp. 157–169). New York: Wiley.

Barnett, R. C. (2003). Reduced hours work/part-time work. *Sloan Work and Family Encyclopedia.* Available at http://wfnetwork.bc.edu/encyclopedia

Barnett, R., & Baruch, G. K. (1985). Women's involvement in multiple roles and psychological distress. *Journal of Personality and Social Psychology, 4*(91), 135–145.

Barnett, R., & Gareis, K. (2004). *Parental after school stress project* (report by the Community, Families and Work Program). Waltham, MA: Brandeis University.

Barnett, R., Gareis, K. C., & Brennan, R. T. (1999). *Fit as a mediator of the relationship between work hours and burnout* (technical report, Women's Studies Program). Waltham, MA: Brandeis University.

Barnett, R. C., & Hall, D. T. (2001, Winter). How to use reduced hours to win the war for talent. *Organizational Dynamics, 29*(3), 192–210.

Barnett, R. C., & Rivers, C. (2004). *Same differences: How gender myths are hurting our relationships, our children, and our jobs.* Cambridge, MA: Perseus.

Barth, M. C., McNaught, W., & Rizzi, P. (1993). Corporations and the aging workforce. In P. H. Mirvis (Ed.), *Building the competitive workforce* (pp. 156–200). New York: Wiley.

Baruch, Y. (2002). The status of research on teleworking and an agenda for future research. *International Journal of Management Reviews, 3,* 113–130.

Belson, K., & Ritchel, M. (2005, December 6). Verizon to halt pension outlay for managers. *New York Times,* p. C1.

Bennis, W. (1989). *On becoming a leader.* New York: Perseus.

Berlew, D. E., & Hall, D. T. (1966). The socialization of managers: Effects of expectations on performance. *Administrative Science Quarterly, 11,* 207–223.

Blank, R. M. (1990). Are part-time jobs bad jobs? In G. Burtless (Ed.), *A future of lousy jobs? The changing structure of U.S. wages* (pp. 123–155). Washington, DC: Brookings Institute.

Blustein, D. L. (1997). A context-rich perspective of career exploration across the life roles. *Career Development Quarterly, 45,* 260–274.

Blustein, D. L., & Noumair, D. A. (1996). Self and identity in career development: Implications for theory and practice. *Journal of Counseling and Development, 74,* 433–441.

Bogden, R., & Biklen, S. K. (1992). *Qualitative research for education: An introduction to theory and methods* (2nd ed.). Boston: Allyn & Bacon.

Bolles, R. (2007). *What color is your parachute? A practical manual for job-hunters and career-changers.* Berkeley, CA: Ten Speed Press.

Bond, J. T., Thompson, C., Galinsky, E., & Prottas, D. (2002). *Highlights of the National Study of the Changing Workforce.* New York: Families and Work Institute.

Boston College Center for Work & Family. (2000). Measuring the impact of workplace flexibility. In R. Pruchno, L. Litchfield, & M. Fried (Eds.), *Study report.* Chestnut Hill, MA: Author.

Boston College Center for Work & Family. (2002). *Bringing work home: The advantages and challenges of telecommuting* (report by E. Hamilton). Chestnut Hill, MA: Author.

Boston College Center for Work & Family & Jandl Associates. (1996). *The displaced family: Job loss, family supportiveness, and the role of outplacement services* (study report). Chestnut Hill, MA: Boston College Center for Work & Family, Carroll School of Management.

Boyatzis, R., McKee, A., & Goleman, D. (2002, April). Reawakening your passion for work. *Harvard Business Review, 80*(44), 86–94.

BPW Foundation. (2004). *101 facts on the status of working women.* Washington, DC: Business and Professional Women/USA and the BPW Foundation.

Branco, K. J., & Williamson, J. B. (1982). Stereotyping and the life cycle: Views of aging and the aged. In A. G. Miller (Ed.), *In the eye of the beholder: Contemporary issues in stereotyping* (pp. 364–409). New York: Praeger.

Brennan, R. T., Barnett, R. C., & Gareis, K. C. (2001, February). When she earns more than he does: A longitudinal study of dual career couples. *Journal of Marriage and Family, 63,* 168–182.

Bridges, W. (1980). *Transitions: Making sense of life's changes.* Reading, MA: Addison-Wesley.

Bridges, W. (1994, September 19). The end of the job. *Fortune,* pp. 62–74.

Bridges, W. (1994). *Job shift: How to prosper in a workplace without jobs.* New York: Perseus.

Bridges, W. (1997). *Creating You & Co.: Learn to think like the CEO of your own career.* New York: Perseus.

Brimhall, D. W., Reaney, L. M., & West, J. (1999). *National Household Education Survey: Participation of kindergartners through third graders in before- and after school care.* Washington, DC: National Center of Education Statistics.

Brockner, J. (1988). *Self-esteem at work: Research, theory, and practice.* Lexington, MA: Lexington Books.

Bronson, P. (2003). *What should I do with my life? The true story of people who answered the ultimate question.* New York: Random House.

Brush, C. (1992). Research on women business owners: Past trends, future directions, and a new perspective. *Entrepreneurship Theory and Practice, 16*(4), 5–30.

Brush, C. (1999). *Women's entrepreneurship.* The Second ILO Enterprise Forum, International Small Enterprise Programmes. Zurich, Switzerland: International Labor Organization.

Business for Social Responsibility. (2004). *Health and wellness.* Retrieved October 7, 2005, from http://www.bsr.org/CSRResources/IssueBriefDetail.cfm?DocumentID=50304

Catalyst. (2001). *The next generation: Today's professional, tomorrow's leaders.* New York. Author.

Chaker, A. M. (2003, December 30). Luring moms back to work: To fight female flight, some companies overhaul leave programs; a five-year break. *Wall Street Journal.*

Champy, J. (1995). *Reengineering management: The mandate for new leadership.* New York: Harper Business.

Chapman, A., Sheeney, N., Heywood, S., Dooley, B., & Coolins, C. (1995). The organizational implications of teleworking. *International Review of Industry and Organizations, 10,* 229–248.

Christensen, K. (1988). *Women and home-based work: The unspoken contract.* New York: Holt.

Christensen, K. (1995). *Contingent work arrangements in family-sensitive corporations* (Policy Paper Series, #R95.03). Boston: Boston University Center on Work and Family.

Clawson, J. G., Kotter, J. P., Faux, V., & McArthur, C. C. (1992). *Self-assessment and career development* (3rd ed.). Englewood Cliffs, NJ: Prentice Hall.

Comfort, D., Johnson, K., & Wallace, D. (2003). *The evolving workplace series. Part-time work and family friendly practices in Canadian workplaces.* Retrieved March 15, 2004, from http://www.hrsdc.gc.ca/en/cs/sp/sdc/pkrf/publications/research/2003-000183/page01.shtml

Committee on Part-Time Career Tracks in Clinical and Investigative Medicine. (2000). *Interim report, April 2000* (unpublished report). Boston: Brigham & Women's Hospital.

Cooper, C. L., & Burke, R. J. (2002). *The new world of work: Challenges and opportunities.* Oxford, UK: Blackwell Business.

Crary, L. M. (1981). *Life maps exercise.* Unpublished exercise. Waltham, MA: Bently College.

Crary, L. M. (1982). *Patterns of life structure: Person–environment designs and their impact on adult lives.* Unpublished doctoral dissertation, Case Western Reserve University, Cleveland, OH.

Dalton, G. W., Thompson, P. H., & Price, R. L. (1977). The four stages of professional careers: A new look at performance. *Organizational Dynamics, 6,* 19–42.

Doherty, S., Andrey, J., & Johnson, L. (2000). The economic and social impacts of telework. In *Telework and the new workplace of the 21st century,* proceedings of a symposium sponsored by the U.S. Department of Labor (pp. 73–97). Xavier University, New Orleans, LA, October 16.

Driver, M. J. (1994). Workforce personality and the new information age workplace. In J. A. Auerbach & J. C. Welsh (Eds.), *Aging and competition: Rebuilding the U.S. workforce* (pp. 185–204). Washington, DC: The National Council on the Aging, Inc., and the National Planning Association.

Drucker, P. F. (1999, March–April). Managing oneself. *Harvard Business Review, 77*(2), 64–74, 185.

Drucker, P. F. (2005, January). Managing oneself. *Harvard Business Review, 83*(1), 100–109.

Dubin, R. (1956). Industrial workers' worlds. *Social Problems, 3,* 131–142.

Dychtwald, K., Erikson, T., & Morrison, B. (2004, March). It's time to retire retirement. *Harvard Business Review, 82*(3), 48–57.

EBRI. (2005, December). *EBRI (Employee Benefit Research Institute) Notes, 26*(12).

Eckblad, J., & Kiel, D. (2003). *If your life were a business, would you invest in it?* New York: McGraw-Hill.

Epstein, C. F., Seron, C., Oglensky, B., & Saute, R. (1999). *The part-time paradox: Time norms, professional lives, family, and gender.* New York: Routledge.

Erikson, E. H. (1963). *Childhood and society* (2nd ed.). New York: Norton.

Erikson, E. H. (1968). *Identity, youth and crisis.* New York: Norton.

Evans, P. A. L., & Bartolome, F. (1984). The changing pictures of the relationship between career and family. *Journal of Occupational Behavior, 5,* 9–21.

Families and Work Institute. (1997). *Study of the changing workforce: Ongoing study of the changing workforce.* New York: Author.

Families and Work Institute. (2004). *Generation and gender in the workplace.* Watertown, MA: American Business Collaboration.

Feldman, D. C. (2002). Second careers and multiple careers. In C. L. Cooper & R. J. Burke (Eds.), *The new world of work: Challenges and opportunities* (pp. 75–94). Oxford, UK: Blackwell Business.

Fetto, J., & Gardyn, R. 2002. You can take it with you. *American Demographics, 24*(2), 10–12.

Fletcher, J. (1994a). *Toward a theory of relational practice in organizations: A feminist reconstruction of "real" work.* Unpublished doctoral dissertation, Boston University.

Fletcher, J. (1994b). Castrating the female advantage: Feminist standpoint research and management science. *Journal of Management Inquiry, 3,* 74–82.

Fletcher, J. (1999). *Disappearing acts: Gender, power, and relational practices at work.* Cambridge: MIT Press.

Fletcher, J. K., & Ragins, B. R. (Forthcoming). Stone center relational theory: A window on relational mentoring. In B. R. Ragins & K. E. Kram (Eds.), *The handbook of mentoring: Theory, research and practice*. Thousand Oaks, CA: Sage.

Fletcher, J. K., & Ragins, B. R. (Forthcoming). *Through the relational theory looking glass: Understanding high-quality mentor relationships*. Thousand Oaks, CA: Sage.

Fried, M. (1998). *Taking time: Parental leave policy and corporate culture*. Philadelphia: Temple University Press.

Friedman, S. D., & Greenhaus, J. H. (2000). *Work and family: Allies or enemies? What happens when business professionals confront life choices*. New York: Oxford University Press.

Frost, R. (1979). *The poetry of Robert Frost: The completed poems, complete and unabridged*. New York: Holt, Rinehart & Winston.

Gabarro, J. J., & Kotter, J. P. (2005, January). Managing your boss. *Harvard Business Review, 83*(1), 91–92.

Galinsky, E., Salmond, K., Bond, J. T., Brumit Kropf, M., Moore, M., & Harrington, B. (2003). *Leaders in a global economy: A study of women and men*. Unpublished report.

Gardella, R. S. (2000). *The Harvard Business School guide to finding your next job*. Boston: Harvard Business Reference.

Gerson, K., & Jacobs, J. A. (2004). *The time divide: Work, family, and gender inequality*. Cambridge, MA: Harvard University Press.

Gerstel, N., & Gallagher, S. K. (2001). Men's caregiving: Gender and the contingent character of care. *Gender and Society, 15*(2), 197–217.

Gil Gordon Associates. (2000). *Financial issues of telecommuting FAQ: Telecommuting tools*. Retrieved June 20, 2002, from http://www.gilgordon .com/telecommuting/faq.htm

Gilligan, C. (1982). *In a different voice: Psychological theory and women's development*. Cambridge, MA: Harvard University Press.

Googins, B. K. (1991). *Work/family conflicts: Private lives—public responses*. New York: Auburn House.

Gordon, G. (2001). *Turn it off: How to unplug from the anytime-anywhere office without disconnecting your career*. New York: Three Rivers.

Green, P. C. (1996). *Get hired: Winning strategies to ace the interview*. Austin, TX: Bard.

Greenhaus, J. H., & Beutell, N. J. (1985). Sources of conflict between work and family roles. *Academy of Management Review, 10*, 76–88.

Greenhaus, J. H., & Parasuraman, S. (1999). Research on work, family, and gender: Current status and future directions. In G. N. Powell (Ed.), *Handbook of gender and work* (pp. 391–412). Newbury Park, CA: Sage.

Grossman, R. J. (2006, January). Developing talent: How to build a skilled promotable workforce. *HR Magazine, 51*(1).

Hakim, C. (1994). *We are all self-employed: The new social contract for working in a changed world*. San Francisco: Berrett-Koehler.

Hall, D. (1993). *Life work*. Boston: Beacon.

Hall, D. T. (1971). A theoretical model of career subidentity development in organizational settings. *Organizational Behavior and Human Performance, 6*, 50–76.

Hall, D. T. (1976). *Careers in organizations.* Glenview, IL: Scott, Foresman.

Hall, D. T. (1986a). Breaking career routines: Midcareer choice and identity development. In D. T. Hall & Associates, *Career development in organizations* (pp. 120–159). San Francisco: Jossey-Bass.

Hall, D. T. (1986b). Dilemmas in linking succession planning to individual executive learning. *Human Resource Management, 25,* 235–265.

Hall, D. T. (1989). Telecommuting and the management of work–home boundaries. In J. Abramson, A. Basu, A. Gupta, D. T. Hall, R. Hinckley, R. Solomon, & L. Waks (Eds.), *The annual review of communications and society.* Queenstown, MD: Institute for Information Studies.

Hall, D. T. (1990, Winter). Promoting work/family balance: An organization-change approach. *Organizational Dynamics, 18,* 5–18.

Hall, D. T. (1999). Accelerate executive development—at your peril! *Career Development International, 4*(4), 237–239.

Hall, D. T. (2002). *Careers in and out of organizations.* San Francisco: Sage.

Hall, D. T., & Associates (1986). *Career development in organizations.* San Francisco: Jossey-Bass.

Hall, D. T., & Associates. (1996). *The career is dead—Long live the career: A relational approach to careers.* San Francisco: Jossey-Bass.

Hall, D. T., & Gordon, F. E. (1973). Career choices of married women: Effects on conflict, role behavior, and satisfaction. *Journal of Applied Psychology, 58*(1), 42–48.

Hall, D. T., & Hall, F. S. (1980). Stress and the two-career couple. In C. L. Cooper & R. Payne (Eds.), *Current concerns in occupational stress* (pp. 243–266). London: Wiley.

Hall, D. T., & Kahn, W. A. (2001). Developmental relationships at work: A learning perspective. In C. Cooper & R. J. Burke (Eds.), *The new world of work* (pp. 49–74). London: Blackwell.

Hall, D. T., & Mirvis, P. H. (1993, October–December). The new workplace: A place for older workers? *Perspectives on Aging,* pp. 15–17.

Hall, D. T., & Mirvis, P. H. (1994a). Careers as lifelong learning. In A. Howard (Ed.), *The changing nature of work.* San Francisco: Jossey-Bass.

Hall, D. T., & Mirvis, P. H. (1994b). The new workplace and older workers. In J. A. Auerbach & J. C. Welsh (Eds.), *Aging and competition: Rebuilding the U.S. workforce* (pp. 58–93). Washington, DC: The National Council on the Aging, Inc., and the National Planning Association.

Hall, D. T., & Mirvis, P. (1995). The new career contract: Developing the whole person at midlife and beyond. *Journal of Vocational Behavior, 47,* 269–289.

Hall, D. T., & Nougaim, K. E. (1968). An examination of Maslow's need hierarchy in an organizational setting. *Organizational Behavior and Human Performance, 3,* 12–35.

Hall, D. T., & Rabinowitz, S. (1988). Maintaining employee involvement in a plateaued career. In M. London & E. Mone (Eds.), *Career growth and human resource strategies: The role of the human resource professional in employee development* (pp. 67–80). Westport, CT: Quorum.

Hall, D. T., & Richter, J. (1988). Balancing work life and home life: What can organizations do to help? *Academy of Management Executive, 2,* 213–233.

Hall, D. T., & Richter, J. (1990). Career gridlock: Baby boomers hit the wall. *Academy of Management Executive, 4,* 7–22.

Hall, D. T., Zhu, G., & Yan, A. (2001). Developing global leaders: To hold on to them, let them go! In W. H. Mobley & M. W. McCall Jr. (Eds.), *Advances in global leadership* (pp. 327–349). New York: JAI/Elsevier Science.

Hall, F. S., & Hall, D. T. (1979). *The two-career couple.* Reading, MA: Addison-Wesley.

Hammer, L., & Barbera, K. (1997). Toward an integration of alternative work: Toward an integration of alternative work schedules and human resource systems. *Human Resources Planning, 20,* 28–36.

Handy, C. (1989). *The age of unreason.* Boston: Harvard Business School Press.

Handy, C. (1994). *The age of paradox.* Boston: Harvard Business School Press.

Harrington, B., & James, J. B. (2005). The standards of excellence in work–life integration: From changing policies to changing organizations. In M. Pitt-Catsouphes, E. Kossek, & S. Sweet (Eds.), *The work and family handbook: Multi-disciplinary perspectives and approaches* (pp. 665–683). Mahwah, NJ: Lawrence Erlbaum.

Hertz, R., & Marshall, N. L. (2001). *Working families: The transformation of the American home.* Berkeley: University of California Press.

Hewitt Associates LLC. (2002). *SpecSummary: United States salaries 2002–2003.* Lincolnshire, IL: Author.

Hewlett, S. A. (2002a). *Creating a life: Professional women and the quest for children.* New York: Hyperion.

Hewlett, S. A. (2002b, April). Executive women and the myth of having it all. *Harvard Business Review,* pp. 66–73.

Higgins, C., Duxbury, L., & Johnson, K. (2000). Part-time work for women: Does it really help balance work and family? *Human Resource Management, 39*(1), 17–32.

Higgins, M. C., & Kram, K. E. (2001). Reconceptualizing mentoring at work: A developmental network perspective. *Academy of Management Review, 26*(2), 264–288.

Hill, J., Vjollca, M., & Ferris, M. (2004). New-concept part-time employment as a work–family adaptive strategy for women professionals with small children. *Family Relations, 53*(3), 282–292.

Hill, L. A. (1994). *Managing your career. Harvard Business School Notes.* Boston: Harvard Business School Press.

Hoffman, E. (2006, July 24). A course in what next? Seminars and workshops can help you clarify what you want. *BusinessWeek.* Retrieved November 30, 2006, http://www.businessweek.com/magazine/content/06_30/b3994408.htm

Howard, A. (1992). Work and family crossroads spanning the career. In S. Zedeck (Ed.), *Work, families, and organizations* (pp. 70–137). San Francisco: Jossey-Bass.

Howard, A., & Bray, D. W. (1988). *Managerial lives in transition: Advancing age and changing times.* New York: Guilford.

Hutchens, R., & Chen, J. (2004, March). *The role of employers in phased retirement: Opportunities for phased retirement amongst white collar workers* (working paper). Ithaca, NY: School of Industrial and Labor Relations, Cornell University.

Ibarra, H. (2003). *Working identity: Unconventional strategies for reinventing your career.* Boston: Harvard Business School Press.

Jacobs, J. A., & Gerson, K. (1998). Who are the overworked Americans? *Review of Social Economy, 56*(4), 442–459.

Jacobs, J. A., & Gerson, K. (2001, February). Overworked individuals or over-worked families? Explaining trends in work, leisure, and family time. *Work and Occupations, 28*(1), 40–63.

Jacobs, J. A., & Gerson, K. (2004). *The time divide: Work, family, and gender inequality.* Cambridge, MA: Harvard University Press.

James, J. (2005, October 28). *The expanding stage that is adult life.* Unpublished presidential address at the biennial meeting of the Society for the Study of Human Development.

Judiesch, M., & Lyness, K. S. (1999). Left behind? The impact of leaves of absence on managers' career success. *Academy of Management Journal, 42,* 641–651.

Kahn, W. A. (1990). The psychological conditions of personal engagement and disengagement at work. *Academy of Management Journal, 33,* 692–724.

Kahn, W. A. (1994). Caring for the caregivers: Patterns of organizational caregiving. *Administrative Science Quarterly, 38,* 539–563.

Kantrowitz, B., Wingert, P., Scelfo, J., Springen, K., Figueroa, A., Brant, M., & Abrams, S. (2001, May 28). Unmarried, with children. *Newsweek,* p. 46.

Kaufman, H. G. (1982). *Professionals in search of work: Coping with the stress of job loss and underemployment.* New York: Wiley.

Kegan, R. (1982). *The evolving self: Problem and process in human development.* Cambridge, MA: Harvard University Press.

Knowdell, R. L. (1998). *Career values card sort planning kit.* San Jose, CA: Career Research and Testing, Inc.

Kossek, E. E., & Lee, M. D. (2005). *Making flexibility work: What managers have learned about implementing reduced-load work.* East Lansing: Michigan State University.

Kossek, E. E., & Lobel, S. A. (Eds.). (1996). *Managing diversity: Human resource strategies for transforming the workplace.* Oxford, UK: Blackwell.

Kossek, E. E., & Ozeki, C. (1998). Work–family conflict, policies, and the job–life satisfaction relationship: A review and directions for organizational behavior–human resources research. *Journal of Applied Psychology, 83,* 139–257.

Kram, K. E. (1985). *Mentoring at work: Developmental relationships in organizational life.* Glenview, IL: Scott, Foresman.

Kram, K. E. (1996). A relational approach to career development. In D. T. Hall & Associates, *The career is dead—Long live the career: A relational approach to careers* (pp. 132–157). San Francisco: Jossey-Bass.

Kram, K. E., & Hall, D. T. (1995). Mentoring in a context of diversity and turbulence. In S. Lobel & E. E. Kossek (Eds.), *Human resource strategies for managing diversity* (pp. 108–136). London: Blackwell.

Kurland, N. B., & Bailey, D. E. (1999). Telework: The advantages and challenges of working here, there and anywhere, and anytime. *Organizational Dynamics, 28*(2): 53–68.

Laslett, P. (1991). *A fresh map of life: The emergence of the third age.* Cambridge, MA: Harvard University Press.

Lee, M. D., & Kossek, E. E. (2006). *Making flexibility work: What managers have learned about implementing reduced-load work* (technical report). Montreal, Quebec, Canada: McGill University.

Levine, J. (1997). *Working father: New strategies for balancing work and family.* New York: Harcourt Brace.

Levinson, D. J. (1986). A conception of adult development. *American Psychologist, 41,* 3–13.

Levinson, D. J., with Darrow, C. N., Klein, E. B., Levinson, M. H., & McKee, B. (1978). *The seasons of a man's life.* New York: Knopf.

Levinson, D. J., with Levinson, J. (1996). *The seasons of a woman's life.* New York: Knopf.

Lincoln, Y. S., & Guba, E. G. (1985). *Naturalistic inquiry.* Beverly Hills, CA: Sage.

Lobel, S. A. (1991). Allocation of investment in work and family roles: Alternative theories and implications for research. *Academy of Management Review, 16,* 507–521.

London, M. (1998). *Career barriers: How people experience, overcome, and avoid failure.* Hillsdale, NJ: Lawrence Erlbaum.

London, M., & Mone, E. M. (1987). *Career management and survival in the workplace.* San Francisco: Jossey-Bass.

Marshall, C. M., Chadwick, B. A., & Marshall, B. C. (1992). The influence of employment on family interaction, well-being, and happiness. In S. J. Bahr (Ed.), *Family research: A sixty-year review, 1930–1990* (Vol. 2, pp. 167–229). San Francisco: New Lexington Press.

McCall, M. W. Jr. (1998). *High flyers: Developing the next generation of leaders.* Boston: Harvard Business School Press.

McCall, M. W. Jr., Lombardo, M. M., & Morrison, A. M. (1988). *The lessons of experience: How executives develop on the job.* Lexington, MA: Lexington Books.

McCullough, D. (2001). *John Adams.* New York: Simon & Schuster.

McGregor, D. (1961). *The human side of enterprise.* New York: Wiley.

McNerney, D. J. (1995). Telecommuting: An idea whose time has come. *HR Focus, 72*(11), 1–3.

Miller, J. B. (1991). The development of women's sense of self. In J. V. Jordan, A. G. Kaplan, J. B. Miller, I. P. Stiver, & J. L. Surrey (Eds.), *Women's growth in connection* (pp. 11–26). New York: Guilford.

Mirvis, P. H. (1995). Mid-life as a consultant. In P. Frost & M. S. Taylor (Eds.), *Rhythms of academic life* (365–380). Newbury Park, CA: Sage.

Mirvis, P. H., & Hall, D. T. (1994). Psychological success and the boundaryless career. *Journal of Organizational Behavior, 15,* 365–380.

Moen, P. (Ed.). (2003). *It's about time: Couples and careers.* Ithaca, NY: ILR Press.

Nilles, J. M. (1998). *Managing telework: Strategies for managing the virtual workforce.* New York: Wiley.

Olmsted, B., & Smith, S. (1994). *Creating a flexible workplace: How to select and manage alternative work options.* New York: AMACOM.

Packard, D. W. (1995). *The HP way: How Bill Hewlett and I built our company.* New York: Harper Business.

Parasuraman, S., & Greenhaus, J. H. (1997). *Integrating work and family: Challenges and choices for a changing world.* Westport, CT: Quorum.

Parker, V. A. (1996). Growth-enhancing relationships outside of work (GROWS). In D. T. Hall & Associates, *The career is dead—Long live the career: A relational approach to careers* (pp. 180–195). San Francisco: Jossey-Bass.

Pitt-Catsouphes, M. (2002). *Family-friendly workplace.* A Sloan Work and Family Encyclopedia Entry. Retrieved November 30, 2006, from http://wfnetwork.bc.edu/encyclopedia

Pitt-Catsouphes, M., Kossek, E. E., & Sweet, S. (Eds.). (2006). *The work and family handbook: Multi-disciplinary approaches and perspectives.* Mahwah, NJ: Lawrence Erlbaum.

Pixley, J. (2003). Presentation at Academic Work–Life Conference, Orlando, FL.

Quinn, J. B. (1992). *Intelligent enterprise: A knowledge and service based paradigm for industry.* New York: Free Press.

Radcliffe Public Policy Center & Harris Interactive. (2000). *Life work: Generational attitudes toward work and life integration.* Cambridge, MA: Radcliffe Public Policy Center.

Rapoport, R., & Rapaport, R. N. (1971). *Dual-career families.* Baltimore, MD: Penguin.

Rapoport, R. N. (1997). *Families, children and the quest for a global ethic.* London: Ashgate.

Rath, L. E. (1966). *Values and teaching: Working with values in the classroom.* Columbus, OH: C. E. Merrill.

Richter, J. (1992). Balancing work and family in Israel. In S. Zedeck (Ed.), *Work, families, and organizations* (pp. 362–394). San Francisco: Jossey-Bass.

Robbins, A., & Wilner, A. (2001). *Quarterlife crisis: The unique challenge of life in your twenties.* New York: Most Tarcher/Putnam.

Roberts, P., & Newton, P. (1987). Levinsonian studies of women's adult development. *Psychology and Aging, 2*(2), 154–163.

Rousseau, D. M. (1990). New hire perceptions of their own and their employer's obligations: A study of psychological contracts. *Journal of Organizational Behavior, 11,* 389–400.

Salzman, A. (1992). *Downshifting: Reinventing success on a slower track.* New York: HarperCollins.

Scharlach, A. E., & Grosswald, B. (1997). The Family and Medical Leave Act of 1993. *Social Service Review, 71,* 335–359.

Schein, E. H. (1988). *Organizational culture and leadership.* San Francisco: Jossey-Bass.

Schor, J. (1992). *The overworked American: The unexpected decline of leisure.* New York: Basic Books.

Sekaran, U. (1992). Middle-class dual-earner families and their support systems in India. In S. Lewis, D. N. Israeli, & H. Hootsman (Eds.), *Dual-earner families: International perspectives* (pp. 46–61). London: Sage.

Sekaran, U., & Hall, D. T. (1989). Asynchronism in dual-career and family linkages. In M. B. Arthur, D. T. Hall, & B. S. Lawrence (Eds.), *Handbook of career theory* (pp. 159–180). Cambridge, UK: Cambridge University Press.

Senge, P. M. (1990). *The fifth discipline: The art and practice of the learning organization.* New York: Doubleday.

Sheehy, G. (1976). *Passages: Predictable crises in adult life.* New York: Dutton.

Sheehy, G. (1996). *The new passages.* New York: Ballantine.

Shellenbarger, S. (1995, February 2). Work & family: When workers' lives are contingent on employers' whims. *Wall Street Journal,* p. B1.

Shellenbarger, S. (2000). *Work & family: Essays from the "Work and Family" column of the* Wall Street Journal. New York: Ballantine.

Shepard, H. A. (1984). On the realization of human potential: A path with a heart. In M. B. Arthur, L. Bailyn, D. J. Levinson, & H. A. Shepard (Eds.), *Working with careers* (pp. 25–46). New York: Center for Research on Careers, Graduate School of Business, Columbia University.

Shilling, S. (1999). The basics of a successful telework network. *HR Focus, 76*(6), 9–11.

Sorensen, A. (2007). The demography of the third age. In J. James & P. Wink (Eds.), *The crown of life: Dynamics of the early post-retirement period.* In K. W. Schaie (Series Ed.), *Annual Review of Gerontology and Geriatrics, 26,* 1–18. New York: Springer.

Sproull, L., & Kiesler, S. (1992). *Connections: New ways of working in networked organizations.* Cambridge: MIT Press.

Story, L. (2002, August 14). Home, condo prices in state still rising. *Boston Globe,* p. B1.

Sull, D. N., & Houlder, D. (2005, January). Do your commitments match your convictions? *Harvard Business Review, 83*(1), 82–91.

Super, D. E. (1992). Toward a comprehensive theory of career development. In D. H. Montross & C. J. Shinkman (Eds.), *Career development: Theory and practice* (pp. 35–64). Springfield, IL: Charles C Thomas.

Super, D. E., Crites, J., Hummel, R., Moser, H., Overstreet, P., & Warnath, C. (1957). *Vocational development: A framework for research.* New York: Teachers College Press.

Survey: CEOs mull quitting their jobs. (2003, December 7). *Boston Globe,* p. C1.

Telecommute Connecticut. (2002). *Getting started.* Retrieved November 30, 2006, from http://telecommutect.com/employers/prog_res.php

Thoreau, H. D. (1949). *Walden.* New York: Houghton-Mifflin.

Time to take another look at telecommuting. *HR Focus.* (2002). *79*(5): 6–7.

Trafford, A. (2004). *My time: Making the most of the rest of your life.* New York: Basic Books.

Uchitelle, L. (2006). *The disposable American: Layoffs and their consequences.* New York: Knopf.

University of Utah Health Sciences Center. (2003). *Home health, hospice & elder care.* Retrieved October 7, 2005, from http://uuhsc.utah.edu/healthinfo/adult/homehealth/elder.html

U.S. Census Bureau. (2001). *2001 statistical abstract of the United States.* Available at http://www.census.gov/prod/2002pubs/01statab/stat-ab01.html

U.S. Department of Labor, Bureau of Labor Statistics. (2006). *Current population statistics.* Table 5. Employment status by sex, presence and age of children, race and Hispanic or Latino ethnicity. Retrieved December 1, 2006, from http://www.bls.gov/cps/wlf-databook2006.htm

U.S. Department of Labor, Employment Standards Administration Wage and Hour Division. (n.d.). *Families and employers in a changing economy.* Retrieved November 4, 2002, from http://www.dol.gov/esa/regs/compliance/whd/fmla/summary.htm

Van Horn, C. E., & Storen, D. (2000). *Telework: Coming of age? Evaluating the potential benefits of telework.* Paper presented at the Telework: The New Workplace of the 21st Century Symposium, New Orleans.

Voyandoff, P. (1988). Work and family: A review and expanded conceptualization. *Journal of Social Behavior and Personality, 3,* 1–22.

Waite, L. J., & Nielsen, M. (2001). The rise of the dual-earner family, 1963–1997. In R. L. Hertz & N. L. Marshall (Eds.), *Working families: The transformation of the American home* (pp. 23–41). Berkeley: University of California Press.

Warren, E., & Tyagi, A. W. (2003). *The two-income trap: Why middle-class mothers and fathers are going broke.* New York: Basic Books.

Watanabe, S., Takahashi, K., & Minami, T. (1997). The emerging role of diversity and work–family values in a global context. In P. C. Earley & M. Erez (Eds.), *New perspectives on international industrial/organizational psychology* (pp. 276–318). San Francisco: New Lexington Press.

Watson Wyatt Worldwide. (2004). *Phased retirement: Aligning employer programs with worker preferences.* Washington, DC: Author.

Weijers, T., Meijer, R., & Spoelman, E. (1992). Telework remains "made to measure": The large scale introduction of telework in the Netherlands. *Futures, 24,* 1048–1055.

Welch, J., & Welch, S. (2005). *Winning.* New York: HarperCollins.

Wells, S. J. (2001). Making telecommuting work. *HR Magazine, 46*(10), 34–46.

Zedeck, S. (1992). Introduction: Exploring the domain of work and family concerns. In S. Zedeck (Ed.), *Work, families, and organizations* (pp. 1–32). San Francisco: Jossey-Bass.

IMPORTANT LINKS

Job Resources

www.Craigslist.com

www.kornferry.com

www.linkedin.com

www.Monster.com

www.russellreynolds.com

Activities and Exercises

BCII/Career Leader: www.careerdiscovery.com

Campbell Interest and Skill Survey: www.profiler.com

Career Portfolio, Florida State: www.wapps.oti.fsu.edu/ais/portfolio

Career Values Card Sort: www.CareerTrainer.com

Strong Interest Inventory (through a career counselor): www.newdream.org

www.thirdpath.org

Index

Employment security, 6
Entrepreneurs, ix, 15, 113
Erikson, E. H., 181
Espoused theory, 25–26
Expatriate assignments, 125–126
Expectations, 5
Extended family support, 5

Families and Work Institute, 106, 107
Family issues, 133–134
  couple styles, career-family involvement
    and, 137–138, 138 (table)
  dependent care supports, 173–174
  domestic tasks, responsibility for, 9,
    108, 134, 135, 136
  dual-career couples and, 136–141,
    138 (table)
  elderly parents, caregiving
    responsibilities and, 5
  extended family supports, 5
  families, changing nature of, 8–9
  family-friendly work policies, 172–176
  family-work balance, male/female
    workers and, 134–136
  globalized corporations and, 6–7
  job loss and, 64–65
  lifestyle factors and, 33–34
  nuclear family stereotype, 5, 9
  parental after-school stress, 173
  working parents, 4–5, 15, 34, 127,
    134–136
  See also Dual-career families; Financial
    planning; Flexible work options
Family and Medical Leave Act (FMLA) of
  1993, 171
Faux, V., 35, 49, 57
Feedback:
  action from feedback, 38
  adult development and, 40
  candid feedback, guidelines for, 43
  class experiences and, 38
  peer feedback, 43–44
  performance evaluations, 38–39
  significant others, input from, 39–42,
    41–42 (table)
  360 degree feedback, 39, 106
Fee work, 115
Feldman, D. C., 189
Fidelity Investments, 199, 200
Financial planning, 126
  aging populations and, 128
  career choices/plans and, 127
  cutting expense vs. increasing income
    and, 129–130

dual-income families and, 127
education costs and, 127–128
financial independence and, 128–129
globalization effects and, 127
healthcare costs and, 128
historical budget, 129
housing costs and, 127
late life careers and, 199–200
look-ahead budget, 129
plan-ahead budget, 129
retirement plans and, 128
transportation costs and, 128
  See also Career development strategies;
    Retirement
Fit, 160, 162–163, 163–164 (box)
Fitness centers, 173
Fletcher, J., 185
Flex force, 6
Flexible work options, 6, 153–154
  Career and Life Orientation
    Index and, 98–101
  compressed work week, 157
  conventional benefits and, 172
  dependent care supports and, 172–174
  development of, 98
  enhanced work life, new forms of
    benefits and, 173
  family-friendly workplace culture,
    174–176
  family-friendly workplace policies,
    172–174
  fit concept and, 160, 162–163,
    163–164 (box)
  flextime, 155–156
  forms of, 154–172
  job sharing, 161–162
  leaves of absence, 170–171
  organizational commitment of workers
    and, 160–161
  part-time/reduced-load
    work, 158–164
  risks/compromises of, 176–177
  sabbaticals, 171–172
  telecommuting, 164–170, 167 (table),
    169 (tables)
  women in the workforce
    and, 7, 9
  work-family climate and, 154
Flextime, 154, 155–156
Formal education, 118
Free-agency. See Individually-driven
  career management
Fried, M., 171
Functional career paths, 102

About the Authors

Brad Harrington: Brad is the executive director of the Boston College Center for Work & Family (CWF) and a research professor of organization studies in the Carroll School of Management at Boston College. CWF is a national leader in helping organizations create effective workplaces that support and develop healthy and productive employees. The center provides a bridge linking the academic community to the some of the world's most progressive companies in the human resource arena.

Before coming to Boston College, Brad spent 20 years with Hewlett-Packard Company, working in a broad range of executive and management positions in quality improvement, human resources, education, management development, and organization development in the United States and Europe. His roles included chief quality officer for HP's worldwide medical products business and head of HP's management and organization development organization. Brad holds a bachelor's degree in business administration from Stonehill College, a master's degree in psychology from Boston College, and a doctorate in human resource development and organization development from Boston University. Brad has consulted with many corporations and healthcare organizations on strategic planning, cultural change, leadership development, career management, and work–life systems. In 2006, Brad was honored as one of the Ten Most Influential Men in the Work–Life Field.

Brad is married to Dr. Annie Soisson, and they have three children: Maggie, Hannah, and Dillon. Brad and his family reside in Winchester, Massachusetts.

Douglas T. Hall: Tim is the director of the Executive Development Roundtable and the Morton H. and Charlotte Friedman Professor of Management in the School of Management at Boston University. He is also faculty director of the MBA program. He has served as acting dean and associate dean of faculty development and faculty director for the master's programs at the School of Management. He received his graduate degrees from the Sloan School of Management at MIT. He has held faculty positions at Yale, York, Michigan State, and Northwestern universities and visiting positions at Columbia, Minnesota, and the U.S. Military Academy at West Point.

Tim's books include *Careers In and Out of Organizations, The Career Is Dead—Long Live the Career: A Relational Approach to Careers, Careers in Organizations, Organizational Climates and Careers, The Two-Career Couple, Experiences in Management and Organizational Behavior, Career Development in Organizations, Human Resource Management: Strategy Design and Implementation,* and *Handbook of Career Theory.* He is a recipient of the American Psychological Association's James McKeen Cattell Award (now called the Ghiselli Award) for research design, the American Society for Training and Development's Walter Storey Professional Practice Award, and the Academy of Management's Everett C. Hughes Award for Career Research. He is a fellow of the American Psychological Association, the Society for Industrial and Organizational Psychology, and the Academy of Management, where he served as a member of the Board of Governors and as president of the Organizational Behavior Division and co-founder and president of the Careers Division.

Tim is married to Marcy Crary, and he has three children and five grandchildren.